"Every pastor needs this resource, which is so [...] and pastorally. The 40-question format makes [...] I've written a few things on church membershi[...] myself learning throughout. An excellent work."
—Jonathan Leeman, Editorial Director, 9Marks

"In this excellent book, Jeremy Kimble provides a well-researched and lucidly written account of church membership and church discipline. It distinguishes itself from similar books by considering both Old and New Testament passages, by showing the connections between ecclesiology and other doctrines such as covenant and kingdom. Highly recommended."
—Bruce Ashford, Professor of Theology and Culture, Southeastern Baptist Theological Seminary

"In recent years, a growing number of evangelicals have shown renewed interest in church membership, church discipline, and related themes. One evidence of this welcome trend is the rash of helpful books, articles, and websites that focus on these key aspects of practical ecclesiology. Jeremy Kimble's contribution to Kregel's fine 40 Question series now ranks as one of the best resources for pastors and students who wish to consider the place of the local church in God's kingdom purposes, as well as his purposes for each of our Christian lives. Kimble offers just the right balance between theory and practice, synthesizing the best of current biblical and theological scholarship with thoughtful, pastorally sensitive application. *40 Questions about Church Membership and Discipline* is an essential resource that deserves a wide reading. Highly recommended."
—Nathan A. Finn, Dean, School of Theology and Missions, Union University

"This handbook concisely explains the *why* and *how* of church membership and church discipline. Jeremy Kimble, who serves as a pastor and who wrote his PhD dissertation on church discipline, is a faithful guide."
–Andy Naselli, Assistant Professor of New Testament and Theology, Bethlehem College & Seminary

"Jeremy Kimble's original work on a biblical theology of church discipline deeply influenced my own thinking on that doctrine. His perspective is sound, expansive, grounded in good ecclesiology, and practical for churches. Add to this his wise and concrete approach to church membership, and you have an immensely helpful book. When pastors and laypeople ask me to recommend resources on church membership and discipline, this book will be at the top of my list!"
—Gregg R. Allison, Professor of Christian Theology, The Southern Baptist Theological Seminary

"Few if any topics are more important to the life, health, and mission of local churches than church membership and church discipline. The treatment of these topics by Jeremy Kimble shows both the knowledge of a scholar and the experience of a pastor. The forty-question format will allow pastors and church leaders to find the help they need for the questions they are asking. It may also prompt them to ask some questions they did not realize they needed to ask. Highly recommended!"

—John S. Hammett, John Leadley Dagg Chair of Systematic Theology,
Southeastern Baptist Theological Seminary

"Jeremy Kimble's contribution to the 40 Questions series is one that brings needed clarity to topics often discussed but rarely discussed together. By asking and answering key questions related to church membership and discipline, Kimble brings into focus how these biblical practices are not mere prescriptions for rightly ordered churches but essential and divinely given preventative medicine for church health and growth. Wonderfully helpful, this book is one we need and one we can use."

—Jason G. Duesing, Provost and Associate Professor of Historical Theology,
Midwestern Baptist Theological Seminary

"Evangelical Christians living in an age of individualist consumerism often find the idea of church membership (and discipline in particular) a foreign concept. Jeremy Kindle's biblically informed book will help people see the church—a people gathered by the Holy Spirit to celebrate freedom under the lordship of Christ—as an aspect of the gospel, church membership as a vital feature of discipleship, and church discipline as a means for making disciples more like Jesus. Everyone who thinks that being a Christian means simply attending church once a week needs to read this book. If they do, they will learn that church membership is less a matter of showing up, and more a matter of growing up: of building and being built up, with others, into the whole measure of the fullness of Jesus Christ (Eph. 4:13). There is no more crucial pastoral, or for that matter theological, task for the people of God today than that."

—Kevin J. Vanhoozer, Research Professor of Systematic Theology,
Trinity Evangelical Divinity School

40 QUESTIONS ABOUT
Church Membership and Discipline

Jeremy M. Kimble

Benjamin L. Merkle, Series Editor

Kregel
Academic

40 Questions about Church Membership and Discipline
© 2017 Jeremy M. Kimble

Published by Kregel Publications, a division of Kregel, Inc., 2450 Oak Industrial Dr. NE, Grand Rapids, MI 49505-6020.

This book is a title in the 40 Questions Series edited by Benjamin L. Merkle.

All rights reserved. No part of this book may be reproduced, stored in a retrieval system, or transmitted in any form or by any means—electronic, mechanical, photocopy, recording, or otherwise—without written permission of the publisher, except for brief quotations in printed reviews.

All Scripture quotations, unless otherwise indicated, are from The Holy Bible, English Standard Version® (ESV®), copyright © 2001 by Crossway, a publishing ministry of Good News Publishers. Used by permission. All rights reserved.

The Hebrew font NewJerusalemU is available from www.linguistsoftware.com/lgku.htm, +1-425-775-1130.

ISBN 978-0-8254-4445-6

Printed in the United States of America

15 16 17 18 19 / 5 4 3 2 1

To my parents, Gerry and Cathy Kimble,
for teaching me the importance and
showing me the beauty of the local church.

Contents

Part 3: General Questions about Church Discipline

Part 4: Concluding Questions about Membership and Discipline

Introduction

This book is intended to assist Christians, pastors, and churches to rightly understand and apply biblical truth regarding church membership and church discipline. My thinking in these areas has been largely shaped by two professors I was blessed to learn from in my seminary days, John Hammett and Gregg Allison. Their encouragement and guidance were essential as I grappled with these matters in my doctoral work. I have also been privileged to serve in both academic and ecclesial contexts where questions are often raised about whether membership is necessary and if church discipline is, in essence, an unloving act. There is a real need for clarity on these matters. It is crucial to the health of the church, and to the ongoing work of sanctification in the lives of Christians, that we approach these practices in the right way.

In the midst of a seeming flood of books about matters of ecclesiology (the doctrine of the church) and, in particular, membership and discipline, this one is unique in several respects. First, whereas many books treat either church membership or discipline—or treat both in a cursory fashion—this book gives a substantive treatment to both. Second, some books have a myopic viewpoint of these doctrines, treating select issues relating either to ecclesial discipline or membership. This book seeks to cover the main issues often discussed, but also attempts to cover a much wider range of topics. This includes topics from biblical, historical, theological, and practical vantage points.

Third, this book aims to help pastors and churches think through the practical ramifications of the practices of church membership and church discipline. It is crucial to be convinced biblically and theologically of the importance of these practices, but one must also consider how to initially pursue, or improve upon, those practices in an ecclesial context. And finally, as with all works in the 40 Questions series, this book is set up to answer specific questions. A quick look at the table of contents will serve as a guide for readers to navigate their way to the answers they are looking for, or they can simply read the book in its entirety. Chapters are relatively brief, but include footnotes and a select bibliography at the end of the book if readers are looking for further resources to go deeper on any topic.

I would like to express my profound appreciation to several colleagues and friends who have read over the contents of this work in manuscript. These include J. R. Gilhooly, John Hammett, Billy Marsh, Andy Naselli, and Ched

Spellman. Thanks also to Ben Merkle for his close editorial work and incisive comments given throughout this process. Finally, to our God, the blessed and only Sovereign, the King of kings and Lord of lords, who alone has immortality, who dwells in unapproachable light, whom no one has ever seen or can see. To him be honor and eternal dominion. Amen (1 Tim. 6:15–16).

Abbreviations

BECNT	Baker Exegetical Commentary on the New Testament
BSac	*Bibliotheca Sacra*
CBQ	*Catholic Biblical Quarterly*
DTIB	*Dictionary of Theological Interpretation of the Bible*
EBC	Expositor's Bible Commentary
EDT	*Evangelical Dictionary of Theology*
FM	*Faith and Mission*
IVPNTC	InterVarsity Press New Testament Commentary
JBL	*Journal of Biblical Literature*
JETS	*Journal of the Evangelical Theological Society*
LW	*Luther's Works*
MSJ	*The Master's Seminary Journal*
NAC	New American Commentary
NDBT	*New Dictionary of Biblical Theology*
NFTL	New Foundations Theological Library
NICNT	New International Commentary on the New Testament
NIGTC	New International Greek Testament Commentary
NIDNTT	*New International Dictionary of New Testament Theology*
NIVAC	New International Version Application Commentary
NSBT	New Studies in Biblical Theology
NTS	*New Testament Studies*
PNTC	Pillar New Testament Commentary
RJ	*Reformed Journal*
RQ	*Restoration Quarterly*
SBJT	*Southern Baptist Journal of Theology*
SBL	Studies in Biblical Literature
SJT	*Scottish Journal of Theology*
STR	*Southeastern Theological Review*
TDNT	*Theological Dictionary of the New Testament*
TJ	*Trinity Journal*
TOTC	Tyndale Old Testament Commentaries

TNTC   Tyndale New Testament Commentaries
WBC   Word Biblical Commentary
WJE   *Works of Jonathan Edwards*
WTJ   *Westminster Theological Journal*
ZECNT   Zondervan Exegetical Commentary on the New Testament

PART 1

GENERAL QUESTIONS ABOUT MEMBERSHIP AND DISCIPLINE

Why Are Church Membership and Church Discipline Important?

Throughout its history the church has experienced both moments of cultural ascendancy, as well as periods of ridicule, ostracization, and persecution. In the West we are currently experiencing what Russell Moore describes as "the collapse of the Bible belt," as Christians find themselves less of a moral majority, and operating more as a prophetic minority.[1] Regardless of how culture views us, the church is called "to contend for the faith that was once for all delivered to the saints" (Jude 1:3), and if this makes the institutional church less appealing and popular in our day and age, we are not surprised (1 Peter 4:12). We know that the world may not resonate with our message and may not join in fellowship with us, seeing such actions as irrelevant and unnecessary.

We expect this kind of posture from the world around us, but when ambivalence and apathy characterize those who would claim to be Christians in regards to the importance of the institutional church, this presents reason for concern and a call for action. Most Christians are not hostile to these concepts, but at times we struggle to understand the importance or relevance of such concepts to our modern-day lives. As Leeman states, although people have a vague sense that Christians should attend and be involved with a local church, "they would also say it's not the most important thing in the world, so we shouldn't make too big a deal about it. If Christians spend several years hopping from church to church, or if they decide to attend one church indefinitely without joining, that's okay too."[2] The aim of this book is to refute

---

1. Russell D. Moore, *Onward: Engaging the Culture Without Losing the Gospel* (Nashville: B&H Academic, 2015), 1–10.
2. Jonathan Leeman, *Church Membership: How the World Knows Who Represents Jesus* (Wheaton, IL: Crossway, 2012), 18.

such thinking and establish the critical importance of church membership and discipline in the life of the Christian.

The Importance of the Church

In terms of "theological triage"—the ordering of doctrine as it relates to its proximity to the gospel—the doctrine of the church can often be overlooked today in comparison to other doctrines.[3] The deity of Christ, justification by faith alone, the inerrancy of Scripture, and the atoning work of Christ are just a few examples of issues that are more tightly tethered to the truths of the gospel. However, given the fact that the doctrine of the church is not the most important, that does not make it unneeded or unimportant. In fact, one should recognize that ecclesiology is connected to the doctrines of God and salvation and, as such, must be factored into our understanding of theology and redemptive history.

John Webster notes that God relates both to himself (immanent Trinity) as well as to his creation (economic Trinity). God is intrinsically perfect in his life and activity.[4] But, continues Webster, "within that life and act there is a movement or turning *ad extra*, in which out of his own perfection God wills and establishes creatures."[5] In other words, God did not remain as a Being merely relating to himself, he also created for his glory and is relationally involved with his creation.[6] In holy love and grace God creates humanity as his image-bearers and the pinnacle of creation (Gen. 1:26–28). Due to the Fall, humanity is in need of saving grace, and the church is "the society of those elected, called, redeemed, sanctified, and glorified in Jesus Christ."[7] In this way, the doctrine of the church is grounded in the perfections of God and the grace of the gospel.

Based on these points, Allison summarizes the necessity and importance of the church in the following way: "[Ecclesiology] is part and parcel of (1) the eternal purpose of God in redeeming his fallen human creatures; (2) the Father's mighty work in regard to the exaltation of his humiliated and crucified Son; (3) the eternal divine counsel with regard to the revelation of himself

---

3. For more on the concept of theological triage, see R. Albert Mohler Jr., "Conservative Evangelicalism," in *Four Views on the Spectrum of Evangelicalism* (Grand Rapids: Zondervan, 2011), 68–96; idem, "The Pastor as Theologian," in *A Theology for the Church*, ed. Daniel L. Akin, rev. ed. (Nashville: B&H Academic, 2014), 725–26.

4. John Webster, "On Evangelical Ecclesiology," *Ecclesiology* 1, no. 1 (2004): 12–13.

5. Ibid., 13. For more on the connection between God as Trinitarian and the church as Christ's bride purchased by the Father see Jonathan Edwards, "Miscellanies (Entry Nos. 501–832)," no. 741, *WJE* 18, ed. Ava Chamberlain (New Haven, CT: Yale University Press, 2000), 367–68.

6. For an extended treatment dealing with God creating for his glory, see Jonathan Edwards, "Dissertation Concerning the End for Which God Created the World," in *WJE* 8, ed. Paul Ramsey (New Haven, CT: Yale University Press, 1989), 405–536.

7. Webster, "On Evangelical Ecclesiology," 10.

and his ways; and (4) prophetic Scripture that assigns an important role to the church in the outworking of salvation."[8] As such, while ecclesiology may not be the doctrine that holds highest importance, it is a necessary area of study due to its close connection to other crucial doctrines (e.g., God and salvation). And this in turn gives credence for understanding the doctrine of church membership and church discipline to also be of great value.

The Importance of Church Membership

Church membership and church discipline are both connected to the realities of community and authority. However, in societies that possess a strong individualist impulse, consumeristic bent, or a resistance to authoritative structures, the call for joining a church formally and submitting to God-given authority is often not well received. The question of authority is relevant to the discussion of local church membership and discipline, because membership and discipline involve a life of submission.[9] This life of submission begins with what we might call the "front door" to the church, namely, church membership.

There are numerous reasons one should consider church membership to be an important doctrine, but three initial reasons are worth surveying here. First, as disciples we are called to persevere in the faith, and this is an ongoing community project. We are called to exhort one another day after day so that we are not hardened by the deceitfulness of sin (Heb. 3:12–13) and not to neglect meeting together so we can stir each other up to love and good works (Heb. 10:23–25). Perseverance in the faith is not something we do merely on our own; it is meant to be pursued with brothers and sisters in Christ gathered around the Word of God, encouraging each other to put off sin and run the race with perseverance (Heb. 12:1–2).

Second, the covenant commitment of the local church makes the invisible new covenant visible.[10] We cannot see, hear, or smell a person being united to Christ and receiving his Spirit by faith, though it is real and eternal. Christ, however, intended for the realities of the gospel as displayed in the new covenant to show up on earth. Christians join a local church in membership, show the initiation of their covenant relationship with Christ through baptism, and demonstrate continual celebration of and submission to the new covenant and that local community through the Lord's Supper.[11] These acts within a local church make the truths of the new covenant manifest for other church members, as well as for an unbelieving world.

---

8. Gregg R. Allison, *Sojourners and Strangers: The Doctrine of the Church* (Wheaton, IL: Crossway, 2012), 59. Allison is quick to point out that the "necessity" of the church is derivative and instrumental, not causative and foundational.
9. Jonathan Leeman, *The Church and the Surprising Offense of God's Love: Reintroducing the Doctrines of Church Membership and Church Discipline* (Wheaton, IL: Crossway, 2010), 68.
10. Question 5 will deal with this point in much more detail.
11. Leeman, *The Church and the Surprising Offense of God's Love*, 268.

Finally, as we conceive of what a church is, we must understand that a church is its membership. In other words, the actual constitution of the church, what its makeup consists of, is people joined in covenant with one another to oversee each other's growth in discipleship.[12] With this understanding, if we take away church membership, we negate the reality of the church as a visible entity.

The Importance of Church Discipline

As one considers the cultural consequences of individualism, consumerism, and aversion to authority, it must also be noted that church discipline is a necessary reality as the "back door" of the church. Again, many more reasons will be enumerated for the importance of ecclesial discipline, but here we offer three. First, the practice of discipline is explicitly mandated in Scripture. Matthew 18:15–20 and 1 Corinthians 5:1–13—along with a number of other passages—specify in detail the methodology and reasoning for such a practice. With such clear warrant and direction from Scripture, it is imperative that we approach this area of church life with care.

Second, as counterintuitive as it sounds, discipline is a proper demonstration of the biblical concept of love. God disciplines those whom he loves (Heb. 12:6–11), and thus a church who claims to love its members without disciplining them contradicts Scripture and offers a different kind of love than God does.[13] Church discipline can potentially be a painful process, but as a spiritual family we are called to work through such matters faithfully and gently. Not only are we called to go through this process in a loving manner, the very act of discipline should be seen as an act of love.

Finally, as with membership, discipline is tied to the call for a persevering faith. Part of the work within membership to encourage one another to endure in the faith includes the process of church discipline. We undergo this process not merely to punish someone, but to call them to repentance. If someone undergoes the final step of church discipline, often referred to as excommunication, the church is essentially saying about that individual that they do not see the fruits of salvation exhibited in their lives in a demonstrative way. Their stubborn refusal to repent of sin does not characterize a Christian, and thus excommunication is a declarative sign of potential end-time judgment.[14] As such, the point of such an action is to call that person to repentance, and if they take that step we lovingly restore them to the body of Christ. Discipline, therefore, is a crucial practice for the life of the church.

---

12. See Leeman, *Church Membership*, 46–47.
13. Thomas White, "The Why, How, and When of Church Discipline," in *Baptist Foundations: Church Government for an Anti-Institutional Age*, eds. Mark Dever and Jonathan Leeman (Nashville: B&H Academic, 2015), 201–2.
14. This point will be receive further elaboration in Question 39.

Summary

Though it can be argued that the doctrine of the church is not the central topic of Scripture, the theme of God's people across the Testaments is of vital significance. God purposed to save a people through the redeeming work of his Son, and thus the church is connected in noteworthy ways to the doctrines of God and salvation. Bearing this in mind, church membership and church discipline define in greater detail key doctrinal truths such as regeneration, perseverance of the saints, God's love and holiness, and end-time judgment. These are not mere cultural monikers dreamt up by people who thought it would be helpful in organizing the church more efficiently. These doctrines have real biblical warrant and theological import, and thus are worthy of further investigation for the good of the church and the fame of God's name.

REFLECTION QUESTIONS

1. Though the doctrine of the church may not be central, why is it still important?

2. What is the concept known as "theological triage"?

3. What is the importance of church membership?

4. What is the importance of church discipline?

5. How is God's love and holiness evident in the practices of church membership and church discipline?

QUESTION 2

What Is a Church?

In conceiving of the essence of what (or who) the church is, understanding the identity of the church as seen in the OT and NT is of great importance. This reflection on the people of God across the Testaments serves as a great test case in considering the continuity and discontinuity that exists within Scripture. It also clarifies what marks identify the church in terms of its origin, orientation, and mission. As such, this section will offer a definition of the church, followed by a brief foray into the way in which the OT and NT identify the people of God, and finally highlight seven marks of the church.

Definition of the Church

The term "church" derives from the Greek word *ekklēsia*, which connotes the idea of "assembly." The term is found in the NT 114 times. Of these occurrences, three refer to a secular assembly, and two refer to the OT people of God. The remaining usage of this term refers to the NT church, at times in a general sense (i.e., universal church) but often describing a gospel-centered assembly in a specific locale (i.e., local church). Thus, to offer a succinct definition, *the church is the people of God who have been saved through repentance and faith in Jesus Christ, and have been incorporated into his body through baptism with the Holy Spirit.*[1] Additionally, these people assemble in local gath-

---

1. See Gregg R. Allison, *Sojourners and Strangers: The Doctrine of the Church* (Wheaton, IL: Crossway, 2012), 29. This definition takes into account the distinctiveness of the new covenant as it relates to the church. Wellum asserts the church "is *new* in redemptive history precisely because she is the community of the *new* covenant." He continues, "the church, unlike Israel, is *new* because she is comprised of a *regenerate, believing* people rather than a 'mixed' group" (Stephen J. Wellum, "Beyond Mere Ecclesiology: The Church as God's New Covenant Community," in *The Community of Jesus: A Theology of the Church*, eds. Kendall H. Easley and Christiopher W. Morgan (Nashville: B&H Academic, 2013), 194. However, one must also rightly note that there are points of continuity between the people of God

erings to worship, hear the preached Word, observe the ordinances, affirm and oversee one another's membership, exercise discipline when needed, and encourage one another to live faithfully as Christians and be on mission in the name of Jesus Christ.

Many images are used to describe the church, but three have been used preeminently: the people of God, the body of Christ, and the temple of the Spirit. This set of images connotes important details regarding the nature of the church. The "people of God" imagery connects us to Israel in the OT (cf. 1 Peter 2:9–10) and reminds us that we are called to live as a family with God as our Father. The "body of Christ" is a picture of the unity in diversity we have within the church as people with different gifts care for one another, all in relation to their union with Christ (1 Cor. 12:1–26). The imagery of the "temple of the Spirit" reminds readers of the dwelling place of God in the OT (e.g., Eden, tabernacle, temple), Jesus as the temple (John 2:13–22), and the fact that believers now operate as the dwelling place of God (1 Cor. 3:16–17), mediating God's presence and worshipping God by offering spiritual sacrifices (Rom. 12:1–2; 1 Peter 2:5). Each of these images contributes to our understanding of the definition of the church.

The People of God across the Testaments

In understanding the nature of the church, one must also consider the people of God in both the OT and NT.[2] The relationship between the OT and NT in general is filled with complexity.[3] While apparent similarities and parallels between the Testaments occur on a number of themes, a degree of

---

(as will be seen). For a brief article on these points of continuity, see D. A. Carson, "When Did the Church Begin?" *Themelios* 41, no. 1 (2016): 1–4.

2. For further detail concerning the relationship between Israel and the Church, see Jeremy M. Kimble, *That His Spirit May Be Saved: Church Discipline as a Means to Repentance and Perseverance* (Eugene: Wipf & Stock, 2013), 16–20.

3. A divide has typically been driven between covenant and dispensational theology. For the covenant position, see Michael Scott Horton, *God of Promise: Introducing Covenant Theology* (Grand Rapids: Baker, 2006); Robert L. Reymond, *A New Systematic Theology of the Christian Faith* (Nashville: Thomas Nelson, 1998), 503–44; O. Palmer Robertson, *The Israel of God: Yesterday, Today, and Tomorrow* (Phillipsburg, NJ: P&R, 2000). A traditional dispensational view would be represented by Charles Caldwell Ryrie, *Dispensationalism*, rev. and expanded (Chicago: Moody Press, 1995). For the progressive dispensationalist position see Craig A. Blaising and Darrell L. Bock, *Progressive Dispensationalism* (Wheaton, IL: BridgePoint, 1993); Robert L. Saucy, *The Case for Progressive Dispensationalism: The Interface between Dispensational & Non-Dispensational Theology* (Grand Rapids: Zondervan, 1993). For a mediating position between covenant and dispensational theology, see Peter J. Gentry and Stephen J. Wellum, *Kingdom through Covenant: A Biblical-Theological Understanding of the Covenants* (Wheaton, IL: Crossway, 2012) and Stephen J. Wellum and Brent E. Parker, eds., *Progressive Covenantalism: Charting a Course between Dispensational and Covenant Theologies* (Nashville: B&H, 2016).

differences also exists.[4] Thus, for our purposes, both continuity and discontinuity between the Testaments must be acknowledged when speaking of Israel, the church, and the subjects of membership and discipline.

One should note that the shape of the visible church today bears a clear continuity—though not identity—with the visible people of God in the Old Testament.[5] Thus, a pattern is seen beginning in the OT where God is interested in blessing a group of people, beginning with the saving of a few families from the flood (Gen. 6–8) and coming into greater focus in the covenant made with Abraham (Gen. 12:1–3). God promises blessing for Abraham's descendants—as well as all the nations—and this promise comes to fruition in the nation of Israel, whom God leads out of Egypt and calls his own people (Exod. 1–20). God shows great interest in calling a particular people to be his own.

In noting further continuity between Israel and the church, one can observe that the two primary terms used to refer to God's people in the OT are *qahal* and *ēdah*. In the NT the word translated "church" is *ekklēsia*, which has three primary usages, all connoting an assembly of people.[6] The translators of the Septuagint used *ekklēsia* to translate *qāhāl* nearly one hundred times, but never to translate *ēdâh*. For *ēdâh* they usually used the Greek term *synagōgē*, which is used only once in the New Testament to refer to the church (James 2:2).[7] Taking this data into consideration, one can see a rich association between the assembly of God in the OT and the NT church by virtue of the etymological connection that exists, as evidenced by the Septuagint.

Another evidence for continuity includes the way in which the NT associates Israel and the church. In Galatians 6:16, Paul referred to "all who walk by this rule" in the Galatian church as "the Israel of God." While some

---

4. For an excellent study on this topic see John S. Feinberg, ed., *Continuity and Discontinuity: Perspectives on the Relationship between the Old and New Testaments: Essays in Honor of S. Lewis Johnson, Jr.* (Wheaton, IL: Crossway, 1988).

5. Millar summarizes: "The entire Bible speaks of God's plan to create his people, in his place, under his rule. He commits himself to working with one people, and follows this commitment through to the end, though he extends the scope of his people through the work of Christ" (J. G. Millar, "People of God," in *NDBT*, ed. T. Desmond Alexander and Brian S. Rosner [Downers Grove, IL: InterVarsity, 2000], 687). See also Elmer A. Martens, "The People of God," Scott J. Hafemann and Paul R. House, eds., *Central Themes in Biblical Theology: Mapping Unity in Diversity* (Grand Rapids: Baker Academic, 2007), 225–53.

6. Walter Bauer, et al., *A Greek-English Lexicon of the New Testament and Other Early Christian Literature* (3rd ed.; Chicago: University of Chicago Press, 2000), 303–04. Hereafter referred to as BDAG.

7. John S. Hammett, *Biblical Foundations for Baptist Churches: A Contemporary Ecclesiology* (Grand Rapids: Kregel, 2005), 27. Hammett derives this data from L. Coenen, "Church," in *NIDNTT*, ed. Colin Brown (Grand Rapids: Zondervan, 1975), 1:292–96.

suggest this title refers to ethnic Jews in the congregation,[8] others believe that earlier Paul referred to all Christians—Jew and Gentile—as "Abraham's seed," and thus the link between Israel and the church is deliberate.[9] Peter also uses OT language specified for Israel to refer to the church as "a chosen race, a royal priesthood, a holy nation, a people for his own possession" (1 Peter 2:9; cf. Deut. 10:15; Exod. 19:5–6; Deut. 7:6). Acts 15 is also a significant passage dealing with this issue. At the Jerusalem Council, James quotes Amos 9:11– 12, a prophecy promising that David's fallen tent would be restored and that Israel would come to possess the nations. Thus, according to the affirmation of the apostles, a prophecy made to Israel in the OT includes in its fulfillment, at least in part, Gentile believers coming into the church.

While one should note that these continuities are present, it is crucial also to consider the differences that exist between Israel and the church. For example, God's people in the OT are ethnically distinct, while the NT church includes both Jew and Gentile. Israel in the OT lived as a separate nation with its own laws; the church in the NT lives among the rulers of the nations, called to obey God's commands, but also subject to the governing authorities (Rom. 13:1–7). A covenant sign for Israel was physical circumcision, while in the NT baptism and the circumcision of the heart marks out the church. Discontinuity also exists because of the coming of Christ and all that he accomplished, as well as the inauguration of the new covenant and the indwelling of the Holy Spirit.[10] Finally, there is a distinct future marked out for the nation of Israel at the end of the ages (Rom. 11:25–28).[11]

Thus, discontinuity must be maintained, even while one can rightly see the relationship between Israel and the church. Though Israel and the church are not identical, they are closely connected through Jesus Christ (Eph. 2:12–13;

---

8. See, for example, S. Lewis Johnson, "Paul and 'the Israel of God': An Exegetical and Eschatological Case-Study," *MSJ* 20, no. 1 (2009): 41–55; John F. Walvoord and Roy B. Zuck, *The Bible Knowledge Commentary* (Wheaton, IL: Victor Books, 1983), 611.

9. So Andreas J. Köstenberger, "The Identity of the *Israel Tou Theou* (Israel of God) in Galatians 6:16," *FM* 19, no. 1 (2001): 3–24. Schreiner states the entirety of the letter to the Galatians is dealing with whether one must become a Jew to be saved. Paul has argued throughout that circumcision is unnecessary and that those who put their faith in Christ belong to the family of Abraham. Seemingly, it would be very confusing to argue for the equality of Jew and Gentile in Christ (3:28), assert that all believers are Abraham's children, and then conclude that only ethnic Jews who believe in Jesus belong to the Israel of God. See Thomas R. Schreiner, *Galatians*, ZECNT 9 (Grand Rapids: Zondervan, 2010), 381–83.

10. For an excellent study on the indwelling of the Spirit as a new reality in the NT, see James M. Hamilton, *God's Indwelling Presence: The Holy Spirit in the Old & New Testaments*, NAC Studies in Bible and Theology (Nashville: B&H, 2006).

11. This final assertion is still debated as a point of theology that affects other areas of biblical intrepretation. Further inquiry goes beyond the purview of this section, but for more detail on the topic see Benjamin L. Merkle, "Romans 11 and the Future of Ethnic Israel," *JETS* 43, no. 4 (2000): 709–21; Douglas J. Moo, *The Epistle to the Romans*, NICNT (Grand Rapids: Eerdmans, 1996), 710–39.

cf. 2 Cor. 1:20) With this in mind, one can affirm that, through the work of Christ, the church has parallels with Israel but is also "new" as the new covenant people of God consisting of both Jews and Gentiles (Eph. 2:11–22).[12]

The Marks of the Church

Traditionally, the marks of the church have come from the Patristic era and the Reformation period. The Patristic marks affirm that the church is one (unity of the church), holy (the church is set apart and called to moral purity), catholic (the church is universal), and apostolic (faithful to apostolic teaching). The Reformation marks of the true church claim that the true church include the right preaching of the Word of God, the right administration of the ordinances, and the right practice of church discipline.

Allison affirms these marks as having relevance for the modern church but also offers seven marks he believes help the church to understand its nature and role in a more comprehensive and biblical manner, taking into account the ontology, or essence, of the church.[13] He affirms that the church is doxological (oriented to the glory of God), logocentric (focused on the Word of God, both Christ and the written Scriptures), pneumadynamic (created, gathered, gifted, and empowered by the Spirit), covenantal (gathered as members of the new covenant community in covenant with one another), confessional (united by confession of the Christian faith), missional (divinely called, divinely sent ministers of the gospel), and spatio-temporal/eschatological (historically located, with a future orientation). These marks give helpful clarity regarding the nature and role of the church, inclusive of historic marks, but offering a more comprehensive vision.

Summary

Defining the reality of the church is an essential task. It invites the reader to consider the nature of the people of God, the imagery associated with the church, the relationship of the people of God across the Testaments, as well as to think through the essential marks of the church. Such reflection helps us to understand the flow of Scripture, from Genesis to Revelation, and offers helpful warrant for the kinds of practices we see in church life on a weekly basis. At root, we do not think of the church in functional and pragmatic categories; rather we begin with the essence of the church as described in Scripture, which will then give rise to the way we are called to operate within local churches.

---

12. To see further elaboration on this last point, see Stephen J. Wellum, "Beyond Mere Ecclesiology: The Church as God's New Covenent Community," in *The Community of Jesus: A Theology of the Church,* eds. Kendall H. Easley and Christopher W. Morgan (Nashville: B&H Academic, 2013), 183–212.
13. See Allison, *Sojourners and Strangers,* 103–6.

REFLECTION QUESTIONS

1. How would you define the term "church" in one sentence?

2. What areas of continuity exist between Israel and the church?

3. What areas of discontinuity exist between Israel and the church?

4. What are the historic marks of the church?

5. What are the seven marks of the church that Allison offers?

What Is Church Membership?

In rightly conceiving of the definition of the church, one must understand that the church is not a building, but a people. God calls for his people to gather corporately (notice, for example, that most of the NT epistles are addressed to specific churches), to submit to qualified leadership (1 Tim. 3:1–7; Titus 1:5–9), to come under the teaching of the Scriptures and faithfully administer the ordinances (Acts 2:37–47; 1 Cor. 11:23–26; 2 Tim. 4:1–2), and to exercise the authority Christ has given to them (Matt. 16:19; 18:17). Thus, a local church gathers for a specific purpose, and they do so as the people of God who have been redeemed through faith in Christ (Col. 1:13–14).

This chapter will show that church life is meant to go beyond mere attendance. When seeking to define church membership, the very definition calls for a certain kind of response. At its root, people are brought into the membership of a local church based on their profession of faith in Jesus Christ, and thereby they become a part of a particular group of people who strive together, by the grace of God and the power of the Spirit, to live in obedience to him. This has a number of implications, but before delving into those details it is crucial to see a more exact definition of membership.

Definition of Church Membership

Leeman offers a helpful definition of church membership: "Church membership is a formal relationship between a church and a Christian characterized by the church's affirmation and oversight of a Christian's discipleship and the Christian's submission to living out his or her discipleship in the care of the church."[1] This definition merits further attention. First, there is a formal relationship between a church and a Christian. This goes beyond occasionally attending a church. Instead, the picture is one of ongoing reciprocal

---

1. Jonathan Leeman, *Church Membership: How the World Knows Who Represents Jesus*, 9Marks (Wheaton, IL: Crossway, 2012), 64.

commitment. Second, this relationship is characterized by the church affirming and overseeing that Christian's discipleship. The front end of this formal relationship is the confirmation of this person's faith in Jesus Christ alone for salvation (more on this in the next section). The ongoing nature of the relationship between church and Christian is one of guidance and support for progressive growth in Christ-likeness. This is the church's responsibility to the member in this formal relationship.

The member agrees in this formal relationship to submit to living out their discipleship in the care and guidance of this particular local church. They recognize that oversight will come from church leadership and fellow church members, and they agree to being formed as Christians within this local church setting. In this way, churches and their members go beyond mere formalities and recognize that there is responsibility and activity involved in this process.

Regenerate Church Membership

One such responsibility inherent in this vision of church membership is the call to ensure, as far as we are humanly able, that those who come into membership are in fact Christians (i.e., regenerate church membership). The concept of the church existing as a "mixed body" of both believers and unbelievers became a well-known theological concept relatively early within the church. Augustine is the most well-known voice defending this ecclesiological framework, which carried over to the medieval era.[2] At the time of the Reformation, however, Avis asserts that the magisterial Reformers were concerned with ecclesiology but more so in redefining the center of the church (i.e., Christ and the gospel). The Anabaptists affirmed this point but also emphasized the importance of defining the circumference of the church (i.e., believers only).[3] This is a crucial point of ecclesiology, and one that can be defended biblically.

The Biblical Case for Regenerate Church Membership

First, regarding church membership as inclusive of only believers, it seems logical that if the Bible conceives of the universal church as consisting of only believers, then the local church would follow suit.[4] While we will make errors and admit unbelievers into membership, we should do all we can to ensure that the local church matches as closely as possible the constitution of the universal church. This also accords with the biblical notion of the kingdom of God. The church, as a community of citizens of the inaugurated—but not yet

---

2. See Gregg R. Allison, *Historical Theology: An Introduction to Christian Doctrine* (Grand Rapids: Zondervan, 2011), 570–78.
3. Paul D. L. Avis, *The Church in the Theology of the Reformers*, NFTL (Louisville: John Knox, 1981).
4. Several of the reasons listed here are derived from John S. Hammett, *Biblical Foundations for Baptist Churches: A Contemporary Ecclesiology* (Grand Rapids: Kregel, 2005), 83–87.

consummated—kingdom of God,[5] aims to live corporately as loyal subjects of the king. Allison argues from Matthew 16:16–19,[6] a key text on rightly understanding the church's relationship to the kingdom, "Specifically, the church is the instrument through which entrance into the kingdom is granted, as the church has been entrusted with and employs 'the keys of the kingdom of heaven' (v. 19)."[7] These keys have to do with the gospel and people's response to it. The church, as the community of the kingdom, provides entrance into the kingdom through the proclamation of the gospel, and its newly born citizens live as kingdom people under the sovereignty of the king. God has allowed the church to exercise the authority of the keys, not only in admission into the church, but also, if needs be, removal from the church (Matt. 18:15–20). This relationship between the kingdom of God and the church assumes a regenerate people exercising the authority of the keys of the kingdom.

Second, the NT recognizes that false teachers and unbelievers will enter the life of the church as members, and the mechanism for dealing with such situations is church discipline. A number of passages teach that a member cannot deny the claim of belief in Jesus by their unrepentant, ongoing sin without experiencing the consequence of discipline. This is so because the church was meant to be a pure (not perfect) body of genuine believers. A third biblical reason to affirm regenerate church membership is that the letters contained in the NT assume that these churches are composed of believers only. For example, letters are written to "those sanctified in Christ" (1 Cor. 1:2), "the saints in Christ Jesus" (Eph. 1:1; Phil. 1:1), and "the holy and faithful brothers in Christ" (Col. 1:2). Clearly, Paul thought he was addressing bodies of Christians.

Fourth, local churches in Acts gathered only those who believed. The church is constituted by those who accepted Peter's message (Acts 2:41, 47; 4:4), people in Antioch who turned to the Lord (11:21), and those who were encouraged by Paul and Barnabas to stay true to their commitment as believers (14:21–23). Paul's regular strategy was to come into a city, preach the gospel, and gather those who responded into churches (e.g., Acts 16:11–40).

---

5. For more detail concerning the kingdom of God, see Craig A. Blaising and Darrell L. Bock, *Progressive Dispensationalism* (Wheaton, IL: BridgePoint, 1993); John Bright, *The Kingdom of God: The Biblical Concept and Its Meaning for the Church* (Nashville: Abingdon, 1953); Graeme Goldsworthy, *The Goldsworthy Trilogy* (Carlisle: Paternoster, 2000); George Eldon Ladd, *A Theology of the New Testament* (Grand Rapids: Eerdmans, 1993); Christopher W. Morgan and Robert A. Peterson, eds., *The Kingdom of God*, Theology in Community 4 (Wheaton, IL: Crossway, 2012); Thomas R. Schreiner, *The King in His Beauty: A Biblical Theology of the Old and New Testaments* (Grand Rapids: Baker Academic, 2013).

6. More detail will be given on this text in answering Question 7.

7. Gregg R. Allison, "The Kingdom and the Church," in *The Kingdom of God*, 189. For further exegetical details and warrant for this interpretation regarding Matthew 16:16–29 and Matthew 18:15–20 as it relates to this topic, see Jeremy M. Kimble, *That His Spirit May Be Saved: Church Discipline as a Means to Repentance and Perseverance* (Eugene, OR: Wipf and Stock, 2013), 37–47.

Finally, regenerate church membership is inherent in the principle that the church, in its essence, consists of its membership.

Because a church "is its members," and because the local church is making visible in a particular milieu a facet of the universal church, one can therefore conclude members of a local church should be regenerate. Thus, when defining the concept of church membership, one must recognize that Scripture discusses it as being regenerate in nature.

The Nature of Regeneration

Having established a case for regenerate church membership, it is also crucial to discuss what constitutes regeneration or, more broadly, salvation.[8] Our God loves his creation (John 3:16–21; 1 John 4:7–12) and is also completely holy, set apart in purity and splendor from the rest of creation (Isa. 6:1–5; Rev. 5:8–11). Humanity, ravaged by sin, has no access to God in their own power (Rom. 3:10–18). In love God sends his Son to be the satisfaction for our sins. In this way God displays his love in justifying us, as well as his holiness in justly upholding his standard of wrath that is due for sin (Rom. 3:21–26). Jesus is the way in which God demonstrates love and holiness in creation.

This truth is known as the gospel. The gospel is news, specifically good news about the person and work of Jesus Christ (1 Cor. 15:1–58). The gospel is the announcement that the crucified and risen Jesus (perfect Son of God, Son of Man), who died for our sins and rose again according to the Scriptures, has been enthroned as the true Lord (Rom. 10:9–10), Savior (Titus 1:3), and Treasure (John 6:35) of the world. When this gospel is preached, God calls people, out of sheer grace, to respond in repentance and faith in Jesus Christ. The church is thus composed of those who have seen and embraced the light of gospel of the glory of Christ, who is the image of God (2 Cor. 4:4).

Meaningful Church Membership

Beyond the idea of church membership as a category for believers only, one should also recognize that there is meaningful activity and responsibility associated with such an office. While advocating for membership rather than mere attendance at a church, it must be noted that meaningful membership does involve regular attendance. If someone does not regularly attend, it will be impossible for the church to know how the person is doing. Meaningful membership also means that a Christian understands that local assembly to be the place where they experience fellowship and engage in ministry.[9] The

---

8. For a thorough and specific study on the doctrine of regeneration, see John Piper, *Finally Alive: What Happens When We Are Born Again* (Ross-shire, Scotland: Christian Focus, 2008).
9. For an excellent work dealing with the concept of fellowship and community, see Mark Dever and Jamie Dunlop, *The Compelling Community: Where God's Power Makes a Church Attractive*, 9Marks Books (Wheaton, IL: Crossway, 2015).

NT envisions Christians fulfilling the many "one another" commands primarily among a concrete group to whom they are accountable (1 Cor. 12).

Finally, meaningful membership is inclusive of certain privileges and responsibilities.[10] For example, members of the church enjoy the Lord's Supper together, which is an amazing privilege. There is also a call to pray for each other (1 Thess. 5:17), use spiritual gifts to build up the body (1 Cor. 12:7), care for and exhort one another (Heb. 3:12–13), promote unity and growth within the body (Eph. 4:3–16), and financially support the church (2 Cor. 8–9; Gal. 6:6). These are just a few examples wherein one can see the meaning of the call for joining a church formally as a member.[11]

Summary

Church membership is an important concept to work through, both on a theological as well as a practical level. It is a formal relationship between a Christian and a local church that involves affirmation, oversight, and submission. And the makeup of this membership, as best as the church can pursue it under God's grace, is to be regenerate in nature. This in turn yields a meaningful membership where the members are more than spectators; rather they are active participants involved in the life and ministry of the church. This is a biblical vision of church membership.

REFLECTION QUESTIONS

1. What is the definition of church membership?

2. What is regenerate church membership?

3. What does it mean to be regenerate?

4. How can church membership be meaningful?

5. What kinds of privileges and responsibilities does membership entail?

---

10. More detail will be given in these two areas in Questions 19 and 20.
11. For further detail on the essence of church membership, see Mark E. Dever, "The Practical Issues of Church Membership," in *Those Who Must Give an Account: A Study of Church Membership and Church Discipline*, eds. John S. Hammett and Benjamin L. Merkle (Nashville: B&H Academic, 2012), 81–101.

What Is Church Discipline?

The practice of church discipline, though not always implemented consistently in contemporary Protestant circles, has deep biblical moorings that must be clearly understood and practiced in order for the church to function properly.[1] Due to misapplications and misunderstandings, discipline has been largely ignored by many congregations, resulting in communities of faith that neglect many of the moral absolutes laid out in Scripture.[2] When one understands, however, that there is a "holiness without which no one will see the Lord" (Heb. 12:14), the church is compelled to use various means to pursue that goal in a corporate manner.

There are a variety of ways one can continue to pursue conformity to Christ, both on an individual and on a corporate level. Often, in Western contexts especially, people think of Christian growth as an individual pursuit. Through the practices of Bible intake, prayer, and other such spiritual disciplines, Christians can see continued growth in their life. However, the Christian life is not just lived out on an individual level; there is also a corporate component that is just as vital to our ongoing progress in sanctification. For the members of a local church, there is a need for teaching, reproof, correction, and training in righteousness (2 Tim. 3:17). As such, church discipline is an essential ingredient to the church's health. Therefore, it is vital that the church come to a coherent,

---

1. This chapter is derived from Jeremy M. Kimble, *That His Spirit May Be Saved: Church Discipline as a Means to Repentance and Perseverance* (Eugene, OR: Wipf and Stock, 2013), 1, 6–9. Used by permission of Wipf and Stock Publishers (www.wipfandstock.com).

2. R. Albert Mohler elaborates on this point, saying, "As a matter of fact, most Christians introduced to the biblical teaching concerning church discipline confront the issue of church discipline as an idea they have never before encountered. At first hearing, the issue seems as antiquarian and foreign as the Spanish Inquisition and the Salem witch trials. Their only acquaintance with the disciplinary ministry of the church is often a literary invention such as *The Scarlet Letter*" (Mark E. Dever, ed., *Polity: Biblical Arguments on How to Conduct Church Life* [Washington, DC: Center for Church Reform, 2000], 43).

robust understanding of ecclesial discipline, knowing that God desires a people who are holy, as he is holy (1 Peter 1:15–16).

The Definition of Church Discipline

Since there are a number of factors involved in the process of discipline, definitions of this practice can vary, but they are typically situated around several common themes. These themes include accountability, exhortation, dealing with sin, authority within the church, excommunication, repentance, and reconciliation. Throughout this study the concept of church discipline will be understood as *divine authority delegated to the church by Jesus Christ to maintain order through the correction of persistently sinning church members for the good of those caught in sin, the purity of the church, and the glory of God.*[3] This definition could use further explanation.

Discipline should be understood as "divine authority delegated to the church by Jesus Christ" in that we act in accordance with his Word, and he has vested those actions with his own ruling power (Matt. 16:13–20). The church maintains order through correcting "persistently sinning members." In other words, this action is not taken for any attendee within the church, but for those who have joined that local church as covenant members. The call is to correct those in persistent, unrepentant sin, as they are not showing forth the fruit of the Spirit with their lack of repentance (Gal. 5:22–24). As such, the confrontation is "for the good of those caught in sin," as they will be called to a persevering, fruit-filled faith. Discipline also aims to maintain "the purity of the church," knowing that a sin like this, gone unchecked, could do serious damage to the church as a whole (1 Cor. 5:6–8). Finally, as with all things, discipline is exacted for "the glory of God" (1 Cor. 10:31; Col. 3:17). With this definition in mind the church must recognize that discipline must be done as it is taught in Scripture, but we are also called to exact such a practice with proper motives and proper goals. Thus, when blatant, habitual, unrepentant

---

3. This definition is derived from a number of sources dealing with the topic of church discipline. Notable contributions to this doctrine include Jay E. Adams, *Handbook of Church Discipline: A Right and Privilege of Every Church Member* (Grand Rapids: Zondervan, 1974); Ken Blue and John White, *Church Discipline That Heals* (Downers Grove, IL: InterVarsity, 1985); Mark E. Dever, ed. *Polity: Biblical Arguments on How to Conduct Church Life* (Washington, DC: Nine Marks Ministries, 2001); Marlin Jeschke, *Discipling the Brother* (Scottsdale, PA: Herald Press, 1979); Roy Knuteson, *Calling the Church to Discipline: A Scriptural Guide for the Church That Dares to Discipline* (Nashville: Thomas Nelson, 1977); J. Carl Laney, *A Guide to Church Discipline* (Minneapolis: Bethany House, 1985); Mark Lauterbach, *The Transforming Community: The Practice of the Gospel in Church Discipline* (Carol Stream, IL: Christian Focus, 2003); Jonathan Leeman, *Church Discipline: How the Church Protects the Name of Jesus*, 9Marks (Wheaton: Crossway, 2012); Thomas C. Oden, *Corrective Love: The Power of Communion Discipline* (Saint Louis: Concordia Publishing, 1995); James T. South, *Disciplinary Practices in Pauline Texts* (Lewistown, NY: Edwin Mellen, 1992); Daniel E. Wray, *Biblical Church Discipline* (Carlisle, PA: Banner of Truth, 1978).

sin occurs within the church, it must be dealt with accordingly, "but always with a view to bringing about repentance."[4]

Formative and Corrective Discipline

The concept of church discipline can be understood as both "formative" and "corrective." Church discipline is one part of the discipleship process, the part where we correct sin and point the disciple toward the better path.[5] As such, churches do well in not separating discipline a great distance from their pursuit of discipleship, recognizing that the former is a crucial aspect of the latter.[6]

Formative discipline means order is maintained in the church through regenerate church membership, the right preaching and teaching of Scripture, proper administration of the ordinances, and observing the many "one another" commands contained in the New Testament.[7] Formative church discipline, according to Don Cox, "is broader than corrective discipline and refers to the nurture of believers through instruction and their shared life in the body."[8] While many churches enact these kinds of practices, it is often not referred to as formative church discipline, though this term may help to give a particular mindset to the life of the church. This type of discipline is exercised in the Christian community as the members express genuine concern for each other and become dynamically involved with one another in deep interpersonal relationships, recognizing that God holds all accountable for their stewardship of life. Thus, the purpose of formative discipline is to enlighten, encourage, support, and sustain one another in the discipline under which they live, and in the fulfillment of their divine mission.

While formative discipline is a crucial component of the disciplinary process, this book will focus on the *corrective* aspect of church discipline, which deals with the direct confrontation of sin. A forthright approach to the process of discipline is elucidated by Jesus, which helps to form a pattern for how one should approach these kinds of situations (Matt. 18:15–20). Jesus states that one should go directly to the person who sinned against them to see if they can restore the relationship. If reconciliation does not take place, two or three witnesses are to be brought along in order to restore fellowship. If there is no reconciliation at this point, the matter is brought before the church so that the sinner can be confronted corporately. If this does not achieve the goal of reconciliation,

4. D. P. Kingdon, "Discipline," in *NDBT*, ed. T. Desmond Alexander and Brian S. Rosner (Downers Grove, IL: InterVarsity, 2000), 450.
5. Leeman, *Church Discipline*, 27.
6. See Thomas R. Schreiner, "The Biblical Basis for Church Discipline," in *Those Who Must Give an Account: A Study of Church Membership and Church Discipline*, eds. John S. Hammett and Benjamin L. Merkle (Nashville: B&H Academic, 2012), 105–6.
7. For a more thorough study of this type of discipline, see Don Cox, "The Forgotten Side of Church Discipline," *SBJT* 4, no. 4 (2000): 44–58.
8. Ibid., 44.

the person is to be removed from the membership of the church and treated as a "Gentile or tax collector." In each of these steps, love and forgiveness are to be extended since the goal of discipline is ultimately reconciliation.

This last step of the discipline process, known as excommunication, is rarer in church settings, since issues typically are dealt with in the first or second step. Nevertheless, this area of discipline demands our attention.

Excommunication does not mean that a person cannot attend a church service; rather, it involves a removal of that person from the membership rolls and the exclusion of the person from partaking of the Lord's Supper. Church members must also know that they are to treat the excommunicant as if that person were an unbeliever, based on their lack of repentance. This understanding of excommunication is needful in embracing both the love as well as the holiness of God, noting that both attributes are exercised in this practice.

Summary

The Christian life constitutes both individual and corporate approaches to growth in godliness, and church discipline is one of the means by which we continue to see growth and development. Discipline is a practice that occurs regularly within the church, and it is intended to keep God's people on the path of perseverance and to exhort the one under discipline to repent. This can be thought of in both formative and corrective terms, the former referring to typical church life and practices intended to help all Christians grow in their faith, the latter referring to specific correction meted out to those involved in ongoing, unrepentant sin. Discipline is necessary and vital for the health of the church.

REFLECTION QUESTIONS

1. How should one define the concept of church discipline, generally speaking?

2. What is formative church discipline?

3. What is corrective church discipline?

4. If a person is excommunicated from the church, what does this mean practically?

5. What does church discipline teach us about the character of God?

PART 2

GENERAL QUESTIONS ABOUT CHURCH MEMBERSHIP

Theological Questions

How Does Church Membership Relate to the New Covenant?

The Bible is the story of God's glory. The Trinitarian God is the main character of all history, and he has created and redeemed a people to put his glory on display (Ps. 19:1; Isa. 43:7; Eph. 1:3–14). The realm in which God's glory is supremely displayed is referred to as his kingdom, God's people in God's place under God's rule and reign. Certainly "kingdom" language can be used to convey the activity of God in exercising his sovereignty over all things (Deut. 2:5, 9, 30; 4:19; 29:25–26; 32:8; Isa. 45:5–7). Most often, however, God's kingdom refers to particular activity in exercising authority over his subjects who, out of their faith in him and love for him, serve only him.[1] One could thus identify the kingdom of God functioning as universal reign and eternal dominion, as God's rule over the nation of Israel (theocracy, Davidic kingship), as inaugurated in the person and work of Christ, as an inaugurated and growing reality in the church (i.e., citizens of the kingdom), and as an eschatological expectation.[2]

In understanding the way in which this kingdom presents itself in Scripture, one must note that the specific outworking of the kingdom within redemptive history is linked to the giving of covenants by God to his people.[3] The term "covenant" (OT, *berith*; NT, *diathēkē*) speaks of an enduring

---

1. See Bruce K. Waltke, "The Kingdom of God in the Old Testament: Definitions and Story," in *The Kingdom of God*, Theology in Community, ed. Christopher W. Morgan and Robert A. Peterson (Wheaton, IL: Crossway, 2012), 49–50.
2. Gregg R. Allison, *Sojourners and Strangers: The Doctrine of the Church* (Wheaton, IL: Crossway, 2012), 89–100. See also Craig A. Blaising and Darrell L. Bock, *Progressive Dispensationalism* (Wheaton, IL: Bridgepoint, 1993), 232–83.
3. This concept is dealt with in detail in Peter. Gentry and Stephen J. Wellum, *Kingdom through Covenant: A Biblical-Theological Understanding of the Covenants* (Wheaton, IL: Crossway, 2012).

agreement which establishes a defined relationship between two parties involving a solemn, binding obligation to specified stipulations on the part of at least one of the parties toward the other, which is taken by oath under threat of divine curse, and ratified by a visual ritual.[4] While a covenant can refer to various agreements between humans (Gen. 21:22–24; 1 Sam. 18:3; 1 Kings 5:1–12; 2 Kings 11:17; Ezek. 16:8; Mal. 2:14), the concept of covenant applies predominantly to divine-human commitments.[5] In terms of ecclesiology and church membership, it is necessary to rightly understand the nature of the kingdom and the covenants so as to see how the NT church is distinct from OT Israel. This distinction is most demonstrably shown in the final covenant discussed in Scripture, which is known as the new covenant.

The Covenants

When studying Scripture one can observe six specific covenants made between God and man. The first covenant God established was with Adam. God gives responsibilities to Adam in the cultural mandate (Gen. 1:28) and provides stipulations about not eating from the tree of the knowledge of good and evil, lest they die (Gen. 2:16–17; cf. Hos. 6:7). The next covenant, made with Noah, holds some similarities to this original Adamic covenant. Described in Genesis 6–9, God restates, after the flood, the cultural mandate to be fruitful, multiply, and fill the earth to subdue it (Gen. 9:1). He also makes a covenant never again to destroy the world by global flood (Gen. 9:11). The sign of the covenant, the "bow in the cloud," serves as a reminder of God's everlasting covenant (Gen. 9:13–16).

The Abrahamic covenant, given in Genesis 12–17, establishes a relationship between God and Abraham. There the patriarch is told he will become a great nation, will be given a land, and will serve as a blessing to the nations (Gen. 12:1–3). The sign of the covenant was the circumcising of the males within this nation when they were eight days old (Gen. 17:10–14). The Mosaic covenant, presented in Exodus 19–24, is founded on the redeeming work of God, rescuing Israel from slavery in Egypt (Exod. 19:4). Based on this redemption, Israel was called to obey God's voice and keep his covenant, and in doing this they would be a kingdom of priests and a holy nation (Exod. 19:5–6). Israel failed to keep this covenant, and thus it is renewed in the book of Deuteronomy for the new generation. However, Israel fails to keep the covenant stipulations, as it was foretold (Deut. 30:1–6), and this demonstrates that "the old covenant itself anticipates a time in which it will fail and will be replaced by a new arrangement with God."[6] The Davidic covenant, told in 2 Samuel 7, promises to

---

4. See Daniel C. Lane, "The Meaning and Use of the Old Testament Term for 'Covenant': With Some Implications for Dispensational and Covenant Theology" (PhD Diss., Trinity International University, 2000), 314.

5. P. R. Williamson, "Covenant," in *NDBT*, eds. T. Desmond Alexander and Brian S. Rosner (Downers Grove, IL: InterVarsity, 2000), 420.

6. Allison, *Sojourners and Strangers*, 67.

David an everlasting house, an everlasting kingdom, and an everlasting throne upon which a son of David will reign (2 Sam. 7:14–16). This Davidic descendant must be faithful as a son, living in obedience to the law of God.[7]

The New Covenant

One must understand the relationship and progression of these covenants. In keeping with the commands associated with the Adamic and Noahic covenant to be fruitful, multiply, and fill the earth with image-bearers of God, one can note that this reality will culminate in the advent of the new heavens and new earth, where "The earth will be filled with the knowledge of the glory of the Lord as the waters cover the sea" (Hab. 2:14). God begins this process with a people (Israel) in a land (Canaan) who would bring blessing to the nations; however, God's people fail to keep the Mosaic covenant. But a king would come, in the line of Abraham, Judah, and David, who would keep the stipulations of the old covenant and, in so doing, usher in a new era for God's people. Thus, all these covenants form the backbone of the Bible's storyline and culminate in the new covenant.

All of the promises of God find their "Yes" in Jesus Christ (2 Cor. 1:20). This means that the covenants culminate in him. He is the Davidic king (Heb. 1:5) who perfectly keeps and fulfills the Mosaic covenant (Matt. 5:17) and, as Abraham's true seed, brings about blessing for the nations (Gal. 3:10–16) and, eventually, restoration of the land (Acts 13:19; Rom. 4:13) that is ultimately consummated in the new heavens and new earth (Rev. 21–22). Jesus also inaugurates the new covenant in his person and work. This covenant is marked by newness, in that it is not like the Mosaic covenant which was external in nature (Jer. 31:32). Instead, this covenant is internal in nature, consisting of a people who have circumcised hearts (Deut. 10:16; 30:1–10), the law written on their hearts (Jer. 31:33), personal and intimate knowledge of the Lord (Jer. 31:34), and forgiveness of iniquity granted by God (Jer. 31:34). This new-covenant people will be cleansed (Ezek. 36:25), have hearts of stone removed and be given hearts of flesh (Ezek. 36:26), and be indwelt by the Spirit of God who will cause them to obey (Ezek. 36:27; cf. Joel 2:28–29; Acts 2:14–21). Jesus tells us that this new covenant was inaugurated in his death and resurrection (Luke 22:20). As God's people who repent and believe in the person and work of Jesus Christ, we are indwelt with the Spirit and now have a ministry of the new covenant (2 Cor. 3:1–18).

The New Covenant's Relationship to Church Membership

It is crucial now to think of how kingdom and (specifically the new) covenant relate to the church and its membership. As has already been noted, there is strong degree of difference between the Mosaic and the new covenants

---

7. For more on the Messiah as the faithful Son and Davidic descendent, see Peter J. Gentry, "Rethinking the 'Sure Mercies of David' in Isaiah 55:3," *WTJ* 69, no. 2 (2007): 283.

respectively. First, there is a structural change in the progression of redemptive history as it relates to these covenants. Wellum explains, "Under previous covenants the genealogical principle prevailed, that is, the relationship between the covenant mediator and his seed was *biological/physical* . . . but now, in Christ, under his mediation, the relationship between Christ and his people is *spiritual*, i.e., born of the Spirit."[8] Thus, whereas Israel was a "mixed community" with a remnant that believed in God (Rom. 9:6), the new covenant community (i.e., the church) is a believing community where everyone knows the Lord, from the least to the greatest (Jer. 31:34).

This change in the structure of the people of God is due to a change in the nature of the new covenant community. All in this community will be regenerate, receive forgiveness of sins, and perhaps most significantly, be indwelt by the Holy Spirit.[9] It is by our union with Christ and the work of the Spirit (Acts 2) that we are regenerated (Titus 3:4–7) and receive forgiveness of sins (Rom. 8:1). These marks apply to all who are a part of the people of God under the new covenant.

These covenantal realities have significant implications for church membership. Where we are located in the realm of redemptive history and based on what covenantal structure we are currently operating under will determine in some measure the way in which we understand the nature of the people of God. As the church, coming after the life, death, resurrection, and ascension of Jesus, and operating under the auspices of an inaugurated new covenant, one must understand the membership of the church to be comprised of believers.[10] This is true since the structure and nature of the new covenant points us to a people who all know the Lord. Church membership is to be a regenerate membership.[11]

---

8. Stephen J. Wellum, "Beyond Mere Ecclesiology: The Church as God's New Covenant Community," in *The Community of Jesus: A Theology of the Church*, eds. Kendall H. Easley and Christopher W. Morgan (Nashville: B&H Academic, 2013), 198.

9. For a full study on the work of the Holy Spirit as it relates to progression of the covenants in redemptive history, see James M. Hamilton Jr., *God's Indwelling Presence: The Holy Spirit in the Old and New Testaments* (Nashville: B&H, 2006).

10. Saucy avers, "Regeneration is the prime requisite for membership in the church (1 Cor. 1:2). . . . [The church] is the fellowship of those who participate with Christ in vital union, who are 'by one Spirit . . . baptized into one body' (1 Cor. 12:13). Only those joined to Christ can be members of his church" (Robert L. Saucy, *The Church in God's Program* [Chicago: Moody, 1972], 103).

11. This is contra Michael Scott Horton, *People and Place: A Covenant Ecclesiology* (Louisville: Westminster John Knox Press, 2008), 119. Here Horton argues, regarding infant baptism, "God commanded the circumcision of every male infant (Gen. 17), so in their case it could not have signified and sealed a response they had already made. Whether administered before or after the act of faith, baptism remains a sign and seal of the righteousness that one has by faith alone (Col. 2:11–12)." This, however, flattens out the distinctiveness and progression of the covenants in Scripture and does not allow the discontinuity the new covenant rightly calls to itself in terms of the status of those who are part of that covenant.

This does not negate the fact that there will be times when the church allows someone into membership who has not truly believed in Jesus Christ. However, we receive people into the church on the basis of their profession that they have trusted in Jesus Christ.[12] This is much different than simply being a part of a nation in the OT or being part of a family as an infant in the NT. The nature and structure of the new covenant demands a certain kind of membership within the new covenant community, namely, a regenerate people in faith union with Christ, born of the Spirit, and declared just by God.

Summary

God manifests his glory through his kingdom, and we see the progression of how God's people relate to God's kingdom through his covenants. In other words, God reigns over God's people in God's place, but it is a reign that is progressively revealed. And God relates to his people by a series of covenants through which he initiates relationship. The new covenant, inaugurated in the person and work of Jesus Christ, shows a people who know the Lord, from the least to the greatest, are regenerate, and are all indwelt by the Spirit.

The existence of God's kingdom and his covenants relates directly to the way in which we think about the way God's people join with the new covenant community. The people of God under the Mosaic covenant were a mixed community, made up of both believers and unbelievers living together as one nation. Under the new covenant, the church is comprised of believers from the various nations of the world. Within this covenantal framework those who join the community must come under the stipulations of the covenant, which in this case means faith in Jesus Christ. As such, church members, as members of the new covenant community, are called to be regenerate if they are seeking to join the church, and churches are called to be vigilant and intentional as they bring in new members.

REFLECTION QUESTIONS

1. How would you define and articulate the reality of the kingdom of God?

2. What takes place biblically in the forming of a covenant?

3. What specific covenants do we see in Scripture?

4. What is the distinctiveness of the new covenant?

5. How does the new covenant give rise to regenerate church membership?

---

12. Wellum, "Beyond Mere Ecclesiology," 212.

Is Church Membership Biblical?

Beyond the theological framework mentioned in the last chapter to argue for church membership being made up of regenerate people, the common question that arises regarding this topic is if it is explicitly biblical. Can you go to a set of verses and passages and prove that church membership is a biblical idea? If not, can I simply attend a church and not worry about going through the process of joining?

These are fair questions and need to be addressed. Much like the Trinity, the term "church membership" cannot be found if you do a search in a concordance. However, the concept of membership and the implications for membership are found in numerous places throughout Scripture, especially the NT. As noted in the previous chapter, there are covenantal differences under the new covenant that must be noted when discussing the people of God. But there are also some OT trajectories to observe when forming the biblical picture of church membership. And more emphatically, we see NT evidence that the norm for the church should not merely be a loosely connected group of uncommitted attenders, but of members in covenant with God and one another.

OT Trajectories

As has been stated previously, while Israel and the church are not synonymous, and there are definite differences between the two, there is also continuity present. Thus one can look at OT trajectories that form a pattern for NT practice while being mindful of covenantal variances that do exist between Israel and the church. Looking at these OT trajectories applies as one examines the biblical pattern of church membership. Therefore, the trajectories will first be noted, followed by the distinct covenantal differences that set Israel and the church apart.

God called Abraham through whom a people as numerous as the stars would come. He promised this people a land and that they would be blessed and serve as a blessing to the nations (Gen. 12:1–3; 15:1–5). God was acquiring a congregation, purchased and redeemed to be his heritage (Ps. 74:2). To be a part of this covenant community, one was either born into the nation—with newborn boys receiving the covenant sign of circumcision (Gen. 17:9–14)—or one could come into the covenant community as a proselyte (Exod. 12:48–49; Deut. 29:10–13; Ezra 6:21). God covenanted with this nation and told them that if they obeyed the law that was given, they would be blessed, but that if they disobeyed that law they would be cursed by God (Deut. 28–30). Thus, the nation of Israel was a community, with a distinct "membership," a people who were in covenant with God and one another to live holy lives in the midst of the nations (Lev. 11:44–45).[1]

However, Israel, as God's covenant people, failed again and again to keep the covenant in the OT. As such, Israel experienced the covenantal curses of Deuteronomy and underwent exile from the land. The OT prophets, therefore, told of future hope wherein a king from the Davidic line would restore the nation (Jer. 23:5–6). There would be rebuilding, forgiveness of sin, and new hearts granted to the people (Ezek. 36:22–36). And this hope was not for the nation of Israel only. In the prophets there is anticipation of the time when non-Israelites would come to worship the Lord and be part of his covenant community (Isa. 49:5–6; Zeph. 2:11).[2] This future covenantal destination would be inclusive of a fully forgiven people (Jer. 31: 33–34) indwelt by the Spirit of God (Ezek. 36:26–27), bought by the shed blood of Jesus Christ (Matt. 26:28; Heb. 9:16–17, 22).

In the old covenant, all are members of a nation, but not all of Israel is truly Israel (Rom. 9:6). In the new covenant, all are members of a community, not by being born spiritually into a particular people group, but by being born again through the work of the Spirit (John 3:1–10). One enters the new covenant community through conversion, attested to by baptism. Thus, while different due to the covenantal expectations under which they operate, OT trajectories are present when noting membership in God's covenant community.

Local vs. Universal

The reader may note that what has just been described relates mainly on a universal level. However, the questions that are asked most often about church membership relate to the church as a local institution. Much more will be said on this topic (see Question 9), but at this point it is sufficient that the signs of the new covenant—namely, the ordinances of baptism and the Lord's

---

1. See Everett Ferguson, *The Church of Christ: A Biblical Ecclesiology for Today* (Grand Rapids: Eerdmans, 1996), 56–59.
2. For an extended treatment of this OT anticipation of Gentiles being part of God's covenant community through the work of Jesus Christ, see Jason S. DeRouchie, "Counting Stars with Abraham and the Prophets: New Covenant Ecclesiology in OT Perspective," *JETS* 58, no. 3 (2015): 445–85. A condensed version is found in "Father of a Multitude of Nations: New Covenant Ecclesiology in OT Perspective," in *Progressive Covenantalism: Charting a Course between Dispensational and Covenant Theologies*, eds. Stephen J. Wellum and Brent E. Parker (Nashville: B&H, 2016), 7–38.

Supper—are what make the church visible and thus local. In other words, God's people have a visible, corporate, political existence on earth.

Bobby Jamieson helpfully elaborates on this point: "By drawing a line between the church and the world, the ordinances make it possible to point to something and say 'church' rather than pointing to many somethings and saying 'Christians.' A church is born when gospel people form a gospel polity, and the ordinances are the effective sign of that polity. They give the church visible, institutional form and order. They knit many into one."[3] Baptism serves as the initiating-oath sign, and the Lord's Supper as the renewing-oath sign, of the new covenant. These are experienced and shared in local church communities operating within the parameters of the new covenant.

New Testament Witness

With this background regarding the universal and local church in mind, one should note that membership in a local church is rooted in the dynamic of shared life in the Spirit. Communing members are born of God, and their fellowship is with the Father and with the Son, Jesus Christ.[4] Church membership goes beyond mere attendance at a weekly gathering; it is participation in a divine reality. Thus, it is a high privilege to assemble with God's people and participate corporately in communing with God and ministering to one another.

Church membership can be defined simply as a formal commitment or covenant between an individual and a local church.[5] God calls for his people to gather corporately (notice, for example, that most of the NT epistles are addressed to specific churches), to submit to qualified leadership (1 Tim. 3:1–7; Titus 1:5–9), to come under the teaching of the Scriptures and faithfully partake of the ordinances (Acts 2:37–47; 1 Cor. 11:23–26; 2 Tim. 4:1–2), and to exercise the authority Christ has given to them (Matt. 16:19; 18:17). In Matthew 16, 18, and 28, Jesus gave the apostles and the apostolic church the power of the keys. This authorized the church to guard the gospel, affirm credible professions, to unite such professors to itself, oversee their discipleship, and exclude

---

3. Bobby Jamieson, *Going Public: Why Baptism Is Required for Church Membership* (Nashville: B&H Academic, 2015), 144.
4. See Mark Lauterbach, *The Transforming Community: The Practise of the Gospel in Church Discipline* (Ross-shire, Scotland: Christian Focus, 2003), 163.
5. Benjamin L. Merkle, "The Biblical Basis for Church Membership," in *Those Who Must Give an Account: A Study of Church Membership and Church Discipline*, eds. John S. Hammett and Benjamin L. Merkle (Nashville: B&H Academic, 2012), 32. Jonathan Leeman, *The Church and the Surprising Offense of God's Love: Reintroducing the Doctrines of Church Membership and Church Discipline* (Wheaton, IL: Crossway, 2010), 234, also helpfully defines church membership as a covenant union between a particular church and a Christian, consisting of the church's affirmation of the Christian's gospel profession (Matt. 16:19), the church's promise to give oversight to the Christian, and the Christian's promise to gather with the church and submit to its oversight (Heb. 3:12–13; 10:24–25; 13:17).

hypocrites.[6] As the people of God under the new covenant, a local church is committed to the truth that God is identifying them as a people for himself, distinguishing them from the world, calling them to righteousness, making them his witness, using them to display his glory, identifying them with one another, and rendering accountability and protection for members.[7] Thus, a local church gathers for a specific purpose, and they do so as the people of God who have been redeemed through faith in Christ (Col. 1:13–14).

While church membership may not be explicitly demonstrative within the NT, there is certainly evidence to the necessity of its existence within a local church. Observing Hebrews 13:17 and 1 Thessalonians 5:12–13, one can deduce that the kind of accountability spoken of demands a commitment made by an individual to formally join a local church.[8] Merkle also makes the simple point that church discipline as advocated in Matthew 18 and 1 Corinthians 5 cannot be properly carried out if a church does not have an official membership roll.[9]

Church members also have particular responsibilities toward one another, most generally that they love each other (John 13:34–35). This love includes watching over one another and holding each other accountable (Rom. 15:14; Gal. 6:1–2; Phil. 2:3–4; 2 Thess. 3:15; Heb. 12:15).[10] These commands to care for one another are given in order that believers would not be hardened by sin but instead would corporately pursue perseverance in the faith (Heb. 3:12–13; 10:24–25).[11] From this evidence one can thus observe the implicit standard of church membership in the NT as a pattern to be followed for today.

---

6. Leeman, *The Church and the Surprising Offense of God's Love,* 180. See also Derek Tidball, *Ministry by the Book: New Testament Patterns for Pastoral Leadership* (Downers Grove, IL: IVP Academic, 2008), 24.

7. See Leeman, *The Church and the Surprising Offense of God's Love,* 236–70.

8. Merkle states, "In order for Christians to give respect and recognition to their leaders, they must place themselves under the authority and accountability of those who will shepherd them. . . . Church membership provides the God-ordained means of providing accountability that all sheep need" ("The Biblical Basis for Church Membership," 36–37).

9. Ibid., 40. In Matthew 18:15–20 we see that the keys of the kingdom (Matt. 16:19) extend to the local church. As a result, Jonathan Leeman, asserts that "the local church has heaven's authority for declaring who on earth is a kingdom citizen and therefore represents heaven." (*Church Membership: How the World Knows Who Represents Jesus,* 9Marks [Wheaton, IL: Crossway, 2012], 61.)

10. Newport asserts, "The church is not a chance collection of people but a community of believers called and united together by the grace of God—a covenant people. Christian believers therefore accept responsibility for each other and agree to exercise such discipline as is necessary to remain faithful to God's covenant. The church should take seriously the Bible's many injunctions to warn, rebuke, exhort, encourage, and build one another up in love" (John P. Newport, "The Purpose of the Church," in *The People of God: Essays on the Believers' Church,* eds. Paul Basden, David S. Dockery, and James Leo Garrett [Nashville: Broadman, 1991], 28).

11. See David Peterson, who aptly observes, "Practical holiness means working out in everyday life and relationships the moral consequences of our union with Christ" (*Possessed*

Summary

Joining a local church is not just an idea someone came up with recently to ensure better attendance on a Sunday morning. As this chapter has demonstrated, church membership is a biblically defensible doctrine. Beginning with the OT one can see that, while taking into account the covenantal differences between Israel and the church, the nation of Israel was a community with a distinct "membership," a people who were in covenant with God and one another to live holy lives in the midst of the nations. This membership was being part of a nation with social and political components that differ from the makeup of the church under the new covenant. Nevertheless, the concept of membership and the people of God begins in the OT and serves as a trajectory for NT understanding.

The NT demonstrates that this membership is not merely in the universal church but is also comprised of belonging to and being in covenant with a local assembly of believers. God calls for believers to gather together locally, administer ordinances, exercise the authority of the keys of the kingdom, fulfill the "one another" commands, hold one another accountable, and exercise church discipline. Thus, while church membership is not explicitly mentioned in numerous places throughout the NT, one can see that all of the items listed previously assume and demand that people are gathered together locally and living out and overseeing one another's discipleship in specific ways. The Bible, therefore, calls us to submit to local church membership.

REFLECTION QUESTIONS

1. What OT trajectories can be noted that point someone toward the reality of membership within the people of God?

2. What is mentioned in this chapter that makes the church visible and thus local?

3. How is church membership defined in this chapter?

4. What other dimensions of church life are connected to church membership?

5. How is church membership connected to growth in sanctification?

---

by God: A New Testament Theology of Sanctification and Holiness, NSBT [Grand Rapids: Eerdmans, 1995], 114). In short, church membership demands that we exhort one another regularly so that we will not be hardened by the deceitfulness of sin (Heb. 3:12–13).

How Does Matthew 16 Speak Specifically to the Matter of Church Membership?

Jesus did not speak in abundant detail about the issue of church membership or discipline.[1] However, there are two key texts to be considered in the Gospels—namely, Matthew 16:13–19 and 18:15–20.[2] These passages have a close linguistic connection, particularly in their use of the term *ekklēsia* ("church"),[3] as well as with the concepts of "binding" and "loosing." While these connections need to be considered, the primary focus in this chapter will be on Matthew 16 and its specific relationship to the concept of church membership.

Context

Matthew 16 begins with a conversation between Jesus and the Pharisees and Sadducees, as these religious leaders ask Jesus to show them a sign from heaven in order to confirm his messiahship (16:1–4). Jesus does not give them what they ask for and later tells his disciples to beware the leaven, or teaching,

---

1. This chapter is derived from Jeremy M. Kimble, *That His Spirit May Be Saved: Church Discipline as a Means to Repentance and Perseverance* (Eugene, OR: Wipf and Stock, 2013), 37–42. Used by permission of Wipf and Stock Publishers (www.wipfandstock.com).
2. One could also look at other passages that speak to this issue more indirectly: Matthew 5:23–24; 7:1–5; Luke 6:37–42; 17:1–4; John 20:23.
3. Due to the rare usage of the term, some have doubted the veracity of its usage in the Gospel of Matthew. Two works that argue for the authenticity and the contextual and cultural fittingness of this term include Edmund P. Clowney, "The Biblical Theology of the Church," in *The Church in the Bible and the World: An International Study*, ed. D. A. Carson (Grand Rapids: Baker, 1987), 16–27; and Benjamin L. Merkle, "The Meaning of *ekklēsia* in Matthew 16:18 and 18:17," *BSac* 167, no. 667 (2010): 281–91.

of the Pharisees and the Sadducees (16:5–12). The disciples and Jesus then arrive in the region of Caesarea Philippi, where Jesus asks his followers the crucial question, "Who do people say that the Son of Man is?" (16:13). The disciples report that many are identifying him with John the Baptist, Elijah, Jeremiah, or one of the prophets (16:14). Jesus then becomes more specific in his questioning and asks his disciples (the "you" in verse 15 is plural) who they believe he is, to which Peter replies with the famous confession, "You are the Christ, the Son of the living God" (16:15–16).

Here the text turns in a direction that is important to our discussion on church membership, particularly as it relates to Matthew 18:15–20. Jesus answers Peter and calls him blessed, acknowledging that this information has not come from men but from God (16:17). He further declares that the man who made this confession is to be called *Petros* and that on this *petra*, or rock, the church would be built, which the gates of hell would not prevail against (16:18).[4] Though Peter is in view specifically in this text, progressive revelation points us to the apostles and prophets in general as being the foundation of the church, with Jesus being the chief cornerstone (Eph. 2:20).

Keys of the Kingdom

The climax of this section culminates with Jesus declaring, "I will give you the keys to the kingdom of heaven, and whatever you bind on earth shall be bound in heaven, and whatever you loose on earth shall be loosed in heaven" (16:19). One must come to terms with what exactly Jesus means when he refers to the "keys of the kingdom of heaven," the issue of "binding and loosing," and how these concepts relate to the kingdom of God, church membership, and discipline.[5] First of all, regarding the keys, Blomberg claims, "'The keys to

---

4. There has been great debate concerning this verse. Roman Catholics have taken this text to refer to Peter as the first pope, as well as the doctrine of apostolic succession. Some have argued that Jesus was speaking of himself as the "rock" in this passage. See R. C. H. Lenski, *The Interpretation of St. Matthew's Gospel* (Minneapolis: Augsburg, 1961), 626; John F. Walvoord, *Matthew: Thy Kingdom Come* (Chicago: Moody, 1974), 121–27. Other have argued that the "rock" refers to Peter's confession. For a thorough treatment of this viewpoint see Chrys C. Caragounis, *Peter and the Rock*, Beihefte Zur Zeitschrift Für Die Neutestamentliche Wissenschaft 58 (Berlin: W. de Gruyter, 1990). Jesus, however, seems to be referring to Peter as the rock upon which the church is built, since he will be a predominant leader of the apostles (as evidenced in Acts 1–12). This best fits the Matthean context, and it also coheres with other NT texts that speak of an apostolic foundation for the church (Eph. 2:20; Rev. 21:14). See BDAG s.v. πέτρα and Πέτρος, 809–10 for support of this interpretation, along with D. A. Carson, "Matthew" in *The Expositor's Bible Commentary*, rev. ed., eds. Tremper Longman and David E. Garland (Grand Rapids: Zondervan, 2006), 368; R. T. France, *The Gospel of Matthew*, NICNT (Grand Rapids: Eerdmans, 2007), 925; David L. Turner, *Matthew*, BECNT (Grand Rapids: Baker Academic, 2008), 400–4.

5. For a helpful article on the relationship between the gates of hell, the keys of the kingdom, and binding and loosing, see Joel Marcus, "The Gates of Hades and the Keys of the Kingdom (Matt. 16:18-19)," *CBQ* 50, no. 3 (1988): 443–55.

the kingdom' (16:19) almost certainly is based on the identical metaphor in Isaiah 22:22."[6] The prophet Isaiah is rebuking an unworthy steward of God's household and saying that authority will be transferred to Eliakim, who will, as a result, possess the key of David, with which he will "open and shut" (Isa. 22:20–22). Motyer notes that contextually and culturally, a key denotes "the power to make and enforce binding decisions."[7]

Connecting Matthew 16:19 to Isaiah 22:22, taking into account the parallel concept of the keys, signifies that Jesus is extending authority to Peter in particular, and later on to the church as a whole (see Matt. 18:18). Peter and the other apostles carry out their foundational ecclesiastical role through handling the keys or exercising kingdom authority (Isa. 22:15, 22; Rev. 1:18; 3:7; 9:1–6; 20:1–3). This authority is exercised through binding and loosing. The disciples are agents of the kingdom of God and, unlike the scribes and Pharisees, they are to use this authority to point others to God's kingdom (cf. Luke 11:52).

Binding and Loosing

Closely tied to the idea of the keys is the statement about "binding and loosing." Certainly there is the idea of authority here, similar to the keys of the kingdom, but the meaning is once again disputed. Some advocate that this phrase refers to authority in exorcism,[8] while others understand authority over entrance into the church to be in view.[9] Others compare Matthew 16:19 and 18:18 and conclude that binding and loosing refer to receiving someone into church membership or either denying them membership by means of not accepting their initial gospel profession, or through church discipline.[10] Turner avers, "Perhaps it is best . . . to combine the ideas of entry into the kingdom (Matt 16:9a, the 'keys') and maintenance of acceptable life within the community (16:9b–c)." If this is so, the "doctrine" and "discipline" are really one; and through the preaching of the gospel, the authorized agent opens the door to the Reign of God or shuts it off.[11] Thus, it appears that Jesus is

6. Craig Blomberg, *Matthew*, NAC 22 (Nashville: Broadman, 1992), 55. See also Carson, "Matthew," 370.

7. J. A. Motyer, *Isaiah: An Introduction and Commentary*, TOTC 18 (Downers Grove, IL: InterVarsity, 1999), 86.

8. Richard H. Hiers, "'Binding' and 'Loosing': The Matthean Authorizations," *JBL* 104, no. 2 (1985): 233–50.

9. See, for example, John Calvin, *A Harmony of the Gospels, Matthew, Mark and Luke* (Grand Rapids: Eerdmans, 1972), 292–93.

10. William David Davies and Dale C. Allison, *Commentary on Matthew VIII-XVIII.*, vol. 2, ICC (Edinburgh: T&T Clark, 1998), 684; J. Andrew Overman, *Church and Community in Crisis: The Gospel According to Matthew* (Valley Forge: Trinity Press International, 1996), 267–75.

11. Turner, *Matthew*, 408. See also R. Albert Mohler, "Church Discipline," in *Polity: Biblical Arguments on How to Conduct Church Life*, ed. Mark E. Dever (Washington, DC: Center for Church Reform, 2000), 53.

giving authority to Peter and the other disciples to admit people into membership and to judge a person within the body of Christ based on the truths of Scripture and that person's adherence (or lack thereof) to the proclamation of the gospel.

An important parallel passage to consider alongside Matthew 16 is John 20:23, where the disciples are told, "If you forgive the sins of any, they are forgiven them; if you withhold forgiveness from any, it is withheld." As we will note in our interaction with Matthew 18 more specifically, there is a similar use of phraseology and verb tenses being utilized here and in Matthew 16.[12] The significance of this linguistic parallel resides in the fact that as the apostles function on the authority of Scripture, what they determine regarding the legitimacy of a person's conversion experience (i.e., fitness for membership) will have already been determined in heaven.

One must be careful not to extract from a text like Matthew 16 more than is actually there. However, one must also observe the linguistic parallels evident in Matthew 16, 18, and John 20. A connection seemingly exists, connoting a progression in understanding, revealing a crucial concept regarding ecclesial authority. In summarizing the importance of Matthew 16 as it relates to church membership, Leeman asserts that text teaches us three principles: first, Jesus authorized the church to be the proclaimer and guardian of the good news of Jesus Christ; second, Jesus authorized his church to affirm any individual who credibly professes the gospel, just as Jesus affirmed Peter for his profession of faith; and, third, Christ authorizes his church on earth to unite such professors in its care-giving embrace.[13] As such, this is a crucial passage to take into account when considering the importance and necessity of church membership.

Summary

Matthew 16 provides somewhat difficult but needful information about church membership. Concepts such as "the keys of the kingdom" and "binding and loosing" must be properly interpreted and applied to local church contexts. In its near context, Matthew 16:16–19 refers to the apostles as the gatekeepers of the kingdom, guiding the authoritative proclamation of Matthew 16:16, permitting entrance to the kingdom through the church for those who

---

12. In Matthew 16:19 and 18:18 one sees that the words for "binding" (*dedemenon*) and "loosing" (*lelymenon*) are perfect passive participles. In John 20:23 the terms *apheōntai* and *kekratēntai* are perfect passive indicatives. Thus, while John 20:23 contains indicatives and not participles, a similar structure still exists in the kinds of terms used. More detail will be given in the chapter dealing with Matthew 18:15–20 regarding the significance of the verb tenses in these passages.

13. Jonathan Leeman, *The Church and the Surprising Offense of God's Love: Reintroducing the Doctrines of Church Membership and Church Discipline* (Wheaton, IL: Crossway, 2010), 192–93.

confess Jesus. Also, in an indirect way, this passage speaks to the authority of the church, an authority that is later shown as sufficient to keep members or expel them through church discipline—potentially demonstrating through lack of repentance that they may be recipients of God's condemnation rather than his forgiveness (see Question 22 regarding Matt. 18:15–20).

This is a crucial foundation when considering the importance of the church as a whole, and the way in which authority is vested by Christ in a gathered congregation to affirm and deny people into membership based on their belief in Jesus Christ for salvation. The ministry of the keys must be properly exercised by the congregation for the membership of the church to operate as it is intended.

REFLECTION QUESTIONS

1. How does Jesus respond to Peter's confession in Matthew 16?

2. What are the keys of the kingdom?

3. What is the meaning of "binding" and "loosing"?

4. How does John 20:23 help us in interpreting Matthew 16:19?

5. How does this vision of membership affect the way we should be approaching it in our churches?

How Has the Church Practiced Membership throughout Its History?

From the earliest days of the Christianity, believers organized themselves into local gatherings called churches.[1] They met together regularly, baptized new converts, participated in the Lord's Supper, and had a specific kind of leadership structure. While belonging to a specific local church and committing to live the Christian life with a particular group of fellow Christians may not have been called "church membership" in the earliest days, the concept is clearly present.

During the past 2,000 years, church membership has been abdicated, recovered, and modified in various ways. Finn rightly observes, "Factors influencing church membership practices include theological convictions, political and social context, and pragmatic considerations."[2] As such, historical consideration of church membership is necessary to understand the direction the church has gone on the topic of membership. This chapter will thus offer a brief look at church membership within the four main eras of church history: Patristic, Medieval, Reformation, and Modern.

Patristic Era (AD 100–500)

This era of church history is important to note as it resides most closely to the times of the NT. However, as one studies the concept of church membership in this era, it is apparent that ecclesiological change came in rather rapid fashion. And the changes that came about for identifying the members of the

---

1. A helpful secondary source on this topic that is utilized in various sections of this chapter is Nathan A. Finn, "A Historical Analysis of Church Membership," in *Those Who Must Give an Account: A Study of Church Membership and Church Discipline*, eds. John S. Hammett and Benjamin L. Merkle (Nashville: B&H Academic, 2012), 53–79.
2. Ibid., 53.

churches were also tied to other key components of ecclesiology, particularly the doctrine of baptism.

In the earliest NT churches, one sees that baptism and church membership apparently followed close on the heels of conversion (Acts 2:41–47; 8:35–39). However, according to second-century sources, such as the Didache and the works of Justin Martyr, by the mid-second century conversion and baptism were separated by a period of moral instruction, prayer, and fasting. This separation between conversion and baptism led to two classes of membership: baptismal candidates and full communicant members.[3] While baptismal candidates were not allowed to participate in communion, which was reserved for full communicant members, they were required to attend church services and were subject to church discipline.[4]

This two-tiered approach to membership continued and progressed throughout this era of church history. In fact, the pre-baptism probationary period expanded to such a degree that some patristic sources call for a period of up to three years prior to being able to join as a full member.[5] These prospective baptismal candidates, now referred to as catechumens, were held to the same standards and restrictions as previously, but obviously for a greater length of time.

This pattern of instructing catechumens persisted into the third century, though the standards for membership lessened in many respects with Constantine's legalization of Christianity in 313. By the sixth century, the idea of the catechumenate was on the decline. The citizens of the Roman Empire increasingly identified with Christianity, at least outwardly. This brought a vast increase to the number of catechumens to be dealt with, and thus the instructional period for candidates for membership decreased from three years to forty days, normally coinciding with Lent.[6] Within this time period, the rise of paedobaptism also contributed to the collapse of regenerate church membership. While credobaptism was practiced by the early church, by the fifth century, infant baptism had emerged as the preferred practice in the church.[7] This doctrinal shift coincided with the belief that the church was in fact a "mixed body." Augustine, for example, in opposition to the Donatists

---

3. For more details on this practice, see Jack P. Lewis, "Baptismal Practices of the 2nd and 3rd Century Church," *RQ* 26, no. 1 (1983): 1–17.

4. See Didache and Justin Martyr, *First Apology*, in *Life and Practice in the Early Church: A Documentary Reader*, ed. Steven A. McKinion (New York: NYU Press, 2001), 7–9.

5. Hippolytus, *Apostolic Tradition*, 17. Available at http://bombaxo.com/hippolytus.html (accessed 3/9/15). For further detail, see also Clinton E. Arnold, "Early Church Catechesis and New Christians' Classes in Contemporary Evangelicalism," *JETS* 47, no. 1 (2004) 39–54.

6. Everett Ferguson, ed., *Encyclopedia of Early Christianity*, vol. 1, 2nd ed. (New York: Garland, 1997), s.v. "Conversion."

7. For an introduction of the transition that took place in regards to baptism, see Steven A. McKinion, "Baptism in the Patristic Writings," in *Believer's Baptism: Sign of the New Covenant in Christ*, eds. Thomas R. Schreiner and Shawn D. Wright (Nashville: B&H, 2006), 163–88.

held that the church is composed of both genuine believers and false members, both wheat and tares.[8]

As infant baptism became increasingly popular, less emphasis was placed on teaching adults prior to baptism. Instead, increasingly churches sought to baptize infants and prepare those children, through confirmation, for full membership. As the church spread into the west, it became a common pattern to baptize and allow someone into membership with no catechetical instruction. In many cases, the only requirements were renunciation of the pagan gods and a willingness to be baptized.[9] As such, church membership, whether initiated through infant baptism or adult confession, had lost its meaning in terms of separating the regenerate from the rest of the world.

Medieval Era (AD 500–1500)

Church membership continued to diverge from NT precedent as infant baptism became the dominant position of the church. Two other factors for change include the Christendom models of church-state relations and a greater emphasis on the universality of the church. Charlemagne was the first in the ninth century to govern his vast territory as a self-consciously divinely appointed ruler. This Holy Roman Empire was to be a political entity like its predecessor, the Roman Empire, but with distinctly Christian rulers.[10] The empire would give recognition to the true church, that is, the Roman Catholic Church, and this relationship of church and state would dominate the ecclesiology of the Middle Ages. As such, infant baptism was a sign tantamount to both church membership and citizenship.[11] This made church membership not a free decision based on conversion, but rather part and parcel of merely living in a certain geographical locale.

Regarding the universality of the church, emphasis was placed here especially as the churches of the East and West continued to vie for authority. After the Great Schism of 1054 which finalized the growing split between Eastern Orthodoxy and Western Catholicism, the Church of Rome placed great emphasis not on local parishes but on the universal church. This is due to the overarching hierarchy of the Roman Church, with the pope being the earthly head of the church. Priests worked under the authority of pope, cardinals, and bishops and administered the seven sacraments—through which saving grace was imparted—with the authority of the Church of Rome. These factors led to a lessened call for any kind of robust regenerate church membership.

---

8. Augustine, *The City of God*, 1.35, in *NPNF*, 3:258; idem, *On Baptism, Against the Donatists*, 1.14, in *NPNF*, 4:418. See also Gregg R. Allison, *Historical Theology: An Introduction to Christian Doctrine* (Grand Rapids: Zondervan, 2011), 570–72.
9. See Richard Fletcher, *The Barbarian Conversions: From Paganism to Christianity* (Berkeley: University of California Press, 1999); Finn, "A Historical Analysis of Church Membership," 57.
10. Allison, *Historical Theology*, 573.
11. Joseph H. Lynch, *The Medieval Church: A Brief History* (New York: Longman, 1992), 158–59.

Reformation Era (AD 1500–1750)

The time of the Reformation led to vast changes within the church, and this included, for some movements, the way in which they approached church membership. Two prominent groups in this time include the Magisterial Reformers and the Free-Church Protestants. The Magisterial Reformers included those reformers who carried out their work of reformation with the power of state authorities backing their efforts.[12] Whether Lutheran, Reformed, or Church of England, the Magisterial Reformers embraced modified versions of the Christendom model, sometimes referred to as the "territorial church." This was very similar to the medieval model, but it allowed the religion of the secular rulers to also be the religion of the citizenry, whether that be Lutheranism, Reformed theology, or Anglicanism.[13] These groups practiced infant baptism (though there were differences in how they conceived of their baptismal theologies) and required a later confirmation as a prerequisite to full membership in the church. All three of these movements believed that the ideal was for all the citizens in their respective territories to be baptized as infants, confirmed, and brought in as full members of the official state church.

Free Church Protestantism similarly rejected the Christendom model but went further in their reforms. One branch of this group, sometimes referred to as the "Radical Reformers,"[14] rejected infant baptism for confessor baptism and espoused a voluntary approach to church membership which was based on genuine conversion. In England, Free Church congregations emerged in the mid-sixteenth century. The Separatists—those who argued for withdrawal from the Church of England and the formation of autonomous churches—agreed with Anabaptists that church membership should be a voluntary decision by a converted adult. However, unlike the Anabaptists, they continued to embrace the Reformed teaching on infant baptism. The Separatists, along with the Congregationalists of the seventeenth century, argued for a membership that was built around a confession of faith and a common covenant that would spell out correct attitudes and actions within the church.[15]

English Baptists are also an important group to consider within this era. While differing on points of doctrine such as Calvinism, the extent

---

12. Timothy George, *Theology of the Reformers*, rev. ed. (Nashville: B&H Academic, 2013), 98.
13. See Allison, *Historical Theology*, 602–4; Finn, "A Historical Analysis of Church Membership," 60–61.
14. The Radical Reformers were a diverse group, but most well known amongst them were the Anabaptists. For further details on this movement, see William R. Estep, *The Anabaptist Story: An Introduction to Sixteenth-Century Anabaptism*, 3rd ed. (Grand Rapids: Eerdmans, 1996); George Hunston Williams, *The Radical Reformation*, Dissent and Nonconformity Series 11 (Paris: Baptist Standard Bearer, 2001).
15. For a discussion of the early Separatist movement in England, see B. R. White, *The English Separatists Tradition: From the Marian Martyrs to the Pilgrim Fathers* (Oxford: Oxford University Press, 1971).

of the atonement, or the proper day of Christian worship, early Baptists agreed on a number of key points. Aside from a minority among English Baptists adopting an open membership policy (i.e., no requirement of confessor baptism for those who wanted to join in membership and had been baptized as infants),[16] the majority of early Baptists rejected infant baptism, affirmed a voluntary membership, and advocated for a free church in a free state.[17]

Modern Era (1750–present)

The beginnings of the modern era in the West revolve, in great measure, around the awakenings of the eighteenth century. In early American life a number of pastors, most notable perhaps Solomon Stoddard, had adopted what came to be known as the "Half-Way Covenant." In this arrangement, unconverted adults were allowed into partial membership, and thus, while they could not vote, they agreed to the church's confession, submitted to the church's discipline, and were able to have their children baptized. However, by the eighteenth and nineteenth centuries there was increasing emphasis on conversion and the new birth as a prerequisite to full church membership. Under the preaching and influence of men like Jonathan Edwards, the Wesleys, Howell Harris, and George Whitefield, the Great Awakening solidified a belief in individual conversion for membership among many branches of Protestantism.[18]

The Second Great Awakening of the nineteenth century brought an increasing emphasis on the new birth, spiritual awakening, and evangelism, and this influenced the approach of churches to membership. In many ways, church worship itself became primarily concerned with evangelism, baptism, and membership. By the mid-twentieth century, many evangelical churches had shifted in viewing themselves preeminently as baptized, covenanted, local assemblies, to functioning primarily as outreach centers and corporate worship services as catalysts for revival. This perspective made the process for joining a church generally much quicker and more accessible. With this emphasis there has also been a slow decline in church discipline that can also be noted.[19] However, there have been a number of voices in recent decades

---

16. See B. R. White, "Open and Closed Membership among English and Welsh Baptists," *Baptist Quarterly* 24 (1972): 330–34.
17. For an excellent study on Baptist history that develops the details of this era and beyond, see Anthony L. Chute, Nathan A. Finn, and Michael A. G. Haykin, *The Baptist Story: From English Sect to Global Movement* (Nashville: B&H Academic, 2015).
18. For further details, see Thomas S. Kidd, *The Great Awakening: The Roots of Evangelical Christianity in Colonial America* (New Haven, CT: Yale University Press, 2007).
19. For one example of this phenomena, see Gregory A. Wills, *Democratic Religion: Freedom, Authority, and Church Discipline in the Baptist South, 1785-1900* (New York: Oxford University Press, 1997).

calling for a renewed emphasis on regenerate church membership and church discipline, and this is has been a very positive development.[20]

Summary

While changing in varying degrees, one can see that church membership has been held up as an important practice throughout church history. Differing in stance on the timing of membership, the amount of information needed to become a member, and the status of one's salvation in joining a church, the discussion has been front and center for some time. It is crucial, therefore, that we understand this is not a peripheral matter, either doctrinally or practically. Church membership has been tied historically to a certain understanding of the nature of the church, and this affects the way one thinks about the makeup of the church as well as the doctrine of salvation. Practically, membership is historically attested in the various eras of church history. While not on the same level of authority as Scripture, tradition should shape our thinking in some measure in understanding the importance of church membership for the life of the church.

REFLECTION QUESTIONS

1. What are the different eras of church history?

2. How did the church think of and practice church membership in the Patristic Era?

3. How did the church think of and practice church membership in the Medieval Era?

4. How did the church think of and practice church membership in the Reformation Era?

5. How did the church think of and practice church membership in the Modern Era?

---

20. See, for example, Mark Dever, *Nine Marks of a Healthy Church* (Wheaton: Crossway, 2004), 147–66; Kevin DeYoung and Ted Kluck, *Why We Love the Church: In Praise of Institutions and Organized Religion* (Chicago: Moody, 2009); John S. Hammett, *Biblical Foundations for Baptist Churches: A Contemporary Ecclesiology* (Grand Rapids: Kregel, 2005), 109–31.

How Does Church Membership Relate to Baptism and the Lord's Supper?

Church membership exists at a local church level, and the local church is identified by a people who covenant together to oversee one another's discipleship in Christ. As the new covenant people of God they live as a community, directed by the Word of God. They seek to fulfill the "one another" commands for one another that are given as directives in the NT. As new members seek to join this community, and as they continue to live in solidarity with one another, there are signs of the new covenant that are administered, namely, baptism and the Lord's Supper.

These ordinances of the church are significant in that they are what make the church visible.[1] As the church is a people called out by God, the ordinances are the means of showing the world where local churches are assembled and united around the gospel of Jesus Christ. This chapter will argue that baptism is the initiating oath-sign of the new covenant, and the Lord's Supper serves as the renewing oath-sign of the new covenant. As was stated previously, the nature of God's kingdom and his covenants relates directly to the way in which we think about how God's people join with the new covenant community. And this new covenant community is a believing community. Thus, to be members of a local church, one must be a member of the new covenant through faith in Christ, and the initiating and renewing signs of that covenant are the ordinances. Therefore, we will look at these ordinances in detail with an eye to their relationship to church membership.

---

1. Bobby Jamieson asserts, "Baptism and the Lord's Supper are effective signs of church membership; they create the social, ecclesial reality to which they point" (*Going Public: Why Baptism Is Required for Church Membership* [Nashville: B&H Academic, 2015], 2).

Baptism

Baptism is the act of immersing a professing Christian in water,[2] and there are several truths this act signifies. First, as this act is done in the name of the Father, Son, and Holy Spirit, this act associates the new Christian with the triune God. This is fitting in that salvation is also a Trinitarian work (Eph. 1:3–14).[3] Second, the mode of baptism (i.e., immersion) connects this act with the saving work of Christ in his death, burial, and resurrection (Rom. 6:1–5). Lowering a person completely under water, and raising them back up symbolically shows their identification with Jesus' death and resurrection and demonstrates that they are new creations in Christ (2 Cor. 5:17). Third, immersing baptism signifies an individual's cleansing from sin. [4]

Finally, baptism symbolizes incorporation into the new covenant community. In reviewing from a previous chapter, one must recognize the covenantal shift that has occurred in Christ. The people of God in the OT (Israel) were a community made up of both believers and unbelievers. The new covenant, however, has a community comprised of those who have placed faith in Jesus Christ. The new covenant sign is applied to new covenant members once they have entered into new covenant status.

Thus, becoming a Christian, while certainly personal, is never a totally private affair. While one recognizes their status before God changes through personal faith in Jesus Christ, salvation also ushers a person into the community of faith. And baptism is the initiating oath-sign of the new covenant wherein a person's faith goes public as they join in covenant membership with a local assembly of believers. This assembly can bring the new member in, as they are functioning with the keys of the kingdom (Matt. 16:18–19; 18:18), which grants authority to the church to publicly affirm those who credibly profess faith in Christ. In this initial authoritative act, the individual speaks to God and the church, and the church speaks for God to the individual in agreeing to baptize them, knowing what that act signifies. Baptism, thus, identifies someone as a member of Christ's kingdom and inaugurates them into kingdom citizenship and church membership.[5]

---

2. Dealing with the debates surrounding infant baptism and believer's baptism is beyond the scope of this chapter. For someone seeking more information on that topic, readers would be well served in reading John H. Armstrong, ed., *Understanding Four Views on Baptism* (Grand Rapids: Zondervan, 2007); Thomas R. Schreiner and Shawn D. Wright, eds., *Believer's Baptism: Sign of the New Covenant in Christ* (Nashville: B&H Academic, 2006); David F. Wright, ed., *Baptism: Three Views* (Downers Grove, IL: IVP Academic, 2009).
3. For more on the Trinitarian shape of salvation, see Fred Sanders, *The Deep Things of God: How the Trinity Changes Everything* (Wheaton, IL: Crossway, 2010).
4. Gregg R. Allison, *Sojourners and Strangers: The Doctrine of the Church* (Wheaton, IL: Crossway, 2012), 355.
5. See Jamieson, *Going Public*, 81–105.

The Lord's Supper

If baptism is the initiating oath-sign of the new covenant, then the Lord's Supper is the renewing oath-sign of the new covenant. This practice is a transformation of the Passover meal, where now we look to Christ, our Passover Lamb, who has been sacrificed for our sins (1 Cor. 5:7). In the Lord's Supper the church observes the elements of bread and wine, remembering Christ's death (Luke 22:19–21), uniting around the beauty of the gospel (1 Cor. 11:17–34), and anticipating the coming marriage supper of the Lamb where we will all partake with our Lord (Rev. 19:6–10).[6] We repeatedly ratify the new covenant, renewing our trust in Christ and commitment to his people. Baptism, therefore, is the initiating sign that makes the church visible in bringing believers in Jesus Christ into the community. And the Lord's Supper is the ordinance that the visible, local church partakes of, as a sign of their mutual commitment to believe in and live out the gospel (Phil. 1:27).

The Anabaptist theologian Balthasar Hubmaier makes some helpful remarks in connecting baptism, the Lord's Supper, and church membership. Hubmaier identifies the church as a body of believers that assembles to observe baptism and the Lord's Supper, and possesses the power to bind and loose with the keys of the kingdom. He states that the church has the power of fraternal admonition because of the baptismal pledge, "in which one has made himself subject to the church and all her members, according to the word of Christ."[7] The church members thus pledge to fulfill the ministry of "fraternal admonition," or mutual exhortation, for one another. While formative in nature, to ensure continued Christian growth, this exhortation can escalate, if necessary, to the point that an individual would undergo "the ban," or corrective church discipline, which, among other restrictions, would include removal from participation in the Lord's Supper.[8]

Hubmaier further maintained, in connection with these doctrines, that Christ assigned to the church two ministerial powers: binding and loosing. This power to bind and loose is linked to the keys of the kingdom, as indicated in Matthew 16:19 and 18:18. And Hubmaier associated the keys with the practice of baptism and the Lord's Supper.[9] He asserts, "For in water bap-

---

6. Again, as with baptism, there are disputes about the Lord's Supper that go beyond the purview of this chapter. For further study, see John S. Hammett, *40 Questions about Baptism and the Lord's Supper* (Grand Rapids: Kregel Academic, 2015); Thomas R. Schreiner and Matthew R. Crawford, eds., *The Lord's Supper: Remembering and Proclaiming Christ until He Comes* (Nashville: B&H Academic, 2010).
7. Balthasar Hubmaier, "A Christian Catechism," in *Balthasar Hubmaier: Theologian of Anabaptism*, eds. H. Wayne Pipkin and John Howard Yoder, Classics of the Radical Reformation 5 (Scottdale, PA: Herald, 1989), 353.
8. See ibid., 353–54.
9. Hubmaier, "On the Christian Ban," 410–11. McMullan concurs and further describes Hubmaier's view: "[The keys] were intricately related to the doctrines of baptism and the Lord's Supper for Hubmaier, and together they authorized the church to receive repentant

tism the church uses the key of admitting and loosing, but in the Supper the key of excluding, binding, and locking away, as Christ promises and gives to it the power of the forgiveness of sins."[10]

In essence, Hubmaier viewed the church as a community of believers who publicly pledged to live the life of a disciple of Christ at baptism and who continued to pledge obedience to Christ at the Lord's Supper, lest they come under the discipline of the church.[11] And this is in keeping with NT practice.[12]

Summary

Baptism, the Lord's Supper, and church membership are tightly linked practices. The new covenant has been enacted through the person and work of Jesus Christ, such that all those who are united to Christ by faith are part of this covenant community. As the church gathers in local assemblies, the church is made visible through baptizing professing believers, bringing them into membership, and then constantly celebrating this solidarity shared around the gospel through the partaking of the Lord's Supper. Baptism is the initiating oath-sign of the new covenant, and the Lord's Supper is the renewing oath-sign of the new covenant.

With these theological points in place, one can understand the importance of such practices for church membership. The local church is to enact these signs as the church possesses the keys of the kingdom. They authorize new members to join and signify their affirmation of a person's profession of faith through the ordinance of baptism. The ongoing sign of affirmation is the continual partaking of the Lord's Supper together. As such, these ordinances should be done within the local church, for the upbuilding of the local church, as the church is responsible to oversee the lives of those they affirm as being true believers in Jesus Christ.

REFLECTION QUESTIONS

1. What is baptism? What does it signify?

2. What is the Lord's Supper? What does it signify?

---

sinners into a local congregation and to exclude those same ones if they were unwilling to behave in a morally upright way" (William E. McMullan, "Church Discipline as a Necessary Function of the Visible Church in the Theology of Balthasar Hubmaier" [PhD diss., Southeastern Baptist Theological Seminary, 2003], 38).

10. Hubmaier, "Dialogue with Zwingli's Baptism Book," 175. See also, Hubmaier, "A Christian Catechism," 341.

11. See Hubmaier, "On Fraternal Admonition," 383–85.

12. For further thoughts on Hubmaier's ecclesiology, see Jeremy M. Kimble, *That His Spirit May Be Saved: Church Discipline as a Means to Repentance and Perseverance* (Eugene, OR: Wipf and Stock, 2013), 76–84.

3. How are the ordinances connected to the reality of the new covenant?

4. How are the ordinances connected to the reality of the church membership?

5. Why should these ordinances be practiced by church members within a local church?

SECTION B

Ministry Questions

How Is Membership Related to Making Disciples?

The great task of the church is often referred to as the Great Commission: "Go therefore and make disciples of all nations, baptizing them in the name of the Father and of the Son and of the Holy Spirit, teaching them to observe all that I have commanded you. And behold, I am with you always, to the end of the age" (Matt. 28:19–20). As we faithfully proclaim the gospel, planting and watering with the truth, we see God draw people to himself and commit themselves to belief in the person and work of Jesus Christ, following him as their Lord (1 Cor. 3:5–9). In other words, we see disciples being made and growing through gospel proclamation, ongoing instruction, and life-on-life modeling.

People often separate the concept of church membership from discipleship because they seldom connect discipleship in any real way to the life of the local church. However, there is a definite connection between membership and discipleship in both the initiation of recognizing the person as a disciple and in dedicating as a body to that person's continued growth as a disciple. As such, an understanding must be attained in terms of what a disciple is definitionally, how discipleship works, and finally, how membership in a local church is connected to those two concepts.

What Is a Disciple?

When someone thinks of a disciple their mind likely goes to the first century, when Jesus walked the earth and had twelve followers he referred to as disciples. However, as we see in the Great Commission, the concept of "disciple" does not end with Jesus' earthly ministry, as his first followers were called to continue to make disciples of Jesus.[1] Therefore, what we see as an

---

1. Ferguson rightly notes, "Jesus' disciples did not function as rabbis, making their own disciples and setting up a train of tradition, but brought others into personal discipleship to

example and model in the Gospels must also translate to our lives as we work to make more disciples of Jesus.

The standard definition of a "disciple" is someone who adheres to the teachings of another; a follower, student, or learner. It refers to someone who takes up the ways of someone else. Applied to Jesus, a disciple is someone who learns from him to live like him—someone who, because of God's awakening grace, conforms his or her words and ways to the words and ways of Jesus. Or, you might say, as others have put it in the past, disciples of Jesus are themselves "little Christs" (Acts 11:26; 26:28). Parnell wisely observes, "We follow Jesus [in conversion] into a new world, not as mere pedagogy, but as fellowship. We come not as objective pupils, but as rebellious creatures made alive for the first time—rebellious creatures now reconciled to God by the death of his Son. Discipleship—following Jesus—is to live before God's face, to dwell in his presence, to be satisfied in all that he is."[2] Most fundamentally, to follow Jesus means to worship and obey him exclusively.

What Is Discipleship?

The task is to make more and more disciples of Jesus, and discipleship is about training for growth in godliness (1 Tim. 4:7). The church wants these disciples to increasingly look like Jesus. When we disciple others, the aim of our efforts is love for God and for others that flows from "a pure heart and a good conscience and a sincere faith" (1 Tim. 1:5). To say it another way, the aim of discipleship is maturity: "Him we proclaim, warning everyone and teaching everyone with all wisdom, that we may present everyone mature in Christ" (Col. 1:28). Or we might talk about being conformed to the image of God's Son (Rom. 8:29). This involves denying self (worldly pleasure to get the greatest treasure, namely, Jesus Christ), taking up your cross, and following Jesus in every aspect of life (Matt. 16:24).

There are a number of means to growth as a disciple: worship, preaching, the church's missional enterprise, baptism, the Lord's Supper, counseling, community groups, and personal mentoring.[3] While all of these aspects merit attention, the focus here will be more general in nature. When looking at the list above, one can observe that there are two distinct aspects of discipleship. First, discipleship involves instruction on the part of the teacher and hearing and thinking on the part of the follower (2 Tim. 2:2, 7). The instruction involved in discipleship is gospel content along with the exhortations, commands,

---

Jesus (Matt. 11:28–30; 23:8; 28:18–20; John 8:31; cf. 1 Cor. 1:12–13)" (Everett Ferguson, *The Church of Christ: A Biblical Ecclesiology for Today* [Grand Rapids: Eerdmans, 1996], 299).

2. Jonathan Parnell, "The Heart of Discipleship," *Desiring God*, May 25, 2012, http://www.desiringgod.org/articles/the-heart-of-discipleship (accessed 3/17/16).

3. See Gregg R. Allison, *Sojourners and Strangers: The Doctrine of the Church* (Wheaton, IL: Crossway, 2012), 441.

warnings, and promises that flow from it. Therefore, discipleship will involve biblical instruction, correction, rebuke, and admonishment (2 Tim. 3:16–17).

Second, discipleship involves modeling on the part of the teacher and seeing and practicing on the part of the disciple (1 Cor. 11:1; Phil. 4:9; 2 Tim. 3:10–11). Paul was not shy about calling people to imitate his faith, as long as they imitated the ways in which he was imitating Christ. In fact, part of Christian leadership is living in such a way that people can look at your life and seek to imitate the facets that are consistently conforming to the character and ways of Christ (Heb. 13:7). So again, for the teacher, discipleship involves modeling; and for the disciple, it involves seeing and practicing, forming habits of virtue that spring from new life in Christ (2 Cor. 3:18) and the indwelling Holy Spirit (1 Cor. 6:18–20).[4]

The Relationship between Membership and Discipleship

This understanding of what a disciple and discipleship is helps pave the way for seeing the significance of church membership. People are brought into the membership of a local church based on their profession of faith in Jesus Christ, and thereby they become a part of a particular group of people who strive together, by the grace of God and the power of the Spirit, to live in obedience to him. Banks further maintains that Christians are to see themselves as members of a divine family. Family terminology is utilized by Paul to demonstrate the kind of membership one inhabits when joining the church as a member (Rom. 16:13; Gal. 6:10; Eph. 2:19; Col 4:7). In viewing the church as family, emphasis is also put on the responsibilities that church members have to one another.[5]

We are a family of fellow disciples, covenanting together to oversee one another's discipleship. Christians too often fail to place discipleship in *submission* to the local church and its leaders. We might enjoy casual fellowship, but we don't deliberately build relationships for the purposes of discipline, equipping, transparency, and accountability.[6] This is crucial in linking discipleship and membership.[7] In recovering a meaningful church membership we are tasked then with creating a culture of discipleship within the church.

---

4. For more detail on this approach to discipleship, see Michael Horton, *The Gospel Commission: Recovering God's Strategy for Making Disciples* (Grand Rapids: Baker, 2012); James G. Samra, *Being Conformed to Christ in Community: A Study of Maturity, Maturation and the Local Church in the Undisputed Pauline Epistles* (New York: T&T Clark, 2006).
5. See Robert J. Banks, *Paul's Idea of Community* (Peabody, MA: Hendrickson, 1994), 54–57.
6. See Jonathan Leeman, "Introduction—Why Polity?" in *Baptist Foundations: Church Government for an Anti-Institutional Age*, eds. Mark Dever and Jonathan Leeman (Nashville: B&H Academic, 2015), 12.
7. Leeman maintains, "The Christian life should be placed inside the accountability and authorizing structures of the local church both because Jesus commands it and because that's how both the individual and the body grow best." Ibid., 13.

Members must be encouraged to submit to and give of themselves in love toward one another. As members, they are called to care for one another in specific ways, not living the Christian life in isolation.

This point is described in texts such as Hebrews 3:12–13 and 10:23–25. Both of these passages assume that one is joined to a local church and under its authority. Hebrews 3:12–13 warns of an evil, unbelieving heart leading any in the church to "fall away from the living God," and as such the author admonishes the church to exhort one another so they will not be "hardened by the deceitfulness of sin." Commenting on this passage, Davis declares that we must live together in close community with such wisdom and spiritual attentiveness that we can see if a brother or sister is developing an "evil, unbelieving heart that departs from the living God." The passage says that sin is deceitful and that it has a gradual hardening effect on our hearts. A healthy church will be filled with people who care about the spiritual well-being of fellow church members, and who "encourage each other daily," warning about the effects of sin.[8] For the community addressed in Hebrews struggling with the problem of spiritual drifting, hardening of the heart was a real danger. Thus, mutual exhortation to flee from sin and pursue righteousness was essential, and this happens in a local church membership dedicated to discipleship.[9]

Similarly, Hebrews 10:23–25 contains an exhortation to God's people to meet together continually and to consider how they can "stir up one another to love and good works." This is the point of discipleship: to flee sin and pursue righteousness. If church membership consists in the church's public affirmation of an individual's profession of faith, nonattendance renders the church incapable of fulfilling its responsibility. The church can no longer claim with integrity to oversee one's discipleship. Therefore, excommunication effectively sets the record straight.[10] Thus, this kind of rigorous discipleship seen in church membership is, at least partially, intended to be one of the means of maintaining the people of God in a state of perseverance, as it relates to their faith.

---

8. See Andrew M. Davis, "The Practical Issues of Church Discipline," in *Those Who Must Give an Account: A Study of Church Membership and Church Discipline*, eds. John S. Hammett and Benjamin L. Merkle (Nashville: B&H Academic, 2012), 162.

9. See George H. Guthrie, *Hebrews*, NIVAC (Grand Rapids: Zondervan, 1998), 130. One can also observe that this call to exhortation sounds much like the first step of the disciplinary process as advocated by Jesus (Matt. 18:15). As such, concerning the seriousness of disciplining church members, Hays asserts, in regards to Matthew 18:15–20, "The final step of expulsion of the unrepentant sinner from the community (18:17) indicates how seriously the imperatives of righteousness are to be taken. One cannot be an unrepentant sinner and remain within the community of Jesus' disciples" (Richard B. Hays, *The Moral Vision of the New Testament: A Contemporary Introduction to New Testament Ethics* [San Francisco: HarperCollins, 1996], 102).

10. See Jonathan Leeman, *Church Discipline: How the Church Protects the Name of Jesus*, 9Marks (Wheaton, IL: Crossway, 2012), 106–7.

The people of God are called, therefore, to exhort one another continually in a local church context in order that we might be holy as God is holy (1 Peter 1:16; cf. Lev. 11:44). If an individual stumbles and becomes involved in continual, unrepentant sin, the church must lovingly confront and, if necessary, remove those who refuse to repent.[11] This ongoing, communal process of discipline must take place,[12] but a robust culture of discipleship will prevent many of these extreme cases. As such, churches must be dedicated to encouraging honesty and mutual exhortation in corporate gatherings, smaller classes, small groups, and one-on-one settings. This may mean a change in the way things are currently done in our churches, but the changes will be worthwhile as we seek to better accord our ways with texts such as Hebrews 3:12–13 and 10:23–25.

Summary

The link between a disciple, the process of discipleship, and local church membership is real and vital. This means shunning the notion that Christian discipleship is something I do alone, via podcasts and books, or with one mentor. While all of these things are good, a disciple grows best in becoming like Jesus Christ within the context of a local church.

It is within the church that a follower of Jesus will experience a Christian community that is covenanted together and dedicated to seeing one another succeed. Sin will not be swept under the rug. Nor will it be pompously condemned. Local church membership shapes Christian discipleship in that the members of a church oversee one another's discipleship, and humbly exhort one another day after day so as to put off sin and put on righteousness. If a person remains anonymous, aloof, and disconnected from their local church, that process simply cannot happen. As such, the need for growth in discipleship is tightly tied to a person joining a church in membership and getting involved in the life of the church so as to receive biblical instruction and observe godly examples from whom they can learn.

---

11. The reader is rightly reminded by Leeman that, "Public accountability [in church membership and discipline] should be the outgrowth of what's already going on in the private lives of church members" (*Church Discipline*, 67). Leeman elsewhere notes, "Again and again Christians are told to keep one another out of harm's way and to bear one another's burdens (Gal 6:1–2; also 1 Cor 4:21; Jude 22–23). . . . The love of Christian accountability best occurs under the authority of the local church, where the ordinances can be distributed in a disciplined manner" (Jonathan Leeman, *The Church and the Surprising Offense of God's Love: Reintroducing the Doctrines of Church Membership and Church Discipline* [Wheaton, IL: Crossway, 2010], 264).

12. See Lauterbach, who asserts, "Church discipline is not something we 'do' to someone in sin. Church discipline is the constant activity of a church where holiness and love are pursued. We should always be watching over each other, encouraging each other daily against the possibility of a hardened heart, stimulating each other toward love and good works" (Mark Lauterbach, *The Transforming Community: The Practice of the Gospel in Church Discipline* [Ross-shire, Scotland: Christian Focus, 2003], 20).

REFLECTION QUESTIONS

1. How would you define the term "disciple"?

2. How would you define the term "discipleship"?

3. How does discipleship relate to church membership?

4. How does family imagery help us understand how we are to relate to one another in the church?

5. What lessons do we learn for membership and discipleship from texts like Hebrews 3 and 10?

How Is Membership Helpful for the Leaders of the Church?

Church membership is a biblical concept and is a key means of growing as disciples of Jesus Christ. Church members, by the empowerment of the indwelling Spirit and the grace of God, exhort one another constantly, flee sin, and pursue righteousness. In this oversight of one another's discipleship within the structure and polity of the church, real growth can occur in community.

This vision of community and discipleship is essential when thinking about the importance of church membership and its relationship to the pastoral leaders of the church. Biblically, there is warrant for saying that pastors are responsible for the spiritual well-being of their people. They will be held accountable for their spiritual condition (Heb. 13:7, 17). Pastors also have to know who they are responsible for because they serve as the stewards and shepherds of the church. Effective stewardship and shepherding are essential in that pastors must care for the souls of their congregation, and this begins the moment they join as members. A robust understanding and implementation of regenerate church membership will give leaders added confidence that they can lead the right people in the right way.

The Biblical Responsibility of Pastors

A variety of titles and images are used in the Scriptures to describe those who commit their lives to serve in pastoral ministry.[1] Those who are called to such a vocation are described as shepherds or pastors (Eph. 4:11), elders (1 Peter 5:1–5), overseers (1 Tim. 3:1), and stewards (Titus 1:7), which are all

---

1. Portions of this chapter are derived from Jeremy M. Kimble, *That His Spirit May Be Saved: Church Discipline as a Means to Repentance and Perseverance* (Eugene, OR: Wipf and Stock, 2013), 154–65. Used by permission of Wipf and Stock Publishers (www.wipfandstock.com).

terms replete with meaning and significance.[2] Through these various titles we receive a more full-orbed understanding of what the role and function of a minister truly is. This is due to the fact that words like this can function as metaphors, describing the tasks of pastoral ministry.[3] The term "elder," which has some loose connection to the elders of the OT, denotes an office of authority held by qualified men who exude specific qualities.[4] "Overseer" is used to represent a variety of different leadership positions in the OT and Greco-Roman society and of a specific office of authority in the NT.[5] Two other terms, one well known, the other receiving less attention, also help give a full picture of the responsibility of a church leader and how they should relate to their members.

Terms such as "steward" and "shepherd" are not always appreciated or utilized in our contemporary milieu to describe pastoral ministry. However, it is important to observe that elders are responsible as stewards for rightly proclaiming the gospel of Jesus Christ, and they function as shepherds for overseeing the souls of the people in their local church. If this is true, implications exist for modern-day pastors as they seek to watch over the spiritual condition of the people within their congregation, knowing they will have to give an account to God as stewards. Thus, while the concepts of "elder" and "overseer" also provide grounding for rightly understanding the pastoral office and its inherent responsibilities, the images of "steward" and "shepherd" will receive focus here, as they can be overlooked, and they give greater depth and clarity to the role and function of one who serves in pastoral ministry.

The Pastor as Steward

Regarding stewardship, in the NT era of the first century, absentee landlords dominated the landscape. These wealthy landowners typically lived in the city and visited their farm estates only occasionally. As a result, these landlords

---

2. Throughout this chapter I will be using the terms of pastor, elder, and overseer interchangeably (cf. Acts 20:17–35; 1 Peter 5:1–5). For a recent argument in favor of elder and overseer being one office in Scripture, see Benjamin L. Merkle, *The Elder and Overseer: One Office in the Early Church*, Studies in Biblical Literature 57 (New York: Peter Lang, 2003). See also Phil A. Newton and Matt Schmucker, *Elders in the Life of the Church: Rediscovering the Biblical Model for Church Leadership* (Grand Rapids: Kregel, 2014); Samuel E. Waldron, "Plural-Elder Congregationalism," in *Who Runs the Church?: 4 Views on Church Government*, ed. Steven B. Cowan (Grand Rapids: Zondervan, 2004), 212–21.

3. For a helpful discussion of metaphors in Scripture, specifically in regard to shepherding, see Timothy S. Laniak, *Shepherds after My Own Heart: Pastoral Traditions and Leadership in the Bible* (Leicester, England: Apollos, 2006), 31–41.

4. See James M. Hamilton Jr., "Did the Church Borrow Leadership Structures from the Old Testament or Synagogue?" in *Shepherding God's Flock: Biblical Leadership in the New Testament and Beyond*, eds. Benjamin L. Merkle and Thomas R. Schreiner (Grand Rapids: Kregel, 2014), 13–31.

5. Benjamin L. Merkle, *40 Questions about Elders and Deacons* (Grand Rapids: Kregel, 2008), 63–65.

utilized people known as stewards to inspect, certify, manage, oversee, and report on the household and its accompanying land.[6] Responsibility belonged to the steward to faithfully maintain what was under his care. Thus, the terms "steward" and "stewardship" have a tangible background to draw from, in elucidating how stewardship was conceived of in that time.

The idea of stewardship is depicted in a literal manner in several places throughout the NT (Matt. 24:45–51; Luke 12:42–48; 16:1–13; Rom. 16:23; Gal. 4:1–2). In summarizing the literal usage, the steward, who was typically a slave himself, held responsibility over the properties belonging to the master, were accountable for the other slaves of that particular estate, performed administrative duties in caring for the estate, at times may even have been involved in the upbringing and education of the children of their master, and would have to give an account for their actions.[7] All of these literal uses of this particular word in the NT give us a helpful interpretive lens to better understand its metaphorical usage.

Of all the NT writers, the apostle Paul uses these terms the most extensively (1 Cor. 4:1–2; 9:17; Eph. 3:2; Col. 1:25; Titus 1:7; 1 Tim. 3:15) though they can also be found in the writings of Peter (1 Peter 4:10). In many of these passages one can observe that Paul considers himself to be a steward of the gospel. As such, Paul is compelled to preach the truth regarding Jesus Christ faithfully so that the grace of God can be revealed to both Jew and Gentile. Paul refers to elders as "stewards of God" (Titus 1:7) who must faithfully oversee the church, which is God's household (1 Tim. 3:15).[8] This is the task of a steward. Thus, the concept of the "steward of God" cited in Titus 1:7 is given greater clarity when one understands the connection to household imagery.[9]

In summary, the language of stewardship refers to the practice in the ancient world of giving to a trusted slave or employee the administration of the owner's property or business. The biblical theme of stewardship derives from the premise that God creates all and so owns all (Gen. 1:1; Deut. 10:14; Ps. 24:1). Hence, human beings are accountable to God for their use of what he

---

6. F. Alan Tomlinson, "The Purpose and Stewardship Theme within the Pastoral Epistles," in *Entrusted with the Gospel: Paul's Theology in the Pastoral Epistles*, eds. Andreas J. Köstenberger and Terry L. Wilder (Nashville: B&H Academic, 2010), 75–77. See also K. H. Rengstorf, '*Hupēretēs*,' *TDNT*, 8:539.

7. See especially Wilfred Tooley, "Stewards of God : An Examination of the Terms *oikonomos* and *oikonomia* in the New Testament," *SJT* 19, no. 1 (1966): 74–86.

8. George W. Knight, *The Pastoral Epistles: A Commentary on the Greek Text* (Grand Rapids: Eerdmans, 1992), 180–81.

9. See Towner: "Theological description of the church is most evident in 1 Timothy where household imagery provides the dominant components. The church is God's household (3:15; Gk. *oikos theou*). This phrase ties together related concepts in key places to describe God's rule in life in terms of household order (1:4; Gk. *oikonomia theou*), and the overseers' leadership in terms of household management (3:4–5)" (P. H. Towner, "The Pastoral Epistles," in *NDBT*, eds. T. Desmond Alexander and Brian S. Rosner [Downers Grove, IL: InterVarsity, 2000], 334).

placed at their disposal (Gen. 1:26–30).[10] As such, the elder is the steward of God overseeing his household, the church, through the means of preaching, teaching, and leadership.

The Pastor as Shepherd

Regarding shepherding, one may observe key details in relation to pastoral ministry in Acts 20:17–38 and 1 Peter 5:1–5. In Acts 20 Paul calls the elders at Ephesus to meet with him (20:17), though these men are later referred to as overseers (20:28).[11] The elders are exhorted to "care for the church of God" (20:28). The term "care" is a verbal form of the term "pastor" (cf. Eph 4:11). The verb in this verse carries the idea of serving as a herder of sheep, protecting, caring, leading, and nurturing.[12] The metaphor of shepherding the flock of God takes up a familiar OT picture of God's people under their rulers (Ps. 100:3; Isa. 40:11; Jer. 13:17; Ezek. 34) and applies it to the task of caring for and directing the church. Therefore, the elders, in continuity with OT leadership, function as overseers who are to care for the people that God has entrusted to their care.

Acts 20:28 is quite similar to the exhortation Peter gives to his fellow elders in 1 Peter 5:1–5. They are told to "shepherd the flock of God that is among you, exercising oversight" (5:2). Laniak elaborates and offers the following assessment of these two passages:

> The elders are to shepherd (*poimanō*) God's flock under their care. Only here and in Acts 20:28 is the imperative form of the verb used in this way. . . . In both contexts the association between shepherding and careful oversight is clear. In Acts the "overseers" (*episkopoi*) are expected to guard or pay close attention to (*prosechō*) the needs of the flock (in the context of wolves; v. 29). Similarly, leaders in Hebrews 13:17 "watch over" (*agrypneō*) your souls as they serve the "great Shepherd of the sheep" (Heb. 13:20). In 1 Peter 5:2 the elders are to oversee (*episkopeō*) the flock. This is the flock of the "Shepherd and Overseer (*episkopon*) of your souls" (2:25). Watching, noted frequently in this study, is a comprehensive summary of shepherding tasks. It is the vigilant attention to threats that can disperse or destroy the flock.[13]

---

10. See Everett Ferguson, *The Church of Christ: A Biblical Ecclesiology for Today* (Grand Rapids: Eerdmans, 1996), 276.
11. It seems safe to conclude, therefore, that elders and overseers are two different designations for the same office. See Thomas R. Schreiner, *New Testament Theology: Magnifying God in Christ* (Grand Rapids: Baker Academic, 2008), 693; Merkle, *The Elder and Overseer*, 129–35.
12. BDAG s.v. ποιμαίνω, 842.
13. Laniak, *Shepherds after My Own Heart*, 232–33.

Therefore, the elders are to watch over the church of God, which is the flock entrusted to them by the Chief Shepherd (1 Peter 5:2, 4). Pastors are the stewards of God's gospel message, as well as the shepherds of God's people, and thus they must labor to see the members of their congregations living lives that are worthy of the gospel of Christ (Phil. 1:27).

Implications for Church Membership

Based on the aforementioned principles, the following principles can be stated regarding the pastor as steward and shepherd of a local church. Pastors are responsible as stewards of the gospel to faithfully preach and teach the whole counsel of God. Practically speaking, it would seem that a pastor should proclaim biblical truths as accurately as possible, which means that exposition through entire books of the Bible would be the primary way in which Scripture would be communicated. This type of preaching will focus most intensely upon the actual words of Scripture and, as such, serves as the greatest possible means to being a faithful steward of God's Word. Another extension of this point is that pastors should exercise leadership in overseeing the overall teaching ministry of the church.

Pastors should lead in overseeing the process of taking in new members as well as in the administration of the ordinances to the church. They must also shepherd their people in such a way as to watch over their lives and assist them in pursuing godliness on a personal level. Pastors, ideally in a plurality of elders, must have a knowledge of each member within their church in order to honestly claim that they are faithfully stewarding the church God has given them.[14] Pastors are accountable for knowing the identity of our flock and understanding their physical and spiritual condition. In these ways, pastors can serve as faithful stewards and shepherds.[15]

Summary

Having examined the relevant texts, it would seem that the concepts of elder, overseer, stewardship, and shepherding are paradigmatic for rightly understanding the task of present-day pastors in relation to their members. God has given pastors a tremendous amount of responsibility, and those who serve in ministry should feel the weight of this calling. It must be noted, therefore,

---

14. Commenting on Acts 20:28 and Hebrews 13:17, Leeman states that, "the plainest way to read these two passages is to say that the elders of a church, collectively, should be able to pay careful attention to every member of the flock, because they will give an account for every member of the flock before God" (Jonathan Leeman, *The Church and the Surprising Offense of God's Love: Reintroducing the Doctrines of Church Membership and Church Discipline* [Wheaton, IL: Crossway, 2010], 308). This is also a pragmatic argument for a plurality of elders serving in a local church, particularly as churches grow.

15. For more on this topic, see Jeremy M. Kimble, "The Steward of God: Exploring the Role and Function of Elders," *STR* 6, no. 1 (2015): 83–111.

that elders are not simply taking on some unimportant leadership position in a local church; rather, they are called to faithfully preach and teach the Word of God and oversee the members of their local church.

REFLECTION QUESTIONS

1. What are the various terms for the leadership of the church? What do all of these terms mean?

2. What is the significance of referring to pastors as stewards?

3. What is the significance of referring to pastors as shepherds?

4. How do these terms shape the way pastors approach their role in ministry?

5. If you serve as a pastor/elder, what specific areas could be improved as a steward and shepherd of your congregation?

What Is the Process of Church Membership?

John Webster is correct when he remarks that a group of people coming to faith is not the "only constitutive moment for ecclesiology."[1] The bricks might have been made, but they still need mortar to call them a wall. Thus, Leeman rightly observes, "A person is included in the universal church through salvation. Yet at this point the church remains an abstract idea without a palpable and public presence. A second constitutive moment is needed in order for 'the church' to show up on planet earth. For that to happen, a group of Christians must gather and organize themselves (or be organized) as a congregation and affirm one another as believers."[2]

Thus, when thinking of church membership, one understands that membership is not something that happens automatically. Christian people who move into a new area will look for a local church to join. Walking through the doors does not make them members. Even regular attendance does not make them members of that particular church. So then the question becomes what is it that moves those people from visitors to attenders to official church members? Four aspects of the process for church membership will be discussed in this chapter: regeneration, baptism, inquiry, and affirmation by church members.

Regeneration

More will be said on this topic at a later point (see Question 16), but this is a key starting point in the process of joining as a member of a local church.

---

1. John Webster, "The 'Self-Organizing' Power of the Gospel: Episcopacy and Community Formation," in *Community Formation: In the Early Church and in the Church Today*, ed. Richard N. Longenecker (Peabody, MA: Hendrickson, 2002), 183.
2. See Jonathan Leeman, *Political Church: The Local Assembly as Embassy of Christ's Rule* (Downers Grove, IL: IVP Academic, 2016), 333.

Regeneration is a work of the Holy Spirit that brings about new life or new birth (John 3:1–10; Titus 3:5). Dever and Alexander rightly maintain that this is an essential mark of a person seeking to join a church in membership: "The health of any local church hangs in large part on the prior question of whether its members are spiritually alive."[3]

This is a key point, in that the church must demonstrate the parameters that exist as a people set apart by God. At the very least we may say that local church membership is a good and necessary implication of God's desire to keep a clear distinction between his own chosen people and the worldly system of rebellion that surrounds them.[4] The people who join a church are those who are part of the new covenant community (Jer. 31:31–34; Ezek. 36:25–27) and citizens of the kingdom of God (Phil. 3:20; 1 Peter 2:11), meaning they are a people who have experienced the regenerating work of the Spirit, repented of their sin, and placed their faith in Christ alone for salvation.

Baptism

A previous chapter discusses this in greater detail (Question 9), but there is a strong cumulative case for baptism as a second requirement of church membership. A. H. Strong rightly argues, "Regeneration and baptism, although not holding to each other the relation of effect and cause, are both regarded in the New Testament as essential to the restoration of man's right relations to God and to his people. They properly constitute parts of one whole, and are not to be unnecessarily separated."[5] Candidates for membership must be converted and have received the initiating sign of their conversion, namely, baptism.[6] To go even further, the idea of an unbaptized Christian is truly foreign to the witness of the NT.[7]

Baptism essentially connected the believing community with the death and resurrection of Christ (Rom. 6:1–4). Baptism symbolized burial with Christ in his death. Baptism also means new life, signifying that believers share in Christ's risen life. It signifies the death of the old self and new life beginning. Baptism serves as a teaching medium for new believers, and the

---

3. Mark Dever and Paul Alexander, *The Deliberate Church: Building Your Ministry on the Gospel* (Wheaton, IL: Crossway, 2005), 59.

4. Ibid., 61.

5. A. H. Strong, *Systematic Theology* (Philadelphia: Judson, 1907), 950.

6. Hammett makes clear this claim "is supported by the order of events in Acts 2:41 (where people are baptized and 'added' to the church) and by the inclusion of baptism as one of the marks of church unity in Ephesians 4:3–6" (John Hammett, "The Why and Who of Church Membership," in *Baptist Foundations: Church Government for an Anti-Institutional Age*, eds. Mark Dever and Jonathan Leeman [Nashville: B&H Academic, 2015], 176).

7. See the argument of Robert Stein, "Baptism in Luke-Acts," in *Believer's Baptism: Sign of the New Covenant in Christ*, eds. Thomas Schreiner and Shawn Wright (Nashville: B&H Academic, 2006), 35–66.

gospel is preached anew to the entire church in understanding the theological meaning reflected in the symbolism. Baptism marks the gathering community and is the sign by which each new believer accepts Jesus as his or her representative, and accepts Jesus' people as his or her people.[8] This is to be done for believers and should be done prior to joining as a member of a local church.[9]

Inquiry

While regeneration and baptism are key prerequisites of church membership, it would also be wise to enact some further investigation, both by the church, as well as the prospective member. The candidate for membership should be fully aware of the stance of the church on doctrine, the process for membership, the ministries of the church, and a host of other details. Joining a church is an important decision, therefore, proper investigation should be done.

The church must seek to do all they can to ensure that the candidate for membership is in fact converted. Saucy affirms, "While the New Testament teaches a regenerate church membership and only those in Christ are in the church as His living body, it is possible for some unsaved individuals to gain entrance into the local congregation. . . . God alone can know the heart of man, but the realization of the possibility of false profession requires the church to do all possible to make the issue of the necessity of the new birth crystal clear."[10] As such, clear lines of demarcation should be drawn in the right preaching of the gospel, calling for sinners to repent.

Beyond this, there are some best practices churches can institute to work toward consistency and integrity in pursuing a regenerate church membership. Churches should have an agreed upon statement of faith and church covenant. Statements of faith unite a church doctrinally, while church covenants guide a church in their conduct.[11] Membership in a local church means that one takes on certain responsibilities, both to know and to guard the doctrine of the church as well as the overall behavior of its members. Without such documents, the process of membership loses a certain amount of authority. Churches should discuss who and what

8. Oliver O'Donovan, *The Desire of the Nations: Rediscovering the Roots of Political Theology* (Cambridge: Cambridge University Press, 1999), 364.
9. See G. R. Beasley-Murray, *Baptism in the New Testament* (Grand Rapids: Eerdmans, 1973); David S. Dockery, "The Church in the Pauline Epistles," in *The Community of Jesus: A Theology of the Church*, eds. Kendall H. Easley and Christopher W. Morgan (Nashville: B&H Academic, 2013), 113–14; Stanley J. Grenz, *Theology for the Community of God* (Grand Rapids: Eerdmans, 1994), 529–31.
10. Robert L. Saucy, *The Church in God's Program* (Chicago: Moody, 1972), 104–5.
11. For a historical account of the application of church covenants, particularly in Baptist contexts, see Charles W. Deweese, *Baptist Church Covenants* (Nashville: Broadman, 1990).

they are as a church and what the Bible demands of them as Christians. Churches can then work to personalize a specific statement so that the covenant is owned as their covenant, not as one imposed upon them.[12] Thus, the church membership process must include a clear notion of what the local church believes and how they will live as believers in community and in the world, and this gives churches right standards as they assess potential members.

The process of church membership should also include some form of membership classes and interview. Membership classes can vary in length and content but should include teaching on the statement of faith, the church covenant, the history of Christianity and of that particular local church, the expectations of members, and the way in which the church operates, including the process of church discipline. The main purpose of the classes is to confirm awareness of the church's expectations and standards for potential members. This offers opportunity for both church leadership and potential church members to learn about one another and ask pertinent questions before proceeding in the process.

An interview should also be conducted to personally ascertain the candidate's understanding of the gospel, their conversion experience, and to ensure baptism as a believer. This interview can be conducted by several elders or other recognized leaders in the church, and it should specifically gauge the potential member's knowledge of the good news of Jesus Christ and the way in which that good news applies to them. This is the best opportunity in many respects to work toward regenerate church membership, and it is a real joy to hear people articulate the details of the gospel. The interviewers can also inquire about why, if applicable, they are leaving their previous church, if they have been baptized, and whether they have ever undergone church discipline.

Affirmation by Church Members

Finally, affirmation by the entire membership of the church should take place. The members of the church exist as a kingdom of priests (i.e., priesthood of the believer; 1 Peter 2:9). Leeman rightly maintains,

> Jesus, the second Adam, new Israel, and Davidic son came to rule obediently by laying down his life for the sins of the nations and rising from the grave. In so doing, he offered a new covenant in his blood, so that all who would repent and believe might receive a pardon from sin and a share in

---

12. For a helpful outline of practical steps that need to be taken for the preparation and implementation of a church covenant, see Charles W. Deweese, *A Community of Believers* (Valley Forge, PA: Judson, 1978), 28–40.

his kingly authority. To that end, he granted them the keys of the kingdom, enabling them to fulfill their covenantal responsibilities to identify themselves with God and one another, distinguish themselves from the world, exercise proper discipline, and pursue together the life of righteousness that rightly represents the Son, the Father, and the Spirit. As such, a local church publicly administers the office responsibilities of the new covenant. And a local church exists wherever a group of saints regularly gather to preach the gospel and exercise the keys by publicly affirming and submitting to one another through baptism and the Lord's Supper. The life of the church, among other things, is a citizen's life, whereby the saints share in kingdom rule together, jointly exercising the keys of the kingdom in one another's lives.[13]

The church, as a kingdom of priests, authorized with the keys of the kingdom, are to take seriously their role of receiving new members. This process would typically take place on a Sunday morning, when most of the members are present. Information would ideally be posted prior to that Sunday so people could read or hear about the person's biography and testimony. It can include a live or video testimony, followed by a vote to affirm or deny the candidates for membership. Taking these steps will further ensure the integrity of the membership process.

Summary

Both churches and individuals should carefully consider the process of church membership. The individual joining a church is submitting to a particular group of leaders, a confession of faith, and other members. Members must gain clarity before they covenant with a church, recognizing the authority they have and the authority under which they place themselves.

The church must do all it can to maintain a regenerate church membership, knowing they will not likely be flawless in this regard. A stringent process for membership will be helpful in attaining this goal. This process can include having a clear statement of faith and church covenant, administering new member classes, conducting membership interviews, and building a culture within the church where members recognize their importance and authority in affirming new members. All of this will contribute to a healthy culture within the church.

---

13. Leeman, *Political Church*, 390. For further evidence regarding a congregational polity as fulfilling NT standards, see idem, *Don't Fire Your Church Members: The Case for Congregationalism* (Nashville: B&H Academic, 2016).

REFLECTION QUESTIONS

1. How can we seek to ensure those who join our church are in fact converted?

2. What should an individual reflect on when looking to join a church?

3. What process should a church go through in bringing in new members?

4. In terms of bringing in new members, of what significance are the concepts of the priesthood of the believer and the keys of the kingdom?

5. Are you a member of a church? If not, what is preventing you?

Does Membership Look the Same in Every Culture and Context?

We live in a global context. Due to Internet connections, cheaper flights, and burgeoning intercultural cities, we are seemingly more connected than ever before. Yet, there remain definite degrees of difference. Such differences can center on longstanding traditions, the way we dress, the food we eat, and the languages we speak. These differences can also impact the way the church functions in various places around the globe.

Worship always has been and always will be the ultimate purpose of God in the universe. God put his people on mission to make disciples of all nations (Matt. 28:19–20), that people from every tribe, tongue, nation, and language might forever praise him (Ps. 67:1–7).[1] The mission to make disciples among all peoples calls for churches to be planted all over the world. Membership within these churches across the globe will be a concept that is (or should be) embraced by all churches.

And so, we must ask the question: Is all that we have been discussing thus far some kind of modern Western construct, or is the concept of church membership universal and transcultural? Won't it look radically different in certain contexts where the church is oppressed, small, and/or home-based? This is an important question to answer, as the church must be faithful in implementing church membership if it is to be biblical, regardless of cultural context. The answer is simple, yet also multifaceted. Therefore, we will look at cultural similarities, differences, and the biblical baseline for church membership across all time and cultures.

---

1. For an extensive treatment of missions, especially to unreached people groups, see John Piper, *Let the Nations Be Glad!: The Supremacy of God in Missions*, 3rd edition (Grand Rapids: Baker Academic, 2010).

How Membership Is the Same Everywhere

Regardless of cultural context, membership is going to be the same wherever you go for a number of reasons.[2] Specifically, the task is to be a distinct people who are a light to the world (Matt. 5:3–16) and who are dedicated to making disciples of Jesus Christ (Matt. 28:19–20). The tools to accomplish that task are embedded in the realm of membership. The church *is* its membership, and the members exercise the authority of the keys of the kingdom in guarding the gospel, affirming credible professions of faith, overseeing Christian discipleship, teaching truth, and excluding false professors (Matt. 16:13–19; 18:15–20). This is true in any church around the globe.

Second, membership will look the same everywhere in that, while cultural contexts differ, we live in enemy territory and fight against a common enemy. The church functions as an embassy of the kingdom of God. An embassy represents the authority, name, reputation, character, and glory of one nation inside another nation. The local church does exactly this, only it represents a kingdom not across geographic space but across eschatological time. It represents the invisible spiritual entities of heaven, heaven's powers and heaven's battles against the cosmic powers of the present darkness and the spiritual forces of evil.[3] As an embassy of God's kingdom we operate in foreign, enemy territory.

Beyond the metaphor of embassy, being a member of a different kingdom is a thoroughly biblical principle. We are told that God is sovereign over all things (Ps. 104:1–30; Isa. 45:5–7). Satan is the prince of this world with whom we are in conflict (Matt. 4:8–9; John 12:31; 14:30; Eph. 6:10–13; 1 Peter 5:8–9). We, however, have already been raised with Christ (Col. 3:1–3), seated in the heavenly places with Christ Jesus (Eph. 2:6), and we are elect exiles and sojourners in this world (1 Peter 1:1; 2:11). While we live as citizens of a particular country on planet earth, we are ultimately citizens of heaven (Phil. 3:20) who desire a better, heavenly country (Heb. 11:13–16).

As it relates to membership, regardless of where we live, we live within the tension of an inaugurated kingdom and a creation that is still in the throes of sin and Satanic oppression. That is the context of our church

---

2. As Leeman asserts, "Membership will look the same everywhere because the Jesus-established local church *is* its membership. And Jesus has given every church everywhere *the same tools* for accomplishing *the same task*" (Jonathan Leeman, *Church Membership: How the World Knows Who Represents Jesus* [Wheaton, IL: Crossway, 2012], 122 [emphasis original]).

3. See Jonathan Leeman, *Political Church: The Local Assembly as Embassy of Christ's Rule* (Downers Grove, IL: IVP Academic, 2016), 368. Horton likewise makes this point and states, "As the gospel claims and renames strangers to the covenant, the kingdom of God spreads in holiness. Yet in this time between the times, there is still the conflict between the holy and the common, the heirs of promise and a world that prefers the darkness to the light" (Michael Horton, *People and Place: A Covenant Ecclesiology* [Louisville: Westminster John Knox, 2008], 192).

membership universally. And as Hansen rightly asserts, commenting on Philippians 3:20, "The implication of asserting our citizenship in the heavenly state is that we are a 'colony of heavenly citizens' here on earth."[4] And this citizenship is most ably expressed in a local church context where the authority of the keys of the kingdom is implemented. Local churches protect the gospel against all kinds of attack, and they are called to assess gospel affirmations and oversee one another's discipleship.

How Membership Can Differ Everywhere

Now, with all of that being said, it should also be clear that churches in different locations face different challenges. As such, certain kinds of strategies and structures to accomplish the overarching mission may differ slightly. First, one must reckon with societal complexity as opposed to overall simplicity. Regarding certain cultures, Leeman observes, "The larger and more complex a society becomes, the more difficult it is to affirm and oversee credible professions of faith. This work is made difficult by job transience, social mobility, church size, urban sprawl, demanding work schedules, religious pluralism, ethnic prejudice, multi-denominationalism, centuries of accumulated heresies, false churches, church hopping, cultural trends such as individualism and consumerism, and much more."[5] The bigger and more complex a society becomes the more difficult it is to efficiently oversee members and membership.

Some societies deal with these issues much more than others. The characteristics described above may resonate with a number of readers who live in the West, but there are other cultures that simply do not live in this manner. Community and interdependence hold greater value, along with living at a more local level, and this can give rise to a more natural oversight in the church. Thus, while the principles of membership remain, the process and general oversight of members can differ in terms of dealing with potential difficulties and obstructions to community.

Another factor that can call for difference in the conception of church membership is the fact that, in some cultures, Christianity and the church are treated with contempt, ostracized, or even persecuted. Allison avers, "The church is *for* the world—encouraging its members to faithfully obey the cultural mandate to build civilization while loving neighbor and making disciples—and *against* the world, helping its members to be compassionately critical of and justly opposed to all that in this fallen world is tainted by sin and in rebellion against Jesus Christ."[6] In standing against the world in this way, the church can be opposed, and this affects a church's ability to affirm and oversee professions of faith.

---

4. G. W. Hansen, *The Letter to the Philippians*, PNTC (Grand Rapids: Eerdmans, 2009), 269.
5. Leeman, *Church Membership*, 124.
6. Gregg R. Allison, *Sojourners and Strangers: The Doctrine of the Church* (Wheaton, IL: Crossway, 2012), 463 (emphasis original).

In fact, when a church lives in a relatively peaceful society that generally embraces Christianity, more work may actually need to be done to ensure that the membership process goes as it should.[7] This is due to the fact that Christianity is so accepted and normative that family expectations, societal patterns, and mere tradition can get us into church, as opposed to actual re-generation. In this setting, membership classes, interviews, and other means of ascertaining proper affirmation of the gospel are necessary in order to be faithful. However, in a simpler society where Christianity is not esteemed, things like membership classes, a record of who the members are, and other such processes may not be as necessary. There is no incentive to submit to baptism and joining a church, and so those who join will likely give a true testimony, knowing that joining a church will cost them. It is also likely that these churches will be small and intimate in nature, since some governments would break up the church if it was discovered.

The Biblical Norm

Regardless of context, several principles hold true for church membership. First, a confession of faith in the gospel of Jesus Christ must be of first pri-ority. This can happen in a pastor's office at a plush church building or while walking the streets of Nairobi, Kenya; but since membership is regenerate in nature, leaders do all they can to ascertain the authenticity of that confession of faith. Second, members are given a chance to hear from the candidate for membership. Again, whether this be on a Sunday morning after hearing a video testimony from the candidate, or at a house church in Afghanistan where the testimony is offered live, followed by a time of question-and-answer, members should exercise the authority of the keys of the kingdom.

Third, if all has gone well, the church affirms the candidate for member-ship. This can be very formal process in a large church or an informal discus-sion amongst fifteen people in a persecuted church, but affirmation should take place at some level. Finally, if it has not yet occurred, the church should welcome the new member in by baptism. This is the sign of the new covenant and can be applied in a baptistery in a church building or a nearby river or lake. This process, while it may look different on certain levels, is a needful part of bringing in new members.

Summary

We live in an increasingly global society. We need to understand the various challenges for churches as one crosses from cultures receptive to Christianity to those that oppress and persecute that kind of affiliation. While

---

7. Leeman asserts, "We're dealing with the realm of prudence here, but generally speaking I think we can say, the more social favor Christianity receives and the more complex society is, the more structure a church may require" (*Church Membership*, 125).

maintaining regenerate membership may prove difficult in different ways, the church is its membership, and thus the bringing in of new members must be done with care. In any given scenario as we seek to uphold the biblical norm for church membership, we seek to proclaim, display, and protect the gospel through the lives of its formally affirmed members.[8]

REFLECTION QUESTIONS

1. How does where we live potentially affect the process of church membership?

2. How does societal complexity affect the membership process?

3. How can cultural oppression of Christianity affect the membership process?

4. Regardless of context, what are the biblical norms for bringing in new members?

5. Depending on where you live, think of others who may live with different realities as it relates to the acceptance of Christianity. How can you pray for the church around the world in terms of doing the process of church membership well?

---

8. Ibid., 129.

Practical Questions

Why Do Some Churches Not Believe in Church Membership?

Several years ago Donald Miller wrote an article that received a large volume of feedback. Miller made comments like "I don't learn much about God hearing a sermon and I don't connect with him by singing songs to him," and "So, do I attend church? Not often, to be honest." All of this is related to the fact that "I worship God every day through my work. It's a blast."[1] Miller further argues that the traditional church is not like the book of Acts and thus to argue that one must be part of a modern church really has no basis. Community, he continues, is needful for the Christian life but can happen outside of the organized church. In all of this he essentially creates a distinct bifurcation between the universal and the local church. In other words, you can belong to the former without having to be involved in the latter.

This kind of view may go beyond the perspective of many self-proclaimed Christians, but there are many who struggle with the notion of formally joining a church in membership. They understand the benefits of attending a local church on a regular or semiregular basis but simply do not see the need for any kind of process. They may think that since they attend a given church, that should be good enough; there is really is no further need for making things so formal. This chapter will focus on the basic reasons why people think no membership or open membership is a correct approach, answer the objections raised about regenerate church membership, and provide a pathway for a proper approach to this issue.

---

1. Donald Miller, "I Don't Worship God by Singing. I Connect With Him Elsewhere," accessed March 24, 2016, http://storylineblog.com/2014/02/03/i-dont-worship-god-by-singing-i-connect-with-him-elsewhere. For a follow-up blog post where Miller answers many detractors to his position, see idem, "Why I Don't Go To Church Very Often, a Follow Up Blog," accessed March 24, 2016, http://storylineblog.com/2014/02/05/why-i-dont-go-to-church-very-often-a-follow-up-blog.

Reasons for No Membership

To be clear, there are two distinct, though related, groups that will be addressed in this section. First, there are those who advocate for no formal membership, saying that attendance and perhaps involvement in ministry is totally sufficient. This view comports with the sentiments of Miller shown above. Some churches or individual Christians hold to this kind of view claiming that Scripture does not explicitly teach the necessity of church membership. However, the intent of this book, along with many others, is to show that membership is indeed a biblical category.

Some in this camp also say a set of requirements for church membership beyond conversion feels fairly intolerant. There is, today, a widespread concern and push for the rights of individuals, freedom from oppression, and equality under the law. Certainly this kind of concern is to be commended in the main, but there can also be abuses and even oppression in the ways tolerance is defined and fought for. When tolerance is absolutized, it would logically be wrong to exclude anyone for any reason. This so-called "tolerance" has had many effects in our cultural milieu, and when this ideology is largely embraced, it casts the concept of closed membership as being close-minded, narrow, and bigoted. If God is love, and we are called to be tolerant of one another, should we not embrace those into membership who may differ in certain ways? That is an important question to answer. While this is a minority view in theological discourse, churches must guard practically against this attitude slipping into their churches.

Reasons for Open Membership

Second are those who would advocate for what is known as "open membership," a more prevalent view historically. This view holds that those who have been baptized as infants do not need to be "rebaptized," but may join the church as a member without any further action. This is a highly contested matter, particularly in Baptist circles, since this view appears to be a deviation from the view often espoused historically by Baptists (namely, regenerate church membership). Specifically, this is the view that members of the new covenant community (i.e., believers in Jesus) are baptized as an initiating sign of the new covenant, and then they are brought into membership.[2]

---

2. While space and intent precludes a prolonged discussion of this issue in Baptist history, it is important to note a relatively recent discussion on this matter between John Piper, Wayne Grudem, Sam Storms, Mark Dever, and several others (for one place that helpfully streamlines this discussion, see http://www.patheos.com/blogs/adrianwarnock/2007/08/sam-storms-john-piper-john-bunyan-vs/, accessed June 2, 2016). This conversation began in 2005 as Bethlehem Baptist Church discussed and eventually ratified an "open membership" position. Specifically, Bethlehem decided to not allow anyone to join as a member who believed in baptismal regeneration; however, if infant baptism took place as a means of being brought into the covenant community (i.e., Reformed/Presbyterian view of paedobaptism), and if the person was regenerate, they could join the church as a member. This view is

Several reasons are given to advocate for an open membership policy.[3] First, church discipline barely exists in many denominational circles. Here one can ask if churches are not in the habit of disciplining anyone from the church, why would we exclude someone over baptism? If a church allows an adulterer to remain in the body, do we really need any kind of structure for church membership in the first place? Another reason some advocate for open membership is that restrictiveness in membership cuts against the grain of evangelical essentialism. With the post-World War II emergence of figures like Carl Henry, Harold Ockenga, and Billy Graham, along with institutions and organizations such as Fuller Seminary, the NAE, Youth for Christ, Campus Crusade for Christ, and InterVarsity Christian Fellowship, evangelicalism came into full bloom in the mid-to-late twentieth century.[4] There is an impulse, in evangelical cooperation, to boil down our doctrinal commitments to a bare minimum, and if we agree on the gospel then membership should be based on the gospel, not mere secondary issues like baptism or the membership process.

Finally, with the rise of secularism and the decline of Christian values in the West, there is a need for Christians to unify. In countries where Christians are persecuted, there is a greater tendency toward unity. As such, it seems logical to present a unified front as Christianity continues to be pushed to the margins of society. And if that is the case, then a church that advocates for believers' baptism and a policy and process of church membership would seem to be mitigating against that unity. If churches begin to close and society continues to go in a direction that opposes the Christian faith, there will continue to be shouts for gospel unity and the forsaking of ecclesiological distinctives.

---

motivated by the belief that the door to local church membership should be roughly the same size as the door to membership in the universal body of Christ, and the fact that typically excluding someone from membership signifies a warranted doubt about the validity of that person's faith. Also, as that prospective member would go through the process of membership they would have to, after significant study, thought, discussion, and prayer, sincerely and humbly believe that it would be contrary to Scripture and conscience to be baptized by immersion and thus see their infant baptism as invalid. There must be continuing teachable openness under the teaching and leadership of the elders. See https://www.hopeingod.org/document/what-elders-are-proposing-amendments-constitution-and-laws; and https://www.hopeingod.org/document/baptism-and-church-membership-recommendation-elders-amending-bethlehems-constitution, both accessed June 3, 2016. This is a thorough and comprehensive ecclesial view of such an issue, taking into account some very needful points, and thus offering a compelling case for "open membership" with this kind of scrutiny and shepherding oversight. My thanks to Andy Naselli for pointing me to these resources.

3. Some of the content for this section was derived from Bobby Jamieson, *Going Public: Why Baptism Is Required for Church Membership* (Nashville: B&H Academic, 2015), 21–32.
4. For a detailed study of the "new evangelicalism," see George M. Marsden, *Reforming Fundamentalism: Fuller Seminary and the New Evangelicalism* (Grand Rapids: Eerdmans, 1987); Owen Strachan, *Awakening the Evangelical Mind: An Intellectual History of the Neo-Evangelical Movement* (Grand Rapids: Zondervan, 2015).

Answers to the Objections

All of these objections to a kind of church membership that is built upon regeneration and believer's baptism are worthy of response. Regarding tolerance, as cited by the "no membership" view, it must be affirmed that we have imbibed a redefined notion of "tolerance." We are to tolerate all things, which means if there are any restrictions put down in a particular area, for whatever reason, that is deemed intolerant. Carson rightly notes, "Although a few things can be said in favor of the newer definition [of tolerance], the sad reality is that this new, contemporary tolerance is intrinsically intolerant. It is blind to its own shortcomings because it erroneously thinks it holds the moral high ground; it cannot be questioned because it has become part of the West's plausibility structure. Worse, this new tolerance is socially dangerous and is certainly intellectually debilitating."[5] As Christians we stand against this "totalitarian tolerance," knowing we serve a God who both judges and saves and indeed saves through judgment.[6]

Further, one must rightly consider what it means when we say that "God is love." Carson highlights the fact that the Bible speaks of God's love in five different ways: the peculiar love shared between divine Father and Son, God's providential love over creation, God's salvific love toward the fallen world, God's particular and elective love toward a chosen people, and God's conditional love toward his people based on obedience.[7] The basic insight here is that Scripture refers to God's love in different ways. As the first of Carson's points about God's love demonstrates, God's love is first centered on himself as the Trinitarian God, the most glorious Being in the universe. Edwards states, "All God's love may be resolved into his love to himself and delight in himself. . . . His love to the creature is only his inclination to glorify himself and communicate himself, and his delight in himself glorified and in himself communicated."[8] God is uppermost in his own affections, and therefore love is truly God-centered.[9]

Through the gospel God displays his glory, redeems, and is transforming an undeserving people, and he calls them to behold his glory, reciprocate his love, and to live out an infinitely delightful God-centered worldview.[10] This

---

5. D. A. Carson, *The Intolerance of Tolerance* (Grand Rapids: Eerdmans, 2012), 2.

6. For more on this theme of God's glory manifested through both love and holiness, see James M. Hamilton, *God's Glory in Salvation through Judgment: A Biblical Theology* (Wheaton, IL: Crossway, 2010).

7. D. A. Carson, *The Difficult Doctrine of the Love of God* (Wheaton, IL: Crossway, 2000), 16–21.

8. Jonathan Edwards, "The Miscellanies: nos. 501–832," in *WJE* 18, ed. Ava Chamberlain (New Haven: Yale University Press, 2000), 239.

9. For more on the concept of God-centered love and the holiness that is inherent in biblical love, see Jonathan Leeman, *The Church and the Surprising Offense of God's Love: Reintroducing the Doctrines of Church Membership and Discipline* (Wheaton, IL: Crossway, 2010), 39–126.

10. The following paragraph from Jonathan Edwards made this point plain: "God is glorified within himself these two ways: (1) by appearing or being manifested to himself in his own perfect idea, or, in his Son, who is the brightness of his glory; (2) by enjoying and

love for God translates to love for neighbor, where we desire their eternal good. This good is not generic; it is the personal God of the Bible. Loving him means having affection for his glory and honor and despising those things that mitigate against that glory. Therefore, God's God-centered love will discriminate between that which is sin and that which is not, and so should we. This is done most prominently in the practices of church membership and discipline wherein we display God's "holy-love" for all to see.[11]

Several points should also be made regarding the "open membership" position. It is true that church discipline does not take a prominent place in many churches today, but that point does not call for us to abandon regenerate church membership. Rather it means we must return to the biblical standards for church discipline. While the second half of this work will deal with this topic in detail, it is hard to deny the patently obvious call for the church to discipline (Matt. 18:15–20; 1 Cor. 5:1–13). The final two issues deal with evangelical cooperation and dealing with the rise of secularism and anti-Christian attitude. For both of these points, it must be noted that neither give us a reason to abandon distinctives for our ecclesiology, even if they are "secondary" matters. The gospel is not the only thing God tells us in his Word, and issues such as church membership and discipline do touch on the implications of the gospel, and therefore we want to ensure we are doing all we can to be biblical in our approach.[12]

---

delighting in himself, by flowing forth in infinite love and delight towards himself, or, in his Holy Spirit. So God glorifies himself towards the creatures also two ways: (1) by appearing to them, being manifested to their understandings; (2) in communicating himself to their hearts, and in their rejoicing and delighting in, and enjoying the manifestations which he makes of himself. Both of them may be called his glory in the more extensive sense of the word, viz. his shining forth, or the going forth of his excellency, beauty and essential glory *ad extra*. By one way it goes forth towards their understandings; by the other it goes forth towards their wills or hearts. God is glorified not only by his glory's being seen, but by its being rejoiced in, when those that see it delight in it: God is more glorified than if they only see it; his glory is then received by the whole soul, both by the understanding and by the heart. God made the world that he might communicate, and the creature receive, his glory, but that it might [be] received both by the mind and heart. He that testifies his having an idea of God's glory don't glorify God so much as he that testifies also his approbation of it and his delight in it. Both these ways of God's glorifying himself come from the same cause, viz. the overflowing of God's internal glory, or an inclination in God to cause his internal glory to flow out *ad extra*. What God has in view in neither of them, neither in his manifesting his glory to the understanding nor communication to the heart, is not that he may receive, but that he [may] go forth: the main end of his shining forth is not that he may have his rays reflected back to himself, but that the rays may go forth" (Jonathan Edwards, "The Miscellanies: nos. a–z, aa–zz, 1–500," in *WJE* 13, ed. Harry Stout [New Haven, CT: Yale University Press, 1994], 495–96).

11. For an excellent work detailing God and his primary attributes of holiness and love, see David F. Wells, *God in the Whirlwind: How the Holy-Love of God Reorients Our World* (Wheaton, IL: Crossway, 2014).

12. Again, as noted above, Piper offers what is currently the most compelling case for "open membership" with making the entry way into the local church the same size as the entry

What Now?

Churches should cooperate as far as they are able. Certainly there are means of demonstrating unity among Christians as we speak out against social injustice, champion the cause of the unborn, and celebrate the truths of the gospel. However, this does not mean that we need to move or acquiesce regarding our position on membership and the process that we uphold. While many objections are raised, none move us to compromise on the position that membership needs theological foundation and a proper process.

Summary

It may "feel" right in many ways to advocate for no membership or open membership in churches. If a person is a Christian that should be good enough, baptism and other issues relating to the process of joining a church really are not that important. However, as we take into account the gospel, God's holy-love, and the call to obey not only some, but all of Scripture's commands, it seems clear that we are called to walk people through a particular process as we seek to uphold regenerate church membership. This is not an unloving act; in fact, we are teaching people what love means as we take them through the process.

REFLECTION QUESTIONS

1. What are some reasons people give for advocating for no membership or open membership?

2. What are the various ways we can speak of God's love?

3. How does God's love inform us regarding church membership?

4. How does God's holiness inform us regarding church membership?

5. If not in membership, what are some ways we can cooperate with churches that differ from our own?

---

way into the universal church. At a practical level, a decade after all this discussion was introduced, it would be helpful to see something about the effect this has had on the church, the way it has shaped the shepherding ministry of the elders, and how often such cases have come up.

What Kind of Church Should Someone Join?

Many people in our day will move to a different location at some point in their life. This could be due to a job relocation, choice of college, or a host of other possibilities. For a Christian, when a move becomes inevitable, so also does the choice of a new local church. Depending on where one relocates, there may be more or fewer churches to choose from, but there will be some kind of process and decision to be made at some point regarding what local body to join.

The process that someone goes through in choosing a church to join with may differ in some regards, but there are some universal principles. When looking for a local church to join in membership, there are certain nonnegotiable principles that one must take into account. This is crucial to point out because often people are looking for certain things and making them of primary importance when they are secondary at best. Ministry to children and students, musical style, aesthetics, and a host of other personal preferences factor in to some degree, but one must know what every church should embrace. As such, one must look for a church that is properly marked, on mission, and ministering effectively.

A Church That Is Marked

Historically, the church has been given definitive characteristics that people can point to in order to rightly identify what a church is. The earliest ecclesiology formed by the early church affirmed the four attributes or essential characteristics of the church: the church is one, holy, catholic, and apostolic.[1] These marks are tied to particular discussions held in the Patristic

---

1. For further discussion on these four attributes, see Richard D. Phillips, Philip Graham Ryken, and Mark Dever, *The Church: One, Holy, Catholic, and Apostolic* (Phillipsburg, NJ: P&R, 2004).

era and are more crucial in understanding the universal nature of the church. Reformation ecclesiology, focusing more on the local church, affirmed the essential marks of the true church as the right preaching of the Word and the right administration of the sacraments.[2] These marks demonstrate how the church is in fact visible, brought in to being by the gospel and marked out locally by proper administration of baptism and the Lord's Supper to members of the church. Again, these marks are shaped by a particular historic moment within which the church found itself.[3] Thus, while these marks are needful and proper in giving us direction, more could be said.

Again, the previous marks (especially the Reformation marks) should be noted when one is looking to join a local church, but Gregg Allison has also presented seven particular marks of the church that are of a more specific nature.[4] The first three marks revolve around God as Trinitarian, with the claim that the church should be doxological, logocentric, and pneumadynamic. As doxological, the church is oriented to the glory of God, living for and proclaiming the greatness of who he is. As logocentric, the church is to be focused on the Word of God, understood both as Jesus Christ and the inspired Scripture. And as pneumadynamic, the church recognizes that they are created, gathered, gifted, and empowered by the Holy Spirit. These marks should remind someone, as Webster asserts, of "the vital consideration that the church is not constituted by human intentions, activities, and institutional or structural forms, but by the action of the triune God, realized in Son and Spirit."[5]

The final four marks focus on the gathering and sending of the church. First, the church is covenantal, gathered as members in new covenant relationship with God and in covenant relationship with one another. This mark puts specificity to the realities inherent in church membership, implying membership should be regenerate and focused on ongoing discipleship and oversight. Next, the church must be confessional, united by

---

2. John Calvin, *Institutes of the Christian Religion*, ed. John T. McNeill, trans. Ford Lewis Battles (Philadelphia: Westminster, 1960), 4.1.9.

3. Hammett remarks, "Both [sets of marks] seem to be responsive to and shaped by the historical contexts in which they were formed. The creedal formulation of 'one, holy, catholic, and apostolic' helped the patristic church fathers respond to the challenges they faced from various heretical groups in their day, and the Reformation marks reflect the Reformers' conviction that much of the Roman Catholic Church of their day had lost the gospel in their preaching and were practicing the sacraments in a way that obscured rather than portrayed the gospel. This responsiveness suggests that perhaps the development of marks of the church is an ongoing task as churches face new challenges" (John S. Hammett, *Biblical Foundations for Baptist Churches: A Contemporary Ecclesiology* [Grand Rapids: Kregel, 2005], 65).

4. For more detail on these particular marks, see Gregg R. Allison, *Sojourners and Strangers: The Doctrine of the Church* (Wheaton, IL: Crossway, 2012), 105–57.

5. John Webster, "The Self-Organizing Power of the Gospel: Episcopacy and Community Formation," in *Word and Church: Essays in Christian Dogmatics* (New York: T&T Clark, 2001), 195.

both personal confession of Christ and common confession of the historic Christian faith. In other words, the church's membership is comprised of those who believe in Christ, and there is a concrete manifestation of commonly held beliefs. Third, the church is missional. While more will be said regarding this mark in the next section, this means the church understands and lives out its identity as divinely called and divinely sent ministers proclaiming the gospel. Finally, while the church is located in space and time, it is also eschatological in its outlook, possessing a certain hope, and a clear destiny. As a person looks for a church, these marks should be prominent in their inquiries.

A Church on Mission

While already noting that the church is missional, it is worthy of further consideration. There has been some debate regarding the definition of the mission of the church, but some key texts and themes must be prominent in the definition. Based on the sin of mankind, God is on a mission to redeem and restore through the person and work of the Son, Jesus Christ. This good news of salvation in Jesus must, therefore, be proclaimed.[6] Gilbert and DeYoung define the mission of the church, based especially on the Great Commission (Matt. 28:19–20): "The mission of the church is to go into the world and make disciples by declaring the gospel of Jesus Christ in the power of the Spirit and gathering these disciples into churches, that they might worship and obey Jesus Christ now and in eternity to the glory of God the Father."[7]

While some would argue for a more holistic definition,[8] the essence of mission is about proclaiming the saving work of Jesus Christ, making disciples, gathering into churches, and going to again proclaim the good news. These disciples are certainly involved in a variety of good works as the church scatters and lives in the world, but this should not be confused with mission. Christians are to be people of both "declaration and demonstration," but the demonstration of love for neighbor is always aimed at declaring the gospel to those who are in need of hearing it.[9] Christ has done a work, and we must endeavor to proclaim that work so as to make disciples who will love others holistically,

6. Köstenberger and O'Brien maintain, "Thus mission is the ingredient that both precedes Christian existence and constitutes a major motivation for Christian living: the saving mission of Jesus constitutes the foundation for Christian mission, and the Christian gospel is the message of mission, a mission that is not optional but mandatory" (Andreas J. Köstenberger and Peter T. O'Brien, *Salvation to the Ends of the Earth: A Biblical Theology of Mission*, NSBT 11 [Downers Grove, IL: InterVarsity, 2001], 19).

7. Kevin DeYoung and Greg Gilbert, *What Is the Mission of the Church?: Making Sense of Social Justice, Shalom, and the Great Commission* (Wheaton, IL: Crossway, 2011), 241.

8. See, for example, Christopher J. H. Wright, *The Mission of God: Unlocking the Bible's Grand Narrative* (Downers Grove, IL: IVP Academic, 2006); idem, *The Mission of God's People: A Biblical Theology of the Church's Mission* (Grand Rapids: Zondervan, 2010).

9. DeYoung and Gilbert, *What Is the Mission of the Church?*, 223–24.

including, most importantly, telling those others about the good news they have embraced. When looking for a church, this mission should be front and center.

A Church That Is Ministering

Beyond the mission of the church, one also needs to consider the ministries of the church. One should look to see if the church is active and brimming with ministry opportunities and should envision as a future member how they might be able to serve. As a people who are gifted by the Spirit (1 Peter 4:10–11), and in keeping with the command to love our neighbors as ourselves (Matt. 22:34–40), a healthy church is one that ministers to and serves one another. Allison maintains that the ministries of the church include worship of the triune God, proclamation of the Word of God, discipleship of church members through education and community life, and care of people through prayer, giving, support of pastors, and assistance for those in need.[10] Regardless of how one summarizes the various ministries of the church, one must recognize that the gospel creates community. And because it points us to the One who died for his enemies, it creates relationships of service rather than selfishness.[11] Ministry is about looking to others and considering them as better than ourselves (Phil. 2:3–4).

It is crucial to also note that if one is to effectively minister in a local church, it must be just that, a local church. In other words, given the propensity to become accustomed to varying degrees of lengthy commutes, it seems more ideal to pursue membership and minister in a church that is actually nearby. The localness of the local church will allow a person to know people in that particular community, share the gospel more effectively, fellowship with other church members more readily, and minister more freely. It will allow us to share our possessions, share our hearts, and endure with and embrace one another as family.[12] As such, this is a factor that should be taken into account.

Summary

Choosing a church to join is a very important decision. Unfortunately, at times, people can tend to focus on surface issues. Potential church members, while recognizing that no perfect church exists, should look for a church that is rightly marked by biblical principles, is on mission, and is focused on ministering to the needs of others. Beyond this, as they join the church, they should commit themselves to contributing to the church in these particular areas, holding firm to right doctrine, living pure lives, evangelizing, and ministering.

---

10. Allison, *Sojourners and Strangers*, 413.
11. Tim Keller, *Center Church: Doing Balanced, Gospel-Centered Ministry in Your City* (Grand Rapids: Zondervan, 2012), 311.
12. See Joseph H. Hellerman, *When the Church Was a Family: Recapturing Jesus' Vision for Authentic Christian Community* (Nashville: B&H Academic, 2009), 144–62.

REFLECTION QUESTIONS

1. What are the various marks of the church one should be looking for?

2. What is the mission of the church?

3. How do good works factor into the life of the church, although they are not *the* mission of the church?

4. How would you summarize the various ministries of the church?

5. In what ways has God called you to minister in your local church?

Who Should Become a Member of a Church?

Not just anyone should join a church in membership. People must first be called by God and believe in the gospel of Jesus Christ. In other words, to join in membership in a local church, one must be a member of the new covenant community by faith. We have already touched on the fact that a person should also be baptized as a believer to join a church in membership, but here we will focus more precisely on the details of conversion. As such, it is imperative that we focus on the gospel and what this good news entails. Once one establishes what the good news is, it must then be understood what our response to this good news is to be and how that relates to church membership specifically. As a people living under the new covenant, pursuing membership that is truly a body of believers, these points are of utmost importance.

The Gospel

Graham Cole helpfully summarizes both the plight and solution for sinful humanity: "God creates the world, the world gets lost; God seeks to restore the world to the glory for which he created it. Central to the divine strategy is Christ, his coming and his cross. The troubles and calamities will end."[1] Christ is the central figure such that God the Father can be both just and justifier (Rom. 3:21–26).

More specifically, when it comes to the gospel, some basic facts must be recognized. First, God created us for His glory: He created us to put his goodness and truth and beauty and wisdom and justice on display and take delight in Him (Isa. 43:6-7). Next, every human should live for God's glory: If God made us for his glory, it is clear that we should live for his glory. Our duty comes from his design (1 Cor. 10:31). Third, all of us have failed to glorify

---

1. Graham A. Cole, *God the Peacemaker: How Atonement Brings Shalom*, NSBT 25 (Downers Grove, IL: InterVarsity, 2009), 19.

God as we should: None of us has obeyed, trusted, or treasured God the way we should (Rom. 3:23). Fourth, all of us are subject to God's just condemnation: We have all belittled the glory of God. So God is just in shutting us out from the enjoyment of his glory forever (Rom. 6:23). Next, God sent His only Son, Jesus, to provide eternal life and joy: Christ died as our substitute and satisfactory sacrifice (1 Tim. 1:15). Finally, the benefits purchased by the death of Christ belong to those who repent and trust in him (Acts 3:19; 16:31).

Thus, in a broad sense, the gospel is news—specifically, good news about the person and work of Jesus Christ (1 Cor. 15:1–58). The gospel is the announcement that the crucified and risen Jesus (perfect Son of God, Son of Man), who died for our sins and rose again according to the Scriptures, has been enthroned as the true Lord, Savior, and Treasure of the world. When this gospel is preached, God calls people, out of sheer grace, to respond in repentance and faith in Jesus Christ. This definition is historical, telling us who Jesus is and what he accomplished. It is also experiential, meaning it is applied to us through the means of repentance (turning from sin) and faith in Jesus as our Lord, Savior, and Treasure.

Union with Christ and Regeneration

When speaking broadly of salvation, one can think of a number of doctrinal truths. We are saved by God's grace, which is his undeserved goodness extended toward us (Eph. 2:8–9). Considering the doctrine of election, we are a chosen people by God the Father in Christ (Eph. 1:3–4). Christ has provided atonement for us, bringing us into right relationship to God (Rom. 5:1). We are called by God to put our faith in the saving work of Christ (Rom. 8:28–30). Justification denotes the reality that in Christ we are not guilty; rather, we are righteous (Phil. 3:9). We have been adopted into God's family (Gal. 4:6–7), definitively sanctified (1 Cor. 1:2), and progressively growing in holiness by the power of the Spirit (Eph. 4:22–24). We are called to persevere in our faith, knowing that God will preserve us (Phil. 2:12–13), and we look forward to the hope of our glorification, where we will ultimately be free from the presence and power of sin.[2]

Some have argued that all of these concepts are encapsulated in the idea that we are united to Christ. Johnson rightly maintains, "Christ is our salvation and that we are the recipients of his saving work precisely and only because we are recipients of the living Christ. Our union with the living Christ is, in other words, what it means to be saved."[3] Many texts of Scripture could

---

2. For detailed analyses on each of these aspects of salvation, see Bruce A. Demarest, *The Cross and Salvation: The Doctrine of Salvation*, Foundations of Evangelical Theology (Wheaton, IL: Crossway, 1997).

3. Marcus Peter Johnson, *One with Christ: An Evangelical Theology of Salvation* (Wheaton, IL: Crossway, 2013), 18.

be cited in reference to this doctrine, but one can look at Ephesians 1:3–11 and see that all the benefits we have in salvation are based on the fact that we are "in Christ" (cf. John 15:1–10; Rom. 5:12–21; Gal. 2:20). Our union with Christ as a person is the means by which we benefit from his work, and union with Christ happens by faith and repentance.

Horton understands union with Christ to consist as a covenantal union with God—a legal union whereby we are justified and adopted, and an organic union as we live in Christ.[4] A believer is united to Christ at the moment of coming to faith; their union is established by the indwelling of the Spirit. The person united to Christ therefore enters into participation with Christ in his death, resurrection, ascension, and glorification. As a participant in Christ's death and resurrection, the believer dies to the world and is identified with the realm of Christ. And, most importantly for the purposes of church membership, as a member of the realm of Christ the believer is incorporated into his body, since union with Christ entails union with its members.[5]

Another important facet of salvation as it relates to the doctrine of church membership is regeneration. Regeneration, according to Demarest, is "that work of the Spirit at conversion that renews the heart and life (the inner self), thus restoring the person's intellectual, volitional, moral, emotional, and relational capacities to know, love and serve God."[6] The noun *palingenesia* ("new birth," "regeneration") occurs only twice in the NT (Matt. 19:28; Titus 3:5). However, the NT also describes regeneration via several descriptive figures and images. Regeneration is presented as re-creation (2 Cor. 5:17), spiritual resurrection (Eph. 2:4–6; Col. 2:13), circumcision of the heart (Deut. 30:1–6; Ezek. 36:25–27; Col. 2:11), washing (1 Cor. 6:11), and new spiritual birth (John 1:13; 3:1–10; 8:23; 11:41). God does this work in us, and the effects are staggering. Piper summarizes this concept and rightly links it up to union with Christ: "In the new birth, the Holy Spirit supernaturally gives us new spiritual life by connecting us with Jesus Christ through faith. Or, to say it another way, the Spirit unites us to Christ where there is cleansing for our sins (pictured by water), and he replaces our hard, unresponsive heart with a soft heart that treasures Jesus above all things and is being transformed by the presence of the Spirit into the kind of heart that loves to do the will of God (Ezek. 36:27)."[7] Salvation is multifaceted in terms of what God does in our lives when we believe in the gospel, but union with Christ and regeneration are a helpful focus in thinking of church membership.

---

4. Michael Scott Horton, *The Christian Faith: A Systematic Theology for Pilgrims on the Way* (Grand Rapids: Zondervan, 2011), 587–92. See also John M. Frame, *Systematic Theology: An Introduction to Christian Belief* (Phillipsburg, NJ: P&R, 2013), 913–17.
5. Constantine R. Campbell, *Paul and Union with Christ: An Exegetical and Theological Study* (Grand Rapids: Zondervan, 2012), 414.
6. Demarest, *The Cross and Salvation*, 293.
7. John Piper, *Finally Alive* (Ross-shire, Scotland: Christian Focus, 2009), 42.

Pursuing a Regenerate Church Membership

The miracle of salvation must occur in the lives of those who wish to join a local church. There must be a clear understanding of who God is, the nature of our sin, the person and work of Christ, and the call to respond to the gospel in repentance and faith. God must shine the light of the gospel of the glory of God in the face of Christ (2 Cor. 4:6) into the heart of an individual. They must see him as Savior, rescuing them from their sins (John 3:16); Lord, submitting to him as their master (Rom. 10:9–10); and as treasure, their all-satisfying joy (John 6:35).

This is the work of salvation in the life of an individual, and churches must do all they can to ensure that those who join are in fact regenerate. This is crucial because, as has been stated earlier, the church *is* its membership. As such, members, who all act as "priests" in the community (1 Peter 2:9)[8] are to be regenerate and conform to the standards set for the new covenant community (Ezek. 36:25–27). And the ongoing oversight of regenerate church membership is the work not only of pastors, but the present membership of the church. Leeman astutely observes the biblical-theological warrant for members as holding authority in this area:

> The office of priest-king given to the federal head or Adam, which involved *working* and *watching* over the place where God dwelled, was further specified in the life of Israel, fulfilled in Christ, and has now been re-conferred on every member of the church. In the new covenant era that means that every member of the church possesses this same office as mediated through Christ. Specifically, church members are charged with *working* on behalf of Christ's kingdom and with *watching over* the membership and the teaching of God's new covenant temple garden, the church. A pastor, presbytery, or bishop that prevents church members from doing this work, therefore, usurps granted authority and prevents them from doing the very work that God has commissioned them to do.[9]

With this biblical-theological trajectory in place, one understands the importance of this task as present members assess potential candidates for membership.

As the living temple of the Spirit (1 Cor. 3:16–17; Eph. 2:19–22), a kingdom of priests (1 Peter 2:9), and members of the new covenant community

---

8. While not personally agreeing with every detail and implication, for a recent study on the priesthood of believers, see Uche Anizor and Hank Voss, *Representing Christ: A Vision for the Priesthood of All Believers* (Downers Grove, IL: InterVarsity, 2016).

9. Jonathan Leeman, *Don't Fire Your Church Members: The Case for Congregationalism* (Nashville: B&H Academic, 2016), 36–37."

(Jer. 31:31–34), we are to exercise an office of authority as members. All members are on equal footing in the sense that they all know the Lord, from the least to the greatest (Jer. 31:34). As every member possesses this knowledge of God, they are capable of identifying the true teaching of the gospel, as well as identifying who is rightly affirming and embracing this saving knowledge of God. If Christians, by virtue of their Spirit-given competence and their Christ-given duties as priest-kings, possess all the training they need to assess whether their teacher's teaching accords with a true knowledge of God in the gospel, surely they are competent to assess one another's professions of faith.[10] This is the duty of members who have experienced the saving work of Christ and have been brought into the wonders of the new covenant, and we must take this responsibility seriously.

Summary
When seeking to understand who should join as a member of a church, a robust understanding of salvation is necessary, both for the candidate and the church. One must understand the details of all that is accomplished through Christ's work on our behalf. The gospel must be explicitly understood and affirmed. As church members, we aim to ensure that those joining in membership have experienced the work of regeneration and are united to Christ as members of the new covenant community. Certainly pastors take a role of leadership in this area, but all members are responsible for this work, and thus involvement by members at some level in bringing in new members is needful.

REFLECTION QUESTIONS

1. What is the gospel?

2. How must one respond to the gospel?

3. What is union with Christ?

4. How would you describe the various doctrines that describe our salvation (e.g., justification, regeneration, sanctification, etc.)?

5. Why should all members be involved in the process of bringing in new members?

---

10. Ibid., 53–54.

At What Age Should Someone Be Admitted to Membership?

Up to this point we have made the case that baptism is the initiating oath-sign of the new covenant and is to be administered to a person who is seeking to enter as a member of the church. And the NT pattern suggests that baptism seemingly took place directly on the heels of a person believing in Jesus Christ. This pattern then raises the question: If a child is converted to faith in Christ, are they then to be immediately baptized and regarded as a full-fledged church member? Most in the history of the church would not affirm member status being placed on a child, but then some questions remain. As Jamieson claims, "We either have to sever baptism from membership, or introduce people into membership who are not yet ready for its responsibilities, or depart from the apparent New Testament pattern of immediate baptism."[1]

This situation requires careful attention and wisdom. One certainly does not want to deny genuine conversion in children, but at the same time consideration must be given to who joins in membership, particularly noting the tasks involved in membership Also, there has been debate in recent days regarding what ages should be minimal to receive baptism, noting that children can merely be acquiescing to the wishes of their parents and not truly be converted. All of these factors must be considered, citing wisdom and individual assessments as it relates to baptism for children, but also noting the responsibilities of membership and the implication of certain age and maturity requirements.

Salvation Is a Prerequisite

As has been previously argued, church membership is comprised of those who are part of the new covenant community through faith in Jesus Christ

---

1. Bobby Jamieson, *Going Public: Why Baptism Is Required for Church Membership* (Nashville: B&H Academic, 2015), 216.

(Rom. 3:21–26; 10:9–13). Salvation is a prerequisite to church membership; church members are representative members of the kingdom of God. This is due to the relationship between the church and the kingdom of God presently. In one sense God has always been exercising his kingdom power and sovereignty over all things (Deut. 2:5, 9, 30; 4:19; 29:25–26; 32:8; 2 Kings 19:15; Ps. 29:10; 145; Isa. 6:5; Jer. 46:18). In another sense, God exercises kingly authority over his subjects who, out of faith in him and love for him, serve him as kingdom subjects (Exod. 15:18; Num. 23:21; Deut. 33:5; Isa. 43:15). It is with these kingdom subjects that God makes certain covenants in order to give them a mandate for creation (Adamic covenant; Gen. 1:26; 2:15–17; cf. Hos. 6:7), deliver them from his wrath (Noahic covenant; Gen. 9:8–13), establish a people with a land (Abrahamic covenant; Gen. 12:1–3), a law (Mosaic covenant; Exod. 19:3–6), and a king (Davidic covenant; 2 Sam. 7:8–16), culminating in the salvation and transformation of that people and ultimately all peoples (new covenant; Jer. 31:31–34; Ezek. 36:25–27).

The storyline of the OT revolves around the call of Israel as God's chosen nation of kingly priests (Exod. 19:5–6) manifesting God's glory to the nations. However, Israel failed in this charge. By God's grace, through the progression of the covenants, and ultimately through the coming Messianic King, God's particular kingdom in Israel breaks into creation in order to have restorative impact on the more general, universal kingdom of God.[2] One must be careful to note the progression of these covenants and where we are presently in redemptive history when considering the kingdom, salvation, the church, and membership.

Thus, the kingdom of God, denoting his rule and reign, is a central motif to the biblical storyline,[3] and is crucial for rightly understanding the doctrine of the church in general, and the membership of the church specifically. Reynolds rightly notes:

> The primary and indispensable qualification for membership in a particular Church, consists in a connection with the general Church, or body of Christ. . . . Each particular Church seeks to represent, in itself, the kingdom of Christ, and ought, therefore, to be composed entirely of spiritual materials. It is no part of its design to embrace unbelievers, and prepare them for the kingdom of heaven. They have no

---

2. This summary was derived mainly from Bruce K. Waltke, "The Kingdom of God in the Old Testament: Definitions and Story," in *The Kingdom of God*, Theology in Community, eds. Christopher W. Morgan and Robert A. Peterson (Wheaton, IL: Crossway, 2012), 49–71.

3. For several works affirming the centrality of the kingdom of God as a theme in Scripture, see John Bright, *The Kingdom of God: The Biblical Concept and Its Meaning for the Church* (Nashville: Abingdon, 1953); Graeme Goldsworthy, *The Goldsworthy Trilogy* (Carlisle: Paternoster, 2000); George Ladd, *A Theology of the New Testament* (Grand Rapids: Eerdmans, 1993); Thomas R. Schreiner, *The King in His Beauty: A Biblical Theology of the Old and New Testaments* (Grand Rapids: Baker Academic, 2013).

right to its privileges and blessings. They are intruders at its ordinances. No ecclesiastical recognition of them as children, can change their relation as aliens and strangers; and they who introduce them contravene the declared will of the great Head of the Church. The gates of his kingdom are open to none but converted men. It is, therefore, the imperative duty of the churches to admit to membership none but such as give satisfactory evidence that they have been born again.[4]

Thus when considering the nature of the kingdom of God, this gives rise to pursuing a membership that is regenerate.

Exercise of the Keys

Typically, when one thinks of the exercise of the keys, two ideas come to mind: membership and discipline.[5] More specifically, the church, as the community of the kingdom, provides entrance into the kingdom through the proclamation of the gospel and affirmation of those who genuinely receive it. Its newly born citizens live as kingdom people under the sovereignty of the king. God has allowed the church to exercise the authority of the keys, not only in admission into the church, but also, if needs be, removal from the church (Matt. 18:15–20).[6]

Therefore, a local church is a gathering of believers who together testify to the name of Jesus and to their shared membership in him. They do this by preaching the gospel and by employing the keys through admission and removal from membership, as well as the ordinances, which are directly tied to membership and discipline.[7] In observing the progression of the covenants

---

4. J. L. Reynolds, "Church Polity or the Kingdom of Christ," in *Polity: Biblical Arguments on How to Conduct Church Life*, ed. Mark E. Dever (Washington, DC: Center for Church Reform, 2000), 323.

5. Keach rightly maintains, "The power of the Keys, or to receive in and shut out of the congregation, is committed unto the Church" (Benjamin Keach, "The Glory of a True Church and its Discipline Display'd," in Dever, *Polity*, 71).

6. See D. A. Carson who claims, "If the church, Messiah's eschatological people already gathered now, has to exercise the ministry of the keys, if it must bind and loose, then clearly one aspect of that will be the discipline of those who profess to constitute it. Thus the two passages are tightly joined: 18:18 is a special application of 16:19. Again, if we may judge from Paul's ministry, this discipline is a special function of apostles, but also of elders and even of the whole church (1 Cor 5:1–13; 2 Cor 13:10; Titus 2:15; 3:10–11)—an inescapable part of following Jesus during this age of the inaugurated kingdom and of the proleptic gathering of Messiah's people. The church of Jesus Christ is more than an audience. It is a group with confessional standards, one of which (viz., 'Jesus is the Christ') here precipitates Jesus' remarks regarding the keys. The continuity of the church depends as much on discipline as on truth. Indeed, faithful promulgation of the latter both entails and presupposes the former" (*Matthew*, EBC 9, rev. ed. [Grand Rapids: Zondervan, 2010], 374).

7. See Jonathan Leeman, *Don't Fire Your Church Members: The Case for Congregationalism* (Nashville: B&H Academic, 2016), 103.

in redemptive history, we see that this work should not be done merely by pastors/elders; rather, this authority of the keys denotes the work of members. The covenant establishes basic equality of political access and privilege among every member of the community. In Jeremiah 31:31–34, a key text about the new covenant, that there is a "democratization of the priesthood." This is so because every believer will be in the knowledgeable position of the priests and thus will have no need to be taught by any leaders or caste of priests.[8] Leeman summarizes and calls this "the democratization of priestly rule."[9] Thus, under the new covenant, the keys of the kingdom are exercised by all members.

In summarizing what members are called to do, Matthew 16 and 18 together answer this question by pointing to the gathered congregation. In these two texts Jesus gives the gathered congregation the authority to guard the *who* and the *what* of the gospel. It means that they have been tasked with receiving and dismissing the members (the *who*), with ensuring that the teachers are teaching biblical doctrine (the *what*), and, by inference, with being involved in any significant decision that sustains or directs the church's existence as a gospel-bearing witness.[10] In other words, church members represent Christ, seeking to expand the reach of Christ's kingdom, and guarding the people of God in holiness.

Having understood who members should be and what they are to exercise in terms of their office, the question remains as to whether a child can aspire to such terms. We by no means wish to discourage a child who is genuinely seeking Christ in repentance and faith, but we also understand that the terms and tasks of membership are vital to the health of the church. As such, careful wisdom must be applied in this situation.

Wisdom Must Speak

Since baptism is the initiating sign of the new covenant, and thus precedes membership, one must consider children in relation to the timing of baptism, as well as joining in membership. First, regarding baptism, one can state the obvious and affirm that there is no explicit biblical command concerning the proper time at which to baptize a child. The data used to support immediate baptism, which may often result in baptizing very young children, lacks real warrant. There are examples of conversions with no mention of baptism (Acts 2:47; 4:4; and 16:5 refer to daily conversions but not daily baptisms); indeed, there is no mention of any baptisms in the entire first missionary journey of Paul (Acts 13–14), though many were converted in numerous cities. Paul himself seemed to separate his ministry of preaching the gospel and that of baptizing (1 Cor. 1:14–17), and there are

---

8. G. K. Beale, *A New Testament Biblical Theology: The Unfolding of the Old Testament in the New* (Grand Rapids: Baker Academic, 2011), 733–34.
9. Leeman, *Don't Fire Your Church Members*, 47.
10. See ibid., 104.

only a handful of references to baptism in the epistles. Therefore, the call for immediate baptism is not the best argument to make in calling for the baptism of young children.

Historically it can be noted that in credobaptist circles, churches generally thought it most wise to delay baptism until the leadership tested the maturity of the conversion.[11] There is wisdom here in that we do not want to give a child or their parents false assurance of the child's regeneration. At the same time, we do want to apply the sign of the new covenant to those who are truly part of the new covenant. As such, there is wisdom in delaying baptism until at least ten or twelve years of age, or perhaps the early teen years. The point is that assessment must be made by the leadership and the congregation on a case by case basis.

Regarding membership, one recognizes from the thoughts previously given on the kingdom of God and the exercise of the keys, membership is a serious office to inhabit. Here we are dealing with affirming the work of the gospel in someone's life, dealing with the details of church discipline, guarding the gospel doctrinally, overseeing one another's discipleship, and contributing in these ways to the overall health of the church. As such, while a person baptized as a young teen can participate in the life of the church in some ways (e.g., the Lord's Supper, accountability in growth as a disciple), full-fledged membership must come at an age of maturity, when they are able to rightly handle the keys of the kingdom. While this does potentially separate conversion and baptism from full membership, the office demands wisdom to discern multiple complexities. With this in mind, many churches have deemed that a minimum age of eighteen is a prerequisite for joining a church in membership.

Summary

The work of a church member is real and vital. As such, age does matter as one considers who can join as a member. Regeneration is an absolute prerequisite, as well as the initiating oath-sign of the new covenant, namely, baptism. Baptism, however, should be applied wisely to members of the kingdom of God, which may require some time and instruction to discern adequately. Members then exercise the keys of the kingdom, overseeing the *who* and the *what* associated with the gospel in membership, discipline, and the administration of the ordinances. This requires maturity and discernment and must be taken into consideration when thinking through the minimum age for membership in the local church.

---

11. See Mark E. Dever, "The Church," in *A Theology for the Church*, rev. ed., ed. Daniel L. Akin (Nashville: B&H Academic, 2014), 662–63, especially n. 171, where Dever offers a brief survey of well-known Baptist preachers and theologians and the fact that they were baptized in their late teens or early twenties.

REFLECTION QUESTIONS

1. What is the relationship between the kingdom of God and the covenants as seen in Scripture?

2. What is the work that is to be done by the members of the church?

3. What should a typical minimum age for baptism be? Why should this be the minimum age?

4. What can churches intentionally do to ensure those they are baptizing are in fact members of the new covenant community (i.e., regenerate)?

5. What should a typical minimum age for membership be? Why should this be the minimum age?

When Should Someone Be Removed from Membership?

It is a great privilege and, as we have seen, involves the exercise of real authority when operating rightly as a church member. At times, however, those who are part of the church in membership begin to show signs of a life that is not in line with gospel truth. At that point they must undergo the process of church discipline and face potential removal from membership unless they repent.

While the second half of this book will deal with the issue of church discipline in detail, it is worth considering here as an entailment of a robust doctrine of membership. Removal from membership is not to be done hastily, haphazardly, or unlovingly. However, we are to exhort one another and confront sin as we see it manifest itself in the lives of members. This is part of overseeing one another's discipleship. Discipline as a process is to be enacted when sin is recognized in the life of a member that is outward, ongoing, and there is no sign of repentance, though the goal is always restoration.

Outward, Ongoing, Unrepentant Sin

Some people emphasize the fact that love covers a multitude of sins (1 Peter 4:8). This is certainly true, and an important point to hold in the Christian life. However, Strauch adds, there is also a legitimate sense in which Christian love is intolerant: "It is not tolerant in the sense of approving or accepting that which is immoral or false as defined by God's Word. Love cannot be tolerant of that which destroys people's lives or spreads lies about the gospel."[1] Discipline, therefore, must take place for unrepentant sin.

---

1. Alexander Strauch, *A Christian Leader's Guide to Leading with Love* (Littleton, CO: Lewis and Roth, 2006), 161.

As such, church members must learn the skill of how to privately and tenderly confront sin. This does not mean you confront someone every time they commit the slightest infraction, but it does set up an attitude of oversight in discipleship, coupled with humility. The church is called to be holy, blameless, and without blemish through the work of Christ (Eph. 5:25–27). Although this reality is complete for the church in its positional standing in Christ, Saucy claims, "It is also a process in the life of the church as the meaning and significance of that complete salvation are continually applied through the operation of the Holy Spirit by means of the Word."[2] The responsibility of the church is to pursue purification in their midst. Thus, before one speaks of disciplining others, one must recognize the discipline of the Father (Heb. 12:5–7) as well as self-discipline in obedience to the numerous commands for purity in the Word (1 Cor. 11:31; 2 Cor. 7:1; 1 John 3:3).

When the health of the body is endangered by the failure of members to discipline themselves, the church as a community is responsible to exercise the needed correction.[3] The importance of the pursuit of holiness cannot be overestimated, for only a church as the temple of the Spirit can be used of God in service to their own church community and the world. That being said, one must also recognize that formal church discipline is reserved for sins of such significance that the church no longer feels able to affirm a person's profession of faith. Thus, there is a call to holiness while also recognizing that everyone sins. Leeman helpfully clarifies, "Somewhere there's a line between sins and sin patterns that you expect of Christians and sins and sin patterns that make you think someone may not be a Christian. Church discipline is warranted, you might say, when an individual crosses from the first domain into the second."[4] This line is crossed when we see sin in a person as outward, ongoing, and unrepentant.

First, sin will have an outward manifestation. This can be tricky, as there are certain sins that can be difficult to perceive, but it should be something that is seen or heard. More specifically, excommunication must come for those who unrepentantly go through the entire process of Matthew 18:15–18, form divisive factions within the church (Rom. 16:17–18; Titus 3:10), live publicly scandalous lives (1 Cor. 5), or reject essential doctrines of the faith (1 Tim. 1:19–20; 6:3–5; 2 John 7–11).[5] Davis similarly maintains that there are four major categories for sins for which church discipline may occur: "(1) private and personal offenses that violate Christian love; (2) divisiveness and

---

2. Robert L. Saucy, *The Church in God's Program* (Chicago: Moody, 1972), 96.
3. Ibid., 97.
4. Jonathan Leeman, *Church Membership: How the World Knows Who Represents Jesus* (Wheaton, IL: Crossway, 2012), 112.
5. Daniel E. Wray, *Biblical Church Discipline* (Carlisle, PA: Banner of Truth, 1978), 8–9. See also Ted G. Kitchens, "Perimeters of Corrective Church Discipline," *BSac* 148, no. 590 (1991): 211.

factions that destroy Christian unity; (3) moral and ethical deviations that break Christian standards; (4) teaching false doctrine."[6] Grudem more generally classifies examples of discipline in the NT, which include divisiveness (Rom. 16:17; Titus 3:10), sexual sin (1 Cor. 5), laziness (2 Thess. 3:6–10), disobedience (2 Thess. 3:14–15), blasphemy (1 Tim. 1:20), and teaching false doctrine (2 John 10–11). Nonetheless, he, along with the aforementioned works, would maintain that "a definite principle is at work: all sins that were explicitly disciplined in the New Testament were publicly known or outwardly evident sins, and many of them had continued over a period of time."[7]

This gets to our second point: namely, that this sin that receives discipline is ongoing. Some sins that are done one time must receive ample attention, due to the nature of the consequences and its effects on others. However, many sins form a pattern to be observed over a period of time, and this includes the period of time Matthew 18 outlines in going to them to seek out their repentance. Sin that comes under discipline is typically something that is observed as a pattern and therefore must be dealt with.

Finally, in this process of discipline, one observes that the sin in this person's life is not repented of. Repentance refers to the radical turning away from anything which hinders one's wholehearted devotion to God, and the corresponding turning to God in love and obedience.[8] In this case, the person involved has been confronted with the truth of Scripture, but he or she refuses to let go of their sin. From all appearances, the person prizes the sin more than Jesus. As such, the church must remove its public affirmation from the person, barring them from the Lord's Supper and announcing they can no longer formally affirm their citizenship in Christ's kingdom.[9] Discipline, therefore, is exacted not for trite matters over difference of opinion or personal slights, but for the issue of unrepentant sin.

---

6. Andrew M. Davis, "The Practical Issues of Church Discipline," in *Those Who Must Give an Account: A Study of Church Membership and Church Discipline*, eds. John S. Hammett and Benjamin L. Merkle (Nashville: B&H Academic, 2012), 173. Benjamin Keach offers a similar list for discipline, which includes private offenses, scandalous immorality, heresy, divisiveness, and disorderliness ("The Glory of a True Church and Its Discipline Display'd," in *Polity: Biblical Arguments on How to Conduct Church Life*, ed. Mark E. Dever [Washington, DC: Center for Church Reform, 2000], 73–84). For similar reasons given for the practice of church discipline, see Benjamin Griffith, "A Short Treatise Concerning a True and Orderly Gospel Church," in ibid., 106–7; Samuel Jones, "A Treatise of Church Discipline," in ibid., 153–56; P. H. Mell, "Corrective Church Discipline," in ibid., 422–25; Eleazer Savage, "Manual of Church Discipline," in ibid., 487–88.
7. Wayne Grudem, *Systematic Theology: An Introduction to Biblical Doctrine* (Grand Rapids: Zondervan, 1994), 896. See also R. Stanton Norman, "The Reestablishment of Proper Church Discipline," in *Restoring Integrity in Baptist Churches*, eds. Thomas White, Jason G. Duesing, and Malcolm B. Yarnell III (Grand Rapids: Kregel, 2007), 206–7.
8. See J. M. Lunde, "Repentance," in *NDBT*, ed. T. Desmond Alexander and Brian S. Rosner (Downers Grove, IL: InterVarsity Press, 2000), 726.
9. See Leeman, *Church Membership*, 112–13.

Restoration to Membership

One other question deals with the procedure for restoring people to church fellowship after they have been disciplined. Is this an immediate reinstatement, or is there some kind of probationary period? As churches become more faithful in implementing the process of discipline, this question will become increasingly relevant and therefore demands thoughtful attention.

While more will be said on this topic at a later juncture, two points should be noted. First, church discipline is meant to have an effect on the individual that is remedial in nature. The hope in this action is that they would come to a place of repentance (Matt. 18:15; 1 Cor. 5:5; 2 Thess. 3:15; 1 Tim. 1:20). The goal is that godly sorrow would come over a person for their sin and that would produce a repentance that leads to salvation (2 Cor. 7:10). The aim, like God's discipline, is to see the peaceful fruit of righteousness brought about in the life of that individual (Heb. 12:11).

Secondly, church discipline is meant to have an effect on the church. Church discipline restores the honor of God, strengthens the testimony of the church, protects the church from further sin, and reminds the rest of the church of their propensity toward sin and the consequences of such sin.[10] Churches must also be willing to receive those who repent into the membership of the church (2 Cor. 2:5–11). While there may be careful deliberation, the church must recognize the beauty of redemption and the point of discipline and thus receive a repentant person into their midst.

Summary

Membership in a local church denotes membership in the kingdom as a member of the new covenant community. If the fruit of one's life does not demonstrate that a person is in fact part of the kingdom, we cannot affirm them as members of the local church. The basis for such an action would be the observation of sin in the life of an individual that is outward, ongoing, and unrepentant. One must recognize that, even as people redeemed by Christ's blood and indwelt by the Spirit, we will sin, and thus there is a recognition of love covering a multitude of sins. However, there are patterns of sin that bring about the question of whether this person truly belongs to the new covenant community. The individual is called by this action of discipline to turn from their sin and believe in Jesus Christ for salvation. The church must be ready both to confront and forgive when someone comes back in repentance.

---

10. See Saucy, *The Church in God's Program*, 126.

REFLECTION QUESTIONS

1. What is outward sin?

2. What is ongoing sin? At what point should someone confront another person when they begin seeing sinful patterns?

3. What is unrepentant sin?

4. How can the church better prepare itself to be a place that lovingly and humbly confronts sin?

5. How can the church better prepare itself to be a community that willingly receives people back with forgiveness in their hearts?

What Are the Benefits of Being a Church Member?

Our culture can be fairly obsessed with benefits that one can receive when joining up with different kinds of institutions. Whether it is credit card points, golf membership perks, free drinks, admission to a theme park, or birthday desserts, we love seeing benefit in our partnerships and affiliations. And this desire can build within us a pattern of pragmatic utilitarianism, always looking to benefit self in any way possible.

This consumeristic mentality can have ill effect on the church.[1] If members are always looking to be served, and not to serve, the health of the church will be low. We ought to come to church as members looking to contribute and enhance, not always to take and be mere recipients. However, there truly are benefits to joining a church as a member. God's people are called to a community, the local church. And in the church there is much that happens for the development and growth of every member who commits themselves in this way. Specifically, one sees the benefits of mutual oversight of discipleship, service, structure for the Christian life, and the building up of an effective witness.

Mutual Oversight of Discipleship

Rigorous discipleship seen in church membership is, at least partially, intended to be one of the means of maintaining the people of God in a state of perseverance, as it relates to their faith. In describing the identity of the church and pursuing a culture of discipleship, Poettecker claims, "Theologically, it is God's community of grace and discipleship, the fellowship of 'sinners saved by grace' but also the community of 'the saints striving after holiness.' It is

---

1. For more on doing ministry in a consumeristic, materialistic culture, see Thomas White and Jon Mark Yeats, *Franchising McChurch: Feeding Our Obsession with Easy Christianity* (Colorado Springs: David C. Cook, 2011).

Christ's 'imperfect body' yet it is also to be His 'holy Bride.' Thus, it is the disciplined church earnestly seeking to be the holy church."[2] To this end, a culture of discipleship is needed to keep us from sin when tempted, and to strengthen us for ongoing sanctification.

The people of God are called, therefore, to exhort one another continually in a local church context, in order that we might be holy as God is holy (1 Peter 1:16; cf. Lev. 11:44). Formative discipleship is typical among members, and corrective discipline occurs to press discipleship even more deeply into the fabric of the church. As Owens states, "The biblical answer for maintaining a godly witness of a pure church to the world is the practice of church discipline. . . . A recovery of proper stress on sanctification would soon yield a recovery of proper, biblical church discipline."[3] This ongoing, communal process of discipline must take place, but a robust culture of discipleship will prevent many of these extreme cases. As such, churches must be dedicated to encouraging honesty and mutual exhortation in corporate gatherings, smaller classes, small groups, and one-on-one settings. This may mean a change in the way things are currently done in our churches, but the changes will be worthwhile as we seek to better accord our ways with texts such as Hebrews 3:12–13 and 10:23–25.

This work of discipleship happens in a variety of ways. Foundational to this is "spiritually intentional relationships," where it is normal to talk about and challenge each other in spiritual things.[4] Formal Christian education is also an important aspect of discipleship, as one looks to convey theologically informed content and design.[5] The church is also called to pray for one another, be hospitable, give as needed, help one another to apply the truths of the Bible, and make the gospel known to those who need to embrace it. In all of these ways, a church can develop a robust culture of discipleship.

---

2. Henry Poettecker, "The New Testament Community," in *Studies in Church Discipline*, eds. Jacob T. Friesen, et al. (Newton, KS: Mennonite Publication Office, 1958), 18. Kreider likewise maintains, "Paul in his letter to the church at Corinth has made it clear that a church to be the church of Christ must indeed have standards. There are spiritual and moral standards of life in the church. The church must possess a distinctive Christian quality. It must manifest Christ to men and radiate His Spirit. . . . The witness of the church, the spirit of its members, and the purity of its teachings are real concerns" (A. E. Kreider, "Standards with Love," in ibid., 108).

3. Wil L. Owens, "The Doctrine of Sanctification with Respect to Its Role in Eternal Salvation" (PhD diss., Southeastern Baptist Theological Seminary, 2008), 195. See also Lauterbach, who asserts, "Church discipline is not something we 'do' to someone in sin. Church discipline is the constant activity of a church where holiness and love are pursued. We should always be watching over each other, encouraging each other daily against the possibility of a hardened heart, stimulating each other toward love and good works" (Mark Lauterbach, *The Transforming Community: The Practise of the Gospel in Church Discipline* [Ross-shire, Scotland: Christian Focus, 2003], 20).

4. Mark Dever and Jamie Dunlop, *The Compelling Community: Where God's Power Makes a Church Attractive*, 9Marks Books (Wheaton, IL: Crossway, 2015), 119.

5. For more on Christian education in the life of the church, see James R. Estep, Michael Anthony, and Greg Allison, *A Theology for Christian Education* (Nashville: B&H Academic, 2008).

Opportunities to Serve and Be Served

Within the church there are a number of ways to exercise the gifts God has given to us, and this is a great privilege. This call to service is grounded in the Trinitarian God who calls us to love as he loves (John 13:12–17; 14:15–21; 17:20–26) and is the one who gives gifts to the church as Spirit, Lord, and God (1 Cor. 12:4–6). Volf claims, "The reciprocity among Trinitarian persons finds its correspondence in an image of the church in which all members serve one another with their specific gifts of the Spirit, imitating the Lord through the power of the Father."[6] The call to ecclesial service is also grounded in eschatological expectations, recognizing the kingdom of God is an others-centered realm, as well as the priesthood of believers, as fellow church members serve one another in the power of the Spirit.[7]

With this foundation in mind, one must recognize the inherent need to limit the scope of service within the church to members. Outsiders may want to come into the church and begin serving in various ministries without committing themselves to the church in membership. This is where a church must emphasize the benefits of membership, recognizing that there is a clear delineation between those within and those outside the church. The doctrinal teachings of the Trinity, eschatology, and priesthood apply to those who are part of the new covenant community, regenerate. Many may argue that service is a great front door to allow unbelievers access to church life wherein the gospel can be rightly proclaimed. But the gospel witness of a faithful membership serving, sharing, and loving one another is a powerful testimony to those who may sporadically attend the church and wonder about embracing the gospel as their own. Thus, as the importance of church membership increases in a church, commitment grows, relationships flourish, and the church becomes that much more attractive to those looking in from the outside.

Structure for Your Christian Life

Often in a Western context people think about their own personal relationship with God, and rightly so. We will have to stand before God in judgment to give an account (2 Cor. 5:10), and thus it is of utmost importance how we relate to God personally. As such, Christians must devote themselves to proper spiritual disciplines, especially Bible intake, prayer, and fellowship with other church members, not because we are saved because of these kinds of efforts, but because they are a means by which God extends his grace for

---

6. Miroslav Volf, "The Trinity and the Church," in *Trinitarian Soundings in Systematic Theology*, ed. Paul Louis Metzger (London: T&T Clark, 2005), 170.

7. For further thoughts on the Trinity, eschatology, and the priesthood of the believer serving as foundational to service within the church, see Brad Harper and Paul Louis Metzger, *Exploring Ecclesiology: An Evangelical and Ecumenical Introduction* (Grand Rapids: Brazos, 2009), 156–58.

our continued growth in love and holiness.[8] The emphasis is often on Bible and prayer for our own personal growth.

However, we must also understand that there is a corporate aspect to the Christian life, as the call to fellowship reflects, and it is not to be neglected. The church is to be full of relationships that are mutually encouraging and helping people grow spiritually. Members are to be joined to a church covenantally, submitting to the doctrine and the leadership in appropriate ways. The church is made up of believers who are Jew and Gentile, slave and free, male and female (Gal. 3:28), and thus we should embrace that the church is cross-cultural and cross-generational.[9] There should also be an intentionality in the life of the believer to prioritize the corporate life of the church. There should be some kind of geographical closeness so that people can be involved in the life of the church, so that they can receive encouragement, receive specific prayer, and benefit from the gifts that are exercised within the church. The Christian life was not meant to be lived alone, so we must embrace the fact that the corporate life of the congregation is central to the life of the believer (John 13:34–35; Eph. 3:10–11; 4:11–16; Heb. 10:24–25; 1 John 4:20–21).

Building a Witness

Dever and Alexander rightly assert, "The ultimate goal of building this kind of community—one built on distinctively Christian love that flows from the distinctively Christian gospel—is to display God's glory throughout our surrounding neighborhoods, our cities, and ultimately the world."[10] What an amazing privilege and benefit to join a church in membership. Our Christlike love for one another serves as a powerful tool for evangelism (John 13:34–35). In other words, the mutually loving relationships in the church are designed by God to be attractive to an unbelieving culture. Evangelism programs and methods are excellent in terms of training our members to share the gospel, but one must also recall that the life of the church is intended to function as a gospel witness, a window into God's love displayed in a people. While we engage in evangelism personally, we also do so as a body, and that is a great benefit to joining a church as a member.

Summary

While it is not right to look at church membership merely for what someone can get out of it, there truly are benefits to joining a church formally. This is the place where people will take responsibility in overseeing

---

8. For an excellent book on the spiritual disciplines with a focus on Bible, prayer, and fellowship, see David Mathis, *Habits of Grace: Enjoying Jesus through the Spiritual Disciplines* (Wheaton, IL: Crossway, 2016).

9. See Mark Dever and Paul Alexander, *The Deliberate Church: Building Your Ministry on the Gospel* (Wheaton, IL: Crossway, 2005), 109–12.

10. Ibid., 112.

your growth as a disciple of Jesus Christ. The church is the people who serve you and with whom you serve. The corporate aspect of the church provides needed structure for the Christian life, and it is also a place and a people who serve as an effective witness to the world through gospel proclamation and Christ-centered love. Indeed, there are benefits to church membership, and, as will be shown, as one benefits there is also an inherent call to responsibility in seeking to serve others in tangible ways.

REFLECTION QUESTIONS

1. Are you open to oversight of your discipleship in a local church context? What holds you back from the benefit of others knowing you that well?

2. How have you seen the church serve others? What effect would it have on a church if service were not a value?

3. Is the corporate aspect of the church a part of the structure of your Christian life? If not, what must change?

4. How does the love of the church for one another serve as a witness to the world?

5. Are you viewing the church as a mere consumer, or recognizing the benefits of membership in a healthy way?

What Are the Responsibilities of Being a Church Member?

The benefits of church membership are numerous and worthy of reflection. However, whereas the last chapter may have spoken more in generalities about benefits, this chapter is intended to get personal about the responsibilities of being a church member. There is a crucial role to play as a member, recognizing that the lives of others are affected by the way in which we carry out these responsibilities.

As John Webster writes, "Church order is the social shape of the converting power and activity of Christ, which is present as Spirit."[1] Proper church order recognizes that there is authority vested not only in the eldership of the church, but also its members (Matt. 18:15–20; Acts 15:6–22; 1 Cor. 5:1–13). The membership, functioning as priest-kings as a result of the work of Christ (1 Peter 2:8–10), are charged with guarding and proclaiming the gospel, working on behalf of Christ's kingdom, and watching over the membership. Thus, in their commitment to the local church, the responsibilities of church members include submission to leadership, working to oversee the spiritual growth of others, specific ministry, and consistent attendance.

Submission to Church Leadership

In observing the teachings of the NT, one can assert that churches are to be elder led and congregationally ruled (Acts 20:17–28; Titus 1:5–7; 1 Peter 5:1–4). More specifically, Leeman affirms, "The elders *lead* in the day-to-day life of the church, while the congregation possesses the final *rule* over its

---

1. John Webster, "The 'Self-Organizing' Power of the Gospel: Episcopacy and Community Formation," in *Community Formation: In the Early Church and in the Church Today*, ed. Richard N. Longenecker (Peabody, MA: Hendrickson, 2002), 183.

decisions and activities."[2] Elders lead by teaching and exercising authority (1 Tim. 5:17).[3] Thus, elders preach the Word of God. They are to shepherd their people (Acts 20:28) and lead them, which takes up a familiar OT picture of God's people under their rulers (Ps. 100:3; Isa. 40:11; Jer. 13:17; Ezek. 34) and applies it to the task of caring for and directing the church.[4] Elders in the church operate under the authority of the Chief Elder (1 Peter 5:4) and the truths of Scripture.

With these truths in mind, however, one cannot simply put all their dependence in church leadership. God has entrusted to members the task of exercising authority as well. There is a balance to be struck here. Churches should trust their leaders to make decisions, particularly in relation to the teaching ministry of the church. Congregations do not need to micromanage the leadership, but they should be involved when decisions involve the basic integrity, direction, and gospel unity of the church. Part of the authority of the congregation is also seen in electing the leadership for the church. These must be men of integrity, above reproach, who can be trusted in their spiritual wisdom and aptitude to teach biblical truth (1 Tim. 3:1–7).

The vast majority of the time, it will be quite easy to submit to the leadership of the elders of the church. But the church's authority remains in that there is always an opportunity to ponder and even question the decisions made by the leadership. Part of our submission is to recognize the authority and spiritual maturity of the elders and have a general disposition of affirming what they affirm. However, this must be balanced with the fact that all of God's people are empowered and gifted with the Holy Spirit; all have access to God, all know God, and all are priests.[5] Christ is the head of the church, authority is vested in the membership, and gifted leaders are called to lead. The church is authoritative in church discipline (Matt. 18:18; 1 Cor. 5:5), the selection of deacons and elders (Acts 6:3–6; 15:22; 1 Cor. 16:3), the collection and distribution of monies (1 Cor. 16:1–4; 2 Cor. 8–9), administration of the

---

2. Jonathan Leeman, *Don't Fire Your Church Members: The Case for Congregationalism* (Nashville: B&H Academic, 2016), 124–25.
3. Regarding teaching, Vanhoozer writes, "To preach is to address people in God's name, and address "directed to men with the definitive claim and expectation that it has to declare the Word of God to them." This is precisely why preaching ought to be an exposition of Scripture, the objective or written form of God's Word. To be sure, the ultimate authority over church proclamation is God in triune communicative action, and those who proclaim the word are not able to coerce the Spirit to accompany it so that it will unfailingly achieve its purpose" (Kevin J. Vanhoozer, *The Drama of Doctrine: A Canonical-Linguistic Approach to Christian Theology* [Louisville: Westminster John Knox, 2005], 74).
4. I. Howard Marshall, "Acts," in *Commentary on the New Testament Use of the Old Testament*, ed. G. K. Beale and D. A. Carson (Grand Rapids: Baker Academic, 2007), 596.
5. Stephen J. Wellum and Kirk Wellum, "The Biblical and Theological Case for Congregationalism," in *Baptist Foundations: Church Government for an Anti-Institutional Age*, eds. Mark Dever and Jonathan Leeman (Nashville: B&H Academic, 2015), 66.

Lord's Supper (1 Cor. 11:20–26), setting apart and sending people to certain responsibilities (Acts 11:19–24; 13:1–3; 14:24–28), and the right preaching of the gospel (Gal. 1:7–8; 2 Tim. 4:3). And members submit to their leaders (Heb. 13:7, 17), whose authority depends in large part on their faithfulness to God's Word both in doctrine and in life.[6]

Overseeing Others for Growth in Discipleship

While much has already been said on this point, the emphasis in this chapter is to recognize that we must work to know, love, and oversee other members in our churches. Historically, with the Puritans for example, there was a call to guard one another closely in walking in a manner worthy of the gospel (Phil. 1:27). Fitzgerald explains, "Maintaining social order was critical for a godly community, and ministers argued that every Puritan had a responsibility for personal piety and public duty."[7] Thus church discipline was not the sole domain of pastors. Every stage of the disciplinary process depended heavily upon lay participation. Disciplinary measures in churches revolved around a system of lay "collective watch-fulness," where members of the congregation agreed to oversee the moral behavior of fellow congregants, resulting in the enactment of discipline if necessary.[8] Cooper points out, "Failure to exercise 'watch' over a fellow churchgoer represented breach of covenant—itself a grave, punishable violation—with the wayward sheep, whose soul stood in danger, and with the church, which stood to suffer corruption should sin seep in undetected and remain unpunished."[9]

Beyond this one historical example, the Bible calls for attentiveness and action in fostering a culture of discipleship and pursuing ongoing sanctification in a corporate manner (Heb. 3:12–13; 10:24–25). All Christians are to guard one another, through difficult conversations, encouragement, modeling, and sometimes church discipline. The commitment is substantial and calls us to not remain at the surface with fellow members but to know them, probe them, encourage them, love them, and contribute to the corporate culture of spiritual growth.[10] This may be practically difficult if a church is large, but in settings like small groups and Sunday School we have opportunity to know the people well and pursue such a vision of oversight. We should have a vision to care for one another in specific ways (Rom. 12:13–16).

---

6. Ibid., 71.
7. Monica D. Fitzgerald, "Drunkards, Fornicators and a Great Hen Squabble: Censure Practices and the Gendering of Puritanism," *Church History* 80, no. 1 (2011): 46.
8. James F. Cooper, *Tenacious of Their Liberties: The Congregationalists in Colonial Massachusetts*, Religion in America (New York: Oxford University Press, 1999), 127.
9. Ibid., 36.
10. See Mark Dever and Jamie Dunlop, *The Compelling Community: Where God's Power Makes a Church Attractive* (Wheaton, IL: Crossway, 2015), 54–67.

Ministry to Edify the Body

Every Christian is given a manifestation of the Spirit (i.e., spiritual gift) for the common good of the body of Christ (1 Cor. 12:7). Part of our responsibility in the church is to exercise those gifts to build up the church (Eph. 4:11–16). Church members should, therefore, be intent to discover how God has gifted them and to serve accordingly. God has gifted people to function as differing parts of the body of Christ (1 Cor. 12:1–31); therefore, if someone abdicates their responsibility in ministry, it hurts the health of the church. As such, members should serve according to their giftedness.

That being said, members should also seek to serve, regardless of their giftedness. While some may possess a gift of evangelism (Eph. 4:11), this does not mean that those who are not gifted in this way are somehow "off the hook." We are commanded to share the gospel with all peoples (Matt. 28:18–20). We pray and trust God as we share our faith. Similarly, while some may have the gift of giving (Rom. 12:8), we are all commanded to be generous people and give according to what we have (2 Cor. 9:6–8; Eph. 4:28). The church is to engage in worship, proclamation, mission, discipleship, and caring, and as people exercise their spiritual gifts and serve humbly (Phil. 2:3–4) the church will have the freedom and ability to function as they are called to do.

Consistent Attendance

Hebrews 10:25 tells us that ours is a life of "not neglecting to meet together, as is the habit of some, but encouraging one another, and all the more as you see the Day drawing near." Thus, according to this verse, as Christians we are to join with other Christians regularly in the context of the local church. Members have a responsibility to gather with the body so that all of the things mentioned above (submission to leadership, oversight of discipleship, exercise of gifts) can happen and all can benefit. When members decide to skip out on these gatherings they are detracting from their own spiritual growth as well as that of others.

Summary

There is great responsibility inherent in church membership. There is a real need for one another as we traverse our way through the Christian life. We are responsible to submit to elected leadership, all the while knowing that God has granted the keys of the kingdom to the entire membership and thus striking a balance in authority. We must be proactive as members in working for others in their progress and joy in the faith (Phil. 1:25). The entire body of believers must exercise their spiritual gifts for the good of others and regularly attend the gatherings of the church so as to edify others and be edified themselves. One could name off other marks as well, noting that members should be good listeners to sermons, biblical theologians, and devoted to prayer.[11] When members recognize these marks and pursue them with vigor, the health of the church is greatly enhanced.

REFLECTION QUESTIONS

1. What are the responsibilities of a church member to their church?

2. What is the balance as it relates to elders leading and congregations ruling? Who makes what decisions, and what kind of trust should be involved?

3. Who are you known by in a deep way in your church? Who are you specifically overseeing in terms of growth in discipleship?

4. What spiritual gifts has God given you? In what ways are you or can you serve in your church presently?

5. Why is consistent attendance so important to the overall health of the Christian, as well as the overall health of the church?

---

11. For more on the qualities that should mark church members, see Thabiti M. Anyabwile, *What Is a Healthy Church Member?* (Wheaton, IL: Crossway, 2008).

PART 3

GENERAL QUESTIONS
ABOUT CHURCH DISCIPLINE

Theological Questions

What Does the OT Say about Church Discipline?[1]

God disciplines his children as a Father in order that they might share in his holiness (Deut. 8:5–6; Prov. 3:11–12; Heb. 12:4–11; Rev. 3:19). While noting that there is not a specific form of "church discipline" in the OT, there are patterns offered in the OT that help to make sense of the NT practice of discipline. Exile from Eden, expulsion from the camp, and ejection from the land serve as trajectories—not as perfect parallels—pointing to NT discipline. The OT pattern often denotes God as the initiator of the discipline, whereas in the NT God has given authority to the church to exercise discipline. Also, OT discipline often had a decisive and definitive end in death, and in NT discipline the process is often drawn out for the purpose of repentance and reconciliation. Finally, NT discipline is exacted in an ecclesial context, not within a sociopolitical milieu, as was the case with Israel. These differences aside, one can also see continuity.

Exile from Eden

The biblical narrative begins with God's creation of the universe, climaxing in the creation of humanity (Gen. 1). Man and woman are created in God's image to reflect his glory and exercise dominion over the face of the earth (Gen. 1:26–28). God blesses Adam and Eve, who are to function as his vice-regents, and places them in a garden where they will experience blessing and God's presence, provided they obey God's command to not eat from one particular tree in the garden (Gen. 2:15–17). They, however, succumb to temptation, rebel, and eat from the tree of the knowledge of good and evil (Gen. 3:1–7). While the prospect of death—along with other negative results

---

1. This chapter is derived from Jeremy M. Kimble, *That His Spirit May Be Saved: Church Discipline as a Means to Repentance and Perseverance* (Eugene, OR: Wipf and Stock, 2013), 20–35. Used by permission of Wipf and Stock Publishers (www.wipfandstock.com).

of the fall—is made clear as a consequence (Gen. 3:8–19), what the reader sees is the exile of Adam and Eve from their garden paradise (Gen. 3:23–24). The rest of the biblical story revolves around the question of eventual restoration of the relationship between God and humanity.

Because of their choice to rebel against his command, God proclaims that humans are now in a sinful state. Consequently, he drives Adam and Eve from the garden of Eden and places an angel at the entrance of the garden to keep people from partaking of the tree of life (Gen. 3:22–24). This passage evidences increasingly intensive language being used. First, God says he will "send" (*shalach*) the man out, and then he actually "drove" (*garash*) them out.[2] Thus, God removes humanity from his blessing, immediate presence, and protection.

If the story ended there it would be a rather morbid conclusion; however, there is hope to be seen in this passage, as well as God's gracious character. With the consequences of sin clearly stated and with a long-term promise of the serpent's defeat in place, God acts in mercy to sustain the fallen couple. God clothes them (3:21). The Lord also removes them from the garden to protect them from eating of the tree of life, which had not been forbidden previously, so that they will not live forever in a sinful condition (3:22–24). Beyond what is mentioned here, God also pronounces the *protoevangelion* (i.e., the first mention of the gospel) in Genesis 3:15, promising a seed of the woman—namely, Jesus Christ (Gal. 3:16)—who would one day crush the head of the serpent, Satan. Thus, Calvin asserts that, for Adam, a "solemn excommunication" was administered not so the Lord would cut him off from all hope of salvation, but rather that this would cause individuals to seek "new assistance" elsewhere. He continues, "From the moment in which he became alienated from God, it was necessary that he should recover life by the death of Christ, by whose life he then lived."[3] God, therefore, demonstrates his justice and grace, showing that sin is a grotesque affront to his holiness, while also providing for humanity in both a temporal and eternal fashion.

This act of discipline on God's part is profound in that it serves as a model of the way in which sin will merit serious consequences. The expulsion of Adam and Eve from the garden of Eden is the archetype of all subsequent exile (Gen. 3:24). Throughout the rest of the Bible, the state of God's people is one of profound exile, of living in a world to which they do not belong and

---

2. Of this latter term, Wenham states, "It is often used in the Pentateuch of the expulsion of the inhabitants of Canaan (e.g., Exod 23:28–31). It is coupled with 'send out' in Exod 6:1; 11:1, and in each case it adds emphasis" (Gordon J. Wenham, *Genesis 1–15*, WBC 1 [Waco, TX: Word, 1987], 85).

3. John Calvin, *Commentaries on the First Book of Moses, Called Genesis*, trans. John King, vol. 1 (Grand Rapids: Eerdmans, 1948), 184.

looking for a world that is yet to come.[4] Adam and Eve face not only exile, but also specific curses.[5] Therefore, the act of expelling Adam and Eve from the garden of Eden serves as a kind of prototype for how God will deal with sin throughout the rest of redemptive history.

Expulsion from the Camp

After the exile of Adam and Eve, as well as a global flood (Gen. 6–8) and the scattering of the peoples of the earth (Gen. 11), God made a covenant with a man named Abram, to give him a land, bless him, and make a great nation of his descendants (Gen. 12:1–3). That nation is Israel, later brought out of captivity from Egypt in the exodus and brought into covenant relationship with God (Exod. 1–20). The Lord made his law known through the Mosaic covenant, covering a variety of subjects, including disciplinary measures that must be exacted upon certain offending sinners within the nation of Israel. One such measure was expulsion from the camp of Israel, which was their temporary abode, prior to their entry into the Promised Land.

Being taken outside of the camp was a way in which Israel sought to maintain its holiness and purity before the Lord.[6] As such, corpses were taken outside the camp (Lev. 10:4–5), along with lepers and those who were unclean (Lev. 13:46; 14:3–9; Num. 5:1–4; 12:15; Deut. 23:10–11). The sacrifice that bears the sin of the nation on the Day of Atonement was also taken outside the camp (Lev. 16:20–22), along with those who were to be punished for blasphemy or breaking the Sabbath (Lev. 24:14, 23; Num. 15:32–36), and those who were foreigners (Josh. 6:23). These kinds of commands were to be taken seriously, since God called his people to be holy because he was holy (Lev. 11:44–45). Being taken outside the camp signified a way in which God sought to keep the people of Israel pure.

The second type of removal still involves expulsion from the camp, but the intensity of that expulsion picks up in these specific instances. Here discipline

---

4. I. M. Duguid, "Exile," in *NDBT*, eds. T. Desmond Alexander and Brian S. Rosner (Downers Grove, IL: InterVarsity, 2000), 475–76. See also Robert Alter, *Genesis: Translation and Commentary* (New York: W. W. Norton, 1996), 18.

5. Thus, the suggestion that the Genesis narrative reflects what Ciampa would describe as a "covenant, sin, exile, restoration structure," which applies to all of creation, obviously entails "reading the early Genesis narratives in the light of the covenantal background of their Pentateuchal context, where blessings or curses in the land and the covenantal curse of exile from the land are well-established explicit elements of the narrative" (Roy E. Ciampa, "The History of Redemption," in *NDBT*, 259).

6. Ortlund elaborates on this point: "In contrast to the moral chaos widely accepted in the nation which God is expelling from the promised land, Israel is to observe the distinctions entailed in God's moral order. To transgress his boundaries is to deny one's consecration to Yahweh, making one indistinguishable from those not covenanted to him, as if he had not bound Israel to himself at all" (Raymond C. Ortlund, *God's Unfaithful Wife: A Biblical Theology of Spiritual Adultery*, NSBT [Downers Grove, IL: InterVarsity, 2002]).

is undertaken, most often, as capital punishment for the purity of the whole community. Verbrugge elaborates:

> There are five major areas of serious deviation from the laws of God, and in each case the punishment to be meted out was death. Those who worshiped false gods, engaged in serious ritual offenses, practiced certain sexual impurities, committed social crimes (murder, disrespect of parents, kidnapping), or scorned Yahweh through blasphemy, forfeited the right to live. The classic example of this type of Old Testament "excommunication" is preserved for us in the story of Achan in Joshua 7. . . . Not only was the individual cast out of the visible nation of Israel; he was also cut off from the covenant of God with all its privileges. Physical death was but a sign of his spiritual death, his removal from the book of life (cf. Deut. 29:18–21).[7]

Thus, it is important to note that in this instance, while the salvation of the sinner may not be in view explicitly, one reason these kinds of laws were designed seems to be for the people to persist in their faith and covenantal obedience.

One should be aware of the crucial link to be made between this type of serious correction and NT discipline. Paul, for example, cites a repeated phrase from Deuteronomy connecting this kind of discipline to what is seen in 1 Corinthians 5. In verse 13 of this passage, one can discern this connection to NT church discipline with the phrase, "Purge the evil person from among you." This phrase is paradigmatic for Paul—a point that will be addressed in more detail when we look at discipline in 1 Corinthians 5—and is a phrase seen several times in Deuteronomy relating to disciplinary measures.

Deuteronomy, the final book in the Pentateuch, is set directly prior to the people of Israel entering the land of Canaan. In essence, this is a book about a holy God who has elected a people for himself and made a covenant with them to bless and multiply them if they put their faith in the Lord and obey his commands. The persevering obedience of his people is a serious matter to the God of Israel. The phrase, "Purge the evil person from among you," should be observed with this background in mind. The first use of this phrase is found in Deuteronomy 13:1–5, which is contained in a passage that speaks of how Israel should respond to false prophets in their midst. Here, and in most other instances of this phrase in Deuteronomy, the people of God are told to put the sinner, in this case the false prophet, to death.

---

7. Verlyn D. Verbrugge, "The Roots of Church Discipline: Israelite and Jewish Practice," *RJ* 30, no. 5 (1980): 18.

A second use of this phrase is found in Deuteronomy 17:2–7 where the text speaks explicitly about the way in which Israel should deal with those who worship other gods. The law required at least two valid witnesses against the accused person in order for a case to be established and the death penalty to be put into effect (17:5–7).[8] Having given true testimony to the idolatry of the accused, the witnesses cast the first stones but shared the responsibility with the whole community.

The next use of this saying is found in connection with false witnesses (19:15–21). If a malicious witness rises up against another person and the witness is found to be speaking lies about the other individual, then *lex talionis* is to be put into effect, which could include death for that individual depending on the specific crime (19:19–21; cf. Exod. 21:23–25; Lev. 24:17–20). In Deuteronomy 21:18–21, this phrase is again used in reference to a rebellious son who refuses to submit to the authority of his mother and father (cf. Exod. 21:15; Lev. 20:9). The parents make known the situation to the leadership of their community and disclose their efforts to bring the son into submission. The men of the city, therefore, are to stone the son to death, and thus purge evil from the midst of Israel. This is done so that others will hear of it and, as a result, turn from their sin and avoid such practices.[9]

This particular expression is seen again in Deuteronomy 22 where it is cited for a number of offenses, all of which deal with the sin of sexual immorality (22:13–24). The final use of this phrase in Deuteronomy can be found in dealing with one who seeks to steal a fellow citizen for the purpose of selling him into slavery (24:7; cf. Exod. 21:16). This offender must also die, as did the other sinners previously noted in the Deuteronomic context. All of this is done in order that the evil might be taken out of Israel and their purity restored and maintained.

Thus, whether speaking of temporal expulsion or capital punishment discipline for sin was an explicit practice within the nation of Israel. As the people of God, Israel was called to be holy as God is holy (Lev. 19:2). They were in covenant with God, and thus he promised to expel wickedness from the nation. Finally, God saw them as being corporately responsible for the sin of an individual, since Israel functioned as a community (Deut. 19:13; 21:9).

---

8. One can see Matthew 18:16, 2 Corinthians 13:1, and 1 Timothy 5:19 for evidence of the principle of establishing a testimony on the basis of two or three witnesses carrying over into the NT.

9. John Sailhamer, *The Pentateuch as Narrative: A Biblical-Theological Commentary*, Library of Biblical Interpretation (Grand Rapids: Zondervan, 1992), 460. This is important to keep in mind, as one of the primary motivations for Paul in addressing the Corinthian church and commanding them to expel the evildoer was to prevent the sin from spreading any further in the community, so that the Christians would effectively persevere in their faith.

Ejection from the Land

One final OT trajectory that points toward NT church discipline is the Babylonian conquest and Israel's exile from the land. God promised that Israel would undergo his discipline for disobedience, but the discipline was aimed at bringing them to the point of repentance and sustained obedience. In the book of Deuteronomy, Israel stands poised to take possession of the land of Canaan, and Moses sets before a new generation of adult Israelites the obligations which they must fulfill in order to enjoy God's blessing there (Deut. 4–28). At the heart of these obligations is the requirement to love the Lord wholeheartedly (Deut. 6:4–5). Significantly, Israel's future in the Promised Land is tied directly to their willingness and ability to fulfill their covenantal duties.[10] As God's people, they were told by God that if they were obedient to his commands they would enjoy his blessing, but if they were disobedient they would undergo his curse and would be cast out of the land (Deut. 28–30). Deuteronomy 30 describes the choice between obedience and disobedience, not only as a choice between blessing and curse but also as a choice between life and death (Deut. 30:15, 19).

That same chapter (Deut. 30:1–6) predicts that Israel will repeat the history of humanity and find itself choosing disobedience and unfaithfulness, resulting in death and exile (cf. Lev. 26:1–45). The problem for Israel was a hardness of heart that led to constant rebellion and disobedience. The solution would come in an eschatological circumcision of the heart at the time of Israel's restoration (Deut. 10:12–16; 30:1–6; cf. Ezek. 36:25–27). Thus, even before God's people entered the land he had promised them under the leadership of Joshua, the prospect of their exile from that land as a punishment for disobedience was in view. They would suffer the loss of the land and God's special presence.

As one continues to read through the history of the OT, it becomes apparent that Israel, while experiencing times of blessing and obedience, eventually comes to a place of continual disobedience to God. God sent prophets to turn a sinful nation back to the Mosaic covenant. Some kings repented at the prophetic rebuke and found blessings (1 Chron. 17:1–15; 2 Chron. 11:1–23; 19:1–11), but those who did not repent suffered (2 Chron. 16:7–10; 18:1–34). Eventually, despite these preventative measures sent by God, the northern tribes were taken into captivity by Assyria in 722 BC (2 Kings 17:7–23), and the Babylonians overtook Judah in 586 BC (2 Chron. 36:15–21). The latter prophets speak a great deal regarding the exile and understand this event not as mere coincidence but as brought about directly by God as a result of Israel's ongoing sin and the breaking of the covenant.

---

10. See John D. Currid, *A Study Commentary on Deuteronomy* (Wyoming, MI: Evangelical, 2006), 421.

One also observes a pattern of grace and forgiveness exuding from God and his covenants. While God is faithful to discipline his children, he is also faithful to his promises to restore his people to the land as they come to a point of repentance. Seventy years after Israel was taken forcibly from their land, they return to rebuild and start afresh. However, while physical restoration begins on the wall and the temple of Jerusalem, there is still a spiritual need that must be addressed for Israel. Israel experiences the exile and then God's restoration, and all the while they anticipate the promises given by God through the prophets.[11]

The Shift in Discipline

Observing the transition from later writings in the OT to the NT, one can perceive a shift in practice as it relates to discipline.[12] After the exile a new development in discipline arose: separation from the community of Israel without the accompanying death motif. In Ezra 10:7–8 the same Hebrew word is used as in Deuteronomy 29:21 for separating a person from the covenant community (*badal*), but with quite a different connotation: The opportunity was given for repentance and restoration of the sinner.

Ezra records the only clear OT example of formal exclusion, in which the offender is neither put to death nor solely given over to the punishment of God. In other words, seemingly at this stage in God's progressive revelation in the OT, the task of expelling rebellious Israelites from the community was no longer necessarily connected with their physical and spiritual death. The reason for this change is not apparent. Perhaps it came as a result of the revelation of God in the exile itself. In Judah's case for example, God's punishment—his casting his people out of the Promised Land—was followed up with the possibility of repentance and restoration. This strand is the one taken up in the NT regarding ecclesial discipline.[13]

---

11. See C. Marvin Pate, et al., *The Story of Israel: A Biblical Theology* (Downers Grove, IL: InterVarsity, 2004), 67. See also Hamilton, who maintains God brought the exiles back to the land as he had promised (in 539 BC), but other new exodus promises were yet to be fulfilled (e.g., Isa. 11:9; Hab. 2:14). Israel was back in the land, but the desert was yet to bloom, the enemies of God were yet to be defeated once and for all, the Spirit was yet to be poured out on all flesh, the new and greater David was yet to sit on the throne (James M. Hamilton, *God's Glory in Salvation through Judgment: A Biblical Theology* [Wheaton, IL: Crossway, 2010], 355–59).

12. This section is largely dependent on Verbrugge, "The Roots of Church Discipline," 18–19.

13. See Verbrugge, who asserts that this trajectory is important to note if one is to understand the shape that discipline takes in the NT: "That strand of the Old Testament which became the established policy in the New Testament church was the [latter] one which removed an individual from the visible community but contained no 'death warrant.' The decision regarding the invisible church, the kingdom of Christ, the book of life, was left completely in the hands of the Lord" (Verlyn D. Verbrugge, "Delivered Over to Satan," *RJ* 30, no. 6 [1980]: 19).

Summary
     As noted previously, one must rightly observe the degree of discontinuity that exists between OT and NT discipline. One cannot simply equate Israel and the church in every way. However, these trajectories—exile from Eden, expulsion from the camp, and ejection from the land—highlight key principles that carry over into NT practice. In rightly understanding God's discipline in the OT, therefore, one can see that he operates in a manner that displays his holiness and deals with sin in a fitting manner, but with the goal that his people would repent, be restored, and endure in their obedience to him. Thus, while "church discipline" is not an explicit teaching in the OT, these trajectories point to that coming practice in the NT and give us helpful background based on the character of God and the calling of his people.

REFLECTION QUESTIONS

1. Why should one not simply equate the church and Israel?

2. What does the exile of Adam and Eve from Eden teach us regarding church discipline?

3. What does expulsion from the camp of Israel teach us regarding church discipline?

4. What does the exile from the land of Israel teach us regarding church discipline?

5. In the latter parts of the OT, what kind of shift do we see regarding the practice of discipline?

What Does Matthew 18 Say about Church Discipline?[1]

When it comes to NT texts that speak to the issue of church discipline, seemingly the best known passage is found in Matthew 18 which elucidates the process for discipline in specific detail. Jesus anticipates the realities of church life and addresses the process for dealing with conflict. Church members are to exact discipline in a loving and ordered manner, exercising the power of the keys.

Context

Contextually, Matthew 18 begins with Jesus telling his disciples that they must be humble in order to inherit the kingdom of heaven (18:1–4). He then goes on to instruct his followers to avoid practices that would cause others to stumble into sin, even to the point of exercising extreme self-discipline such as cutting off a sinning hand (18:5–9). Jesus then tells a parable in verses 10–14, describing the effort made by a shepherd and his rejoicing over the recovery of a lost sheep (a sinner who had turned aside from the teachings of God). After the text in view, Jesus also tells a parable dealing with the issue of forgiveness (18:21–35). Based on this discussion of sin, and how followers of Jesus are to respond to sin in their life and the lives of others, Jesus moves into one of the central texts regarding church discipline, Matthew 18:15–20.

---

1. This chapter is derived from Jeremy M. Kimble, *That His Spirit May Be Saved: Church Discipline as a Means to Repentance and Perseverance* (Eugene, OR: Wipf and Stock, 2013), 42–47. Used by permission of Wipf and Stock Publishers (www.wipfandstock.com).

Exegetical Details

Beginning in Matthew 18:15, Jesus states that if someone sins against another[2] there should be a private conversation aimed at addressing the sin issue.[3] Thus, church discipline begins in the private sphere, allowing the offender a chance to hear his sin and have an opportunity to repent and seek forgiveness of the one they sinned against.[4] One can see from this verse, therefore, that the overall goal of this kind of confrontation is not condemnation of sinners, but growth in sanctification through repentance of sin and the expressing of forgiveness by the one against whom they sinned.

Jesus continues his teaching in verse 16 because a person is not always won over in this first step, and thus one should go again and take two or three witnesses. The concept of two or three witnesses is based on Deuteronomy 19:15, which appears to be in a judicial context in relation to the nation of Israel. In Deuteronomy it would seem that the witnesses had seen the actual crime committed, whereas in Matthew 18:17 the witnesses bear testimony to the actual confrontation in the second step of church discipline.[5] However, it seems wise

---

2. One should take note of the textual variant in this verse, where the shorter reading simply says "sins" (*hamartēsē*), while the longer reading adds "against you" (*hamartēsē eis se*). Turner observes that the shorter reading is supported by ℵ, B, and 579, while the longer reading garners support from D, L, Δ, θ, 078, *Byz*, and most Latin MSS. He continues, "A complicating factor is that the phrase in question, *eis se*, sounds much like the verb ending -*ēsē*, which could lead to accidental omission if the text was being dictated to the copyist by a reader." When one takes this into consideration, along with the context of the passage and Peter's use of the phrase "against me" in 18:21, it appears that the longer reading is plausibly authentic (David L. Turner, *Matthew*, BECNT [Grand Rapids: Baker Academic, 2008], 444, 447). Ultimately, according to White and Blue, "although the phrase is missing in some early manuscripts, the fact is unimportant. Other passages urge us to go whether the sin is directed against us or not" (John White and Ken Blue, *Church Discipline That Heals: Putting Costly Love into Action* [Downers Grove, IL: InterVarsity, 1992], 88).

3. Concerning this practice, Adams wisely states, "Anything that creates an unreconciled state between us and another must be brought up and dealt with" (Jay Edward Adams, *Handbook of Church Discipline* [Grand Rapids: Ministry Resources Library, 1986], 55).

4. Chamblin points out the importance of such a first step: "In the church's intense fellowship, such sin [against one another] is perilous indeed, regardless of its exact nature (v. 18a). Whereas in [Matthew] 5:23–24 Jesus instructed the offending brother, here he speaks of the offended party's responsibility" (J. Knox Chamblin, "Matthew," in *Baker Commentary on the Bible*, ed. Walter Elwell [Grand Rapids: Baker, 2000], 744). Carson concurs, "The proper thing is to confront the brother privately and 'show him his fault.' The verb *elenchō* probably suggests 'convict' the brother, not by passing judgment, but by convicting him of his sin. The aim is not to score points over him but to win him over (same verb as in 1 Cor 9:19–22; 1 Pet 3:1) because all discipline, even this private kind, must begin with redemptive purposes (cf. Luke 17:3–4; 2 Thess 3:14–15; James 5:19–20; cf. Ecclus 19:13–17)" (D. A. Carson, *Matthew*, EBC, rev. ed. [Grand Rapids: Zondervan, 2010], 402).

5. Norman agrees with this interpretation when he claims, "The witnesses are to assist in the attempted restoration of the errant church member, but if the attempt fails, they will serve as witnesses, not of the original transgression, but of the failure to repent" (R. Stanton Norman, "The Reestablishment of Proper Church Discipline," in *Restoring Integrity in*

to involve one or two people who have at least some kind of knowledge of the sin that has been committed and that at least one of these witnesses be a church leader (i.e., elder), though this is not dictated by the text itself.

Hopefully at this stage the offender has repented of his or her sin and reconciled with the person they offended. If still they refuse, however, Jesus gives a final exhortation in verse 17 to tell the offense to the church. If at this point the sinner still refuses to admit their wrongdoing and remain unrepentant, that person should be considered as a "Gentile or tax collector." In essence, if the person refuses to repent after being called out by the church, Jesus commands the congregation to view that individual as an outsider of the new covenant community. Such an individual is to be cut off from church fellowship and suspended from typical social relations with other Christians. This last step may seem harsh,[6] but the intention in treating others as nonbelievers is not to injure them or punish them, but rather to help them see the seriousness of their sin and their need for repentance. If repentance does not occur, the person is potentially displaying evidence that he or she was never truly a part of the new covenant community; as such, that person needs to confess his or her sin and place faith in Christ for salvation.

In Matthew 18:18 one can see linguistic connections that lead back to 16:19, as Jesus uses the exact same phraseology in regard to "binding and loosing."[7] The tenses are the same as in 16:19, as is the terminology; the only difference is in the fact that the text is addressed to the church and not just to Peter or the rest of the disciples. Daniel Wallace refers to these terms in Matthew 16:19, 18:18 ("will have been bound" and "will have been loosed") as proleptic perfect participles and defines that concept in the following way: "The perfect can be used to refer to a state resulting from an antecedent

---

Baptist Churches, eds. Thomas White, Jason G. Duesing, and Malcolm B. Yarnell [Grand Rapids: Kregel, 2008], 214). See also Carson: "It is not at first clear whether the function of the witnesses is to support the one who confronts his erring brother by bringing additional testimony about the sin committed (which would require at least three people to have observed the offense) or to provide witnesses to the confrontation if the case were to go before the whole church. The latter is a bit more likely, because Deuteronomy 19:15 deals with judicial condemnation (a step taken only by the entire assembly), not with attempts to convince a brother of his fault" (*Matthew*, 402–3).

6. Strauch points out just the opposite when he says, "A critical test of genuine love is whether we are willing to confront and discipline those we care for. Nothing is more difficult than disciplining a brother or sister in Christ who is trapped in sin. It is always agonizing work—messy, complicated, often unsuccessful, emotionally exhaustive, and potentially divisive. This is why most church leaders avoid discipline at all costs. But that is not love. It is a lack of courage and disobedience to the Lord Jesus Christ, who himself laid down instructions for the discipline of an unrepentant believer" (Alexander Strauch, *A Christian Leader's Guide to Leading with Love* [Littleton, CO: Lewis and Roth, 2006], 152).

7. In Matthew 16:19 and 18:18 the words used for "binding" and "loosing" are *dedemenon* and *lelumenon*.

action that is future from the time of speaking."[8] In other words, these perfect passive participles are communicating to the disciples that the heavenly decision to admit into or exclude from the kingdom preceded their declaration of it on earth.[9] He is not stating that the church has the power to determine what will later be decided in heaven. The verb tense indicates that as the church functions on the authority of Scripture, what it determines will have already been determined in heaven.[10] Thus, the authority given to Peter as an apostle is applied in a particular way to the church as it relates to ecclesial discipline.[11]

Carson demonstrates the conceptual connection between Matthew 16:19 and 18:18 by saying:

> If the church, Messiah's eschatological people already gathered now, has to exercise the ministry of the keys, if it must bind and loose, then clearly one aspect of that will be the discipline of those who profess to constitute it. Thus the two passages are tightly joined: 18:18 is a special application of 16:19. Again, if we may judge from Paul's ministry, this discipline is not a special function of apostles, but also of elders and even of the whole church (1 Cor. 5:1–13; 2 Cor. 13:10; Titus 2:15; 3:10–11)—an inescapable part of following Jesus during this age of the inaugurated kingdom and of the proleptic gathering of Messiah's people. The church of Jesus Christ is more than an audience. It is a group with confessional standards, one of which (viz., "Jesus is the Christ") here precipitates Jesus' remarks regarding the keys. The continuity of the church depends as much on discipline as on truth. Indeed, faithful promulgation of the latter both entails and presupposes the former.[12]

8. Daniel B. Wallace, *Greek Grammar Beyond the Basics: An Exegetical Syntax of the New Testament* (Grand Rapids: Zondervan, 1996), 581.

9. See Carson, *Matthew*, 371–72 for detailed discussion on the tenses of "will have been bound," and "will have been loosed" being periphrastic future perfect passive participles. Also see Julius Robert Mantey, "Distorted Translations in John 20:23; Matthew 16:18–19 and 18:18," *RE* 78 (1981): 409–16.

10. R. Albert Mohler, "Church Discipline," in *Polity: Biblical Arguments on How to Conduct Church Life*, ed. Mark E. Dever (Washington, DC: Center for Church Reform, 2000), 52.

11. See John Hammett, *Biblical Foundations for Baptist Ecclesiology: A Contemporary Ecclesiology* (Grand Rapids: Kregel, 2005), 147; R. T. France, *The Gospel of Matthew*, NICNT (Grand Rapids: Eerdmans, 2007), 928; Benjamin Keach, "The Glory of a True Church and Its Discipline Display'd," in *Polity: Biblical Arguments on How to Conduct Church Life*, ed. Mark E. Dever (Washington, DC: Center for Church Reform, 2000), 71.

12. Carson, *Matthew*, 374 (cf. Calvin, *Institutes*, 4.11.2).

This understanding corresponds with Jesus' words in 18:19–20, which states that if two or three agree about these types of matters on earth, their prayers will be heard by the Father. Practically, it should be affirmed that when the church deals with serious issues relating to church discipline, prayer should be offered constantly concerning the situation. This allows the ecclesial body to move forward with humble boldness, knowing that the matter has already been bound or loosed in heaven, and that they are acting in the authority of the Father and the Son.

Implications

This process of discipline must be exacted in a spirit that is ready to forgive, as evidenced by the parable Jesus tells immediately following his teaching (Matt. 18:21–35). Contextually, it seems that Jesus is commanding the people of God to forgive a person who confesses and repents of his or her sin in matters of church discipline.[13] Thus, church discipline has specific regulations not only for the one who has committed a sin, but also for those within the church who are called to be forgiving.[14]

In concluding this significant section on church discipline, it should be noted that God has given the church authority to render judgment concerning an individual if it comes to that point. This judgment is authoritative only insomuch as it abides by the standards given in the Scriptures, which are the words God has given to us for such matters. The goal for the offender is repentance, and the aim for the offended church is forgiveness. All of humanity has sinned, and through the practice of discipline church members are seeking to persevere in their faith to the end, and thus stand before God at the final judgment and receive mercy in Christ (2 Cor. 5:10; Heb. 10:32–39).

---

13. Chamblin asserts, "Failure to forgive fellow believers (none of whose debts to each other could compare with those incalculable debts that God has canceled) shows that one has never really understood God's forgiveness. The judgment threatening such a person is just as real and final (v. 34) as that which threatens the offender (cf. vv. 14-20)—strong incentive for offering genuine, not just apparent, forgiveness (v. 35b)" (*Matthew*, 745).

14. This call to forgiveness brings to mind a passage such as Matthew 6:14–15. There Jesus warns his followers, "For if you forgive others their trespasses, your heavenly Father will also forgive you, but if you do not forgive others their trespasses, neither will your heavenly Father forgive your trespasses." It appears that these verses are citing forgiveness as a fruit by which we know that we belong to God. If we are an unforgiving people toward repentant sinners, we are proving that we are not truly forgiven by God, and thus we ourselves could be subject to church discipline based on that particular sin. A person who has been forgiven by God through salvation must certainly confront and judge others who disobey the commands of God, but it is also very clear that we must forgive the repentant. For further thoughts on this particular subject see Everett Ferguson, *The Church of Christ: A Biblical Ecclesiology for Today* (Grand Rapids: Eerdmans, 1996), 372; Thomas R. Schreiner and Ardel B. Caneday, *The Race Set Before Us: A Biblical Theology of Perseverance and Assurance* (Downers Grove, IL: InterVarsity, 2001), 77.

REFLECTION QUESTIONS

1. Why is Matthew 18 such an important text regarding church discipline?

2. What is the church discipline process described in Matthew 18?

3. What is Jesus saying when he describes the church as "binding" and "loosing?"

4. How is forgiveness tied to church discipline in the context of Matthew 18?

5. How does the practice of church discipline reflect both the loving and holy character of God?

What Does 1 Corinthians 5 Say about Church Discipline?[1]

Paul addresses a number of sinful issues with the church at Corinth, one of which involves church discipline, as he rebukes the church for not dealing with a specific issue of sexual immorality in the proper way. There is a kind of sexual immorality occurring within the church that is not even acceptable among the pagans, namely, that a man "has his father's wife" (1 Cor. 5:1). This is a somewhat ambiguous phrase, which makes it difficult to know for certain what has happened to the father and if there has been a death or divorce. However, in either case what had been forbidden by all the ancients, both Jewish and pagans, is the cohabiting of father and son with the same woman,[2] and as such the church should have immediately dealt with this issue.

1 Corinthians 5:1–5

Paul recognized this sexually immoral man was involved in a knowingly sinful relationship and committing an offense that should certainly be recognized and rebuked by a Christian church. This action, however, had not taken place, as Paul indicted the Corinthians for being arrogant rather than mourning over this serious issue (v. 2). When Paul tells the Corinthians that they ought to mourn rather than be arrogant, some take that to mean a mourning over the impending loss of the sinning brother.[3] However, the word

---

1. This chapter is derived from Jeremy M. Kimble, *That His Spirit May Be Saved: Church Discipline as a Means to Repentance and Perseverance* (Eugene, OR: Wipf and Stock, 2013), 47–53. Used by permission of Wipf and Stock Publishers (www.wipfandstock.com).
2. Gordon D. Fee, *The First Epistle to the Corinthians*, NICNT (Grand Rapids: Eerdmans, 1987), 200. See also Richard B. Hays, *First Corinthians*, Interpretation (Louisville: Westminster John Knox, 1997), 80–81.
3. So G. G. Findlay, "St. Paul's First Epistle to the Corinthians," *The Expositor's Greek Testament* (London: Hodder and Stoughton, 1910), 808.

is only used elsewhere in the NT in 2 Corinthians 12:21, where its sense closely parallels the concept of godly sorrow or repentance (cf. 2 Cor. 7:8–11). Paul, therefore, appears to be imploring the church to mourn over this man's sin, as well as their own sin of arrogance because they are culpable and corporately responsible for the actions of individuals within their covenant community.[4] The Corinthian church must take action and exclude this person from the community of believers and, in so doing, maintain their corporate holiness.

Paul then exhorts the Corinthians to take care of this issue in a corporate fashion (1 Cor. 5:3–5; cf. Lev. 24:14; Num. 15:35; Deut. 19:16–20). Bargerhuff asserts, "For the discipline to be enacted properly and fully in accordance with Jesus' teaching, the formal assembly of the church, along with its communal power and authority to bind and loose, must be formally instigated."[5] Thus, when they assemble in the name of the Lord Jesus and the power of the Lord Jesus is with them (v. 4), they are to deliver this man to Satan for the destruction of the flesh in order that he might ultimately be saved in the day of the Lord (v. 5).

The content of 1 Corinthians 5:5 has been the subject of much debate as to its proper interpretation. While some believe the "destruction of the flesh" refers to a curse that leads to physical death, it seems more persuasive to read this text as referring to the man's sinful nature being destroyed as he is excluded from the community of faith, an edifying and caring environment that contends for one another's sanctification, and put back out into Satan's domain.[6] South contends for the latter interpretation and states, regarding the connection between 1 Corinthians 5:5 and 1 Timothy 1:20, "Here is the only

---

4. The OT is replete with examples of this. In Exodus 16:27–28 after some of the people had broken the Sabbath, God addresses the nation and asks how long they will refuse to keep His commandments and instructions. In Numbers 16:20–27 the people are warned to keep their distance from Korah, Dathan, and Abiram, lest they also be swept away because of all their sins (note especially Moses' prayer in 16:22). In Deuteronomy 19:13—a passage already considered—the nation of Israel is instructed to purge a sinning individual from their midst so that it may go well with them in the land. Other such examples can be found in Deuteronomy 29:19–21; Joshua 7:1–26; 22:16–18; 1 Samuel 14:37–38; and Nehemiah 13:18. See Roy Ciampa and Brian Rosner, "1 Corinthians," in *Commentary on the New Testament Use of the Old Testament* (Grand Rapids: Baker Academic, 2007), 706; and Rosner, "'Ouchi Mallon Epenthēsate': Corporate Responsibility in 1 Corinthians 5," *NTS* 38, no. 3 (1992): 470–71.

5. Eric J. Bargerhuff, *Love That Rescues: God's Fatherly Love in the Practice of Church Discipline* (Eugene, OR: Wipf & Stock, 2010), 161–62. This assertion is in keeping with Matthew 18:15–20.

6. Lampe comments, "The 'destruction of the flesh' and 'his spirit may be saved' are to be understood according to Paul's usual contrast of flesh and spirit, according to which flesh refers to the sinful nature, the life lived according to human desires, and spirit refers to the spiritual nature, life lived according to the Spirit of God (cf. Gal 5:16–25)" ("Church Discipline and the Interpretation of the Epistles to the Corinthians," in *Christian History and Interpretation: Studies Presented to John Knox*, eds. William Reuben Farmer, C. F. D. Moule, and Richard R. Niebuhr [Cambridge: Cambridge University Press, 1967]).

true verbal parallel to 1 Cor 5.5 in the NT and it clearly excludes the idea of the offenders' deaths, since both Hymenaeus and Alexander are not expected to die but to learn something and correct their behavior."[7] The discipline enacted upon this man is, therefore, restorative in nature and aimed at ensuring the salvation of the offender, hoping he will not remain in unrepentant sin.

1 Corinthians 5:6–13

In the final two sections of 1 Corinthians 5 the reader begins to see Paul's rationale for such a seemingly harsh call to discipline. The apostle begins by reiterating that the Corinthians' boasting is not good, and asks rhetorically whether or not they know that "a little leaven leavens the whole lump" (v. 6). Paul then commands the Corinthians to cleanse out the old leaven,[8] and he grounds this command in the fact that Christ, our Passover lamb, has already been sacrificed (v. 7). Thus, they should "celebrate the festival" in the appropriate way (v. 8). The Corinthians, therefore, must repent of their sin and celebrate the festival with sincerity and truth by removing this sinful individual, who is considered "the old leaven, the leaven of malice and evil" (v. 8).[9]

---

7. James T. South, "A Critique of the 'Curse/Death' Interpretation of 1 Corinthians 5.1–8," *NTS* 39, no. 4 (1993): 551. Verbrugge concurs and cites important OT background for rightly understanding this phrase: "Various suggestions have been made, but the most natural is an Old Testament text where the identical words are used. In the Greek version of Job 2:6, Satan is conversing with God, and God says, 'I deliver him [Job] over to you; only spare his life.' God permitted Satan to do as he wished with Job, to afflict him in any way he desired. He had free play over him, short of taking his life. Satan's goal was clear: to get Job to curse God to his face. In this he failed, for Job did not reject God. He cursed the day of his birth, but he did not curse the Lord. The final result of Job's having been delivered to Satan was a stronger, more deeply committed Job, not someone whom Satan was able to take to his realm of the abyss. This is probably why this phrase appealed to Paul, for the motivation behind his instruction in both passages under discussion is wholly positive" (Verlyn D. Verbrugge, "Delivered Over to Satan," *RJ* 30, no. 6 [1980]: 17). One may not find this argument as convincing, but there are linguistic parallels to take into consideration, and one should observe that this is one piece of the cumulative evidence that supports this interpretation of 1 Corinthians 5:5.

8. Ciampa and Rosner explain, "Leaven is a little portion of a previous week's batch of dough that had been allowed to ferment. When added to the next batch, the leaven made the bread rise. It carried with it the slight risk of infection, especially if the process was left to go on indefinitely without starting afresh with a completely new batch" ("1 Corinthians," 708). Paul emphasizes that although in only a "little" part of the church—one person in fact—the evil would inevitably, slowly but surely, spread through the whole community if left unchecked. Thus, Paul is pointing to a pattern of cleansing, which in this case, connotes cleansing the church of sin.

9. Wall notes that such a removal "delivers the congregation from the threat of sin and death" (Robert W. Wall, "Reading Paul with Acts: The Canonical Shaping of a Holy Church," in *Holiness and Ecclesiology in the New Testament*, eds. Kent E. Brower and Andy Johnson [Grand Rapids: Eerdmans, 2007], 134). Thus, Paul is concerned not only for the individual sinner, but the spiritual condition of the entire community.

Paul concludes this passage, noting that in his previous correspondence he did not intend for them to separate themselves completely from those outside of the church who are engaged in sinful practices. Rather, they were to separate from unrepentant offenders from within the church (vv. 9–13). Regarding the list of sins Paul provides in this particular context, Rosner asserts that a distinct connection can be made between the sins recorded in v. 11 and the OT quotation given in v. 13, saying,

> The representative list of sinners that the church is to judge (5:12b) is in one sense a list of covenantal norms that, when broken, automatically exclude the offender. Paul lists "sexual immorality" first, since that is the issue at hand. But what governs his choice of the next five vices in the catalog? Paul gives a clue in 5:13b: the sins to which the Deuteronomic formula "Expel the wicked person from among you," which Paul quotes, is connected in Deuteronomy form a remarkable parallel to the particular sins mentioned in 5:11.[10]

It appears that Paul is exhorting the Corinthians to deal with the sin in their midst—while allowing God to judge those who are outside the church (vv. 11–12)—by expelling the unrepentant sinner from their midst. This exhortation is in keeping with an OT pattern of exclusion, as seen earlier from the texts in Deuteronomy, from which Paul is quoting in v. 13. Therefore, while God commanded Israel to rid themselves of unrepentant sinners through capital punishment in the OT, he now calls the church to remove the wicked person from their midst by excluding them from the community of faith. What was once dealt with through physical death is now achieved through a declaration of potential eschatological judgment, should the individual under discipline fail to repent. This action serves to exhort the offender and the congregation to persevere in their faith.[11]

Summary

First Corinthians 5 is a key text regarding our call to exercise church discipline. In it one finds crucial details regarding the nature of sin, the need

---

10. Ciampa and Rosner, "1 Corinthians," 709. These authors also produce a helpful chart that compares this text with the various citations of the phrase, "Purge the evil person from among you," in Deuteronomy (ibid.).

11. See Roetzel, who, in commenting on 1 Corinthians 5:13, asserts, "It hardly needs saying that Paul is calling for these rigorous measures to equip the church to stand in the final Day. The first fruits of the Kingdom are tasted in the present, but these preliminary signs summon the church to special watchfulness" (Calvin J. Roetzel, *Judgement in the Community* [Leiden: Brill, 1972], 119). See also Thomas Schreiner and Ardel Caneday, *The Race Set Before Us* (Downers Grove: IVP Academic, 2001), 230.

for perseverance in the faith, and the contaminating effect sin can have on the community. Paul makes very clear that this is a non-negotiable matter. Gross, unrepentant immorality cannot go unchecked. Sin can corrupt and kill a church, and thus it is imperative to root out unrepentant sin. This is always done with the hopes that the person under discipline will repent and ultimately be restored. As such, church discipline is rooted in the holiness and love of God which yields the proper motivation for practicing ecclesial discipline. We act in love, in hope that disciplinary measures will awaken an individual from their sinful propensities and call them to repentance and a renewed pursuit of holiness.

REFLECTION QUESTIONS

1. What was the sin issue being dealt with in 1 Corinthians 5?

2. What was the response by the church to the man's sin, and why was it wrong?

3. Why did Paul deem it so necessary to expel the sinful man from their midst?

4. What does "destruction of the flesh" refer to in 1 Corinthians 5:5?

5. How has the application of the key phrase ("expel the wicked person from among you") in 1 Corinthians 5:13 changed since it was first cited in Deuteronomy?

Are There Other NT Passages That Speak about Church Discipline?

Outside of Matthew 18 and 1 Corinthians 5, there are some other, more minor texts that deal with church discipline.[1] Some briefly discuss avoiding the unruly and having nothing to do with factious behavior (Rom. 16:17–18; Titus 3:9–11), knowing that such talk and action can lead to the downfall of a church (2 Tim. 2:16–17). There are, however, two other passages that deserve further attention regarding the practice of church discipline, namely Galatians 6:1 and 2 Thessalonians 3:6–15.

Galatians 6:1

In addressing the churches of Galatia, Paul makes a brief admonition to the Christians there to handle the issue of discipline in a fitting manner. Leading up to this point in the letter, Paul dealt with the issue of the Galatians deserting the gospel (1:1–2:21), reminding them that justification was by faith alone, not by works such as circumcision (3:1–4:11). Paul then calls the Galatians to live in freedom, not under the Law, but by walking in the Spirit (4:12–5:12). He defines this freedom as walking in love for the sake of others (5:13–15), not by living under the bondage of sin, but in bearing the fruit of the Spirit (5:16–24). As such, church members are to care for and do good to one another in the power of the Spirit (5:25–6:18).

While Paul advocates for justification by faith alone in earlier chapters, he also certainly emphasizes living by the Spirit as of utmost importance. As such, one is saved through faith, but, as has been demonstrated elsewhere, believers are saved to do good works by the power of the Spirit. Paul is advocating that

---

1. This chapter is derived from Jeremy M. Kimble, *That His Spirit May Be Saved: Church Discipline as a Means to Repentance and Perseverance* (Eugene, OR: Wipf and Stock, 2013), 53–58. Used by permission of Wipf and Stock Publishers (www.wipfandstock.com).

obedience springing from faith be manifest in the Galatian churches. In the near context, this involves walking according to the Spirit (5:16–25) which, explained more concretely, means not becoming conceited, envious, or provoking one another (5:26). Paul then states that, if anyone among them is overtaken in sin, those who are spiritual should look to restore that person in a spirit of gentleness, while they watch themselves so they will not also be tempted (6:1). The idea of "overtaken" (*prolēmphthē*) appears to connote that one has been overtaken in surprise. This is not to suggest that the sinner is an unwilling victim; they bear full responsibility for their sins. However, while believers live their lives in the Spirit, sin can still attack in unanticipated ways.

Those who are "spiritual" (*pneumatikoi*) are the ones called upon to restore the sinner. Paul is not here referring to a group of spiritual elitists, but rather to all Galatian believers who received the Spirit when they heard the gospel (Gal. 3:2, 5, 14; 4:6) and are called to continue to walk in the Spirit (5:16, 18, 25). In light of this truth, it seems likely that what Paul describes here generally accords with the first step of church discipline in Matthew 18:15–20. One who becomes aware of another's sin should privately speak to the offender in order to restore him or her to fellowship with Christ.[2] This restoration to spiritual health and vitality should be done in a humble manner.[3] One who truly loves others and is walking in the Spirit approaches another person with firmness in dealing with sin and humility in seeking to treat them with gentleness.

Humility and gentleness are crucial aspects of correcting a sinning member of the church, as Paul exhorts the "spiritual" to look to themselves in this process so they will not be tempted. Some believe the temptation is to commit the same sin as the one who has fallen, whereas others argue that the temptation is to become proud. It seems this warning is general enough to include both ideas. Christians should possess an attitude of self-discernment and critical self-appraisal, as Paul is concerned not only with the restoration of the sinner but also the spiritual fruit of the one working to restore the sinner.

A call to perseverance in one's faith (i.e., walking in the Spirit) is key to note in this text, both for the sinner and those who are spiritual. Instead of becoming arrogant and envying one another, believers should exercise concern and love for others so that their goal is to build one another up. This effort to build one another up will involve the mortification of sin and the pursuit of righteousness as believers walk by the Spirit. As members of a community, they are to pursue corporate holiness. Essentially, Paul is calling the churches to be watchful for those who fall into sin, looking to take necessary steps of

---

2. See Thomas R. Schreiner, *Galatians*, ZECNT (Grand Rapids: Zondervan, 2010), 357.

3. Obenhaus agrees and states, "Instead of conceit, competition, and envy (the terms in Gal. 5:26 that echo certain works of the flesh in 5:20–21), Paul urges the churches to pursue a life that evidences the fruit of the Spirit by, for example, restoring transgressors with a spirit of gentleness" (Stacy R. Obenhaus, "Sanctified Entirely: The Theological Focus of Paul's Instructions for Church Discipline," *RQ* 43, no. 1 [2001]: 1–12).

discipline but always with a view to restoration. As such, the sinner is called to repentance and restoration, and the church is reminded of the need to continually walk in the Spirit in a humble and persevering manner.

2 Thessalonians 3:6–15

One other important text from the NT to consider regarding discipline within the church is found in Paul's second letter to the Thessalonians. When Paul was in Thessalonica, he instructed the church in the basic manner of the Christian life, which included teaching on the Christian ethic of work (1 Thess. 4:11; cf. 2 Thess. 3:10). The church is to keep away from anyone who is walking in "idleness" or "disorderly" (3:6).[4] Paul further instructed the Thessalonians to work with their own hands and also gave them a tangible demonstration of this type of work, leaving the church an example to follow (3:7–9). In spite of this teaching and example, some in the congregation ignored them, possibly due to an over-realized eschatology, and as a result Paul referred to this theme in his first letter (1 Thess. 4:11–12; 5:14) as well as the second as the situation deteriorated further (2 Thess. 3:11). Paul directly addresses the offenders who were not working as well as the entire church, apprising them of what their response should be to such people.

The apostle commands the church in verse six to "keep away"[5] from any believer who does not obey this practice of laboring with one's own hands. Paul gives what appears to be a rather harsh and abrupt command in this instance; however, the Thessalonians had already received the apostolic tradition on more than one occasion, and now more drastic measures were necessary in light of their continued disobedience. Concerning the use of the term "brother," Green notes, "As we will see further on, the community should not consider this person to be an 'enemy' or somehow outside the fold but should 'warn him as a brother' (v. 15)." This would imply these persons continue to be members of the family of faith, "although they are subject to the correction and discipline of the community."[6] However, the best way to understand the connection between the disassociation of 3:14 and the warning of 3:15 is to see Paul intending his instructions in 3:15 ("Do not regard him as an

---

4. Beale asserts, "We have already seen (in the first epistle) that the rendering of *atakōs* as *idle* is misleading (see comments on 1 Thess 5:14) and the same holds true for this passage. The notion that best fits the usage in the ancient world and in the present context is 'unruly' or 'disorderly'" (G. K. Beale, *1–2 Thessalonians*, IVPNTC 13 [Downers Grove, IL: InterVarsity, 2003], 249). Seemingly, idleness could be a direct cause of disorderliness, and thus these ideas may overlap.

5. As noted by Morris, "[Paul's] verb (*stellesthai*) was earlier used for activities such as furling sails. It signifies a drawing into oneself, a holding aloof. But such a withdrawal is not to be made in a spirit of superiority" (Leon Morris, *The Epistles of Paul to the Thessalonians: An Introduction and Commentary*, rev. ed., TNTC 13 [Grand Rapids: Eerdmans, 1984], 144).

6. Gene L. Green, *The Letters to the Thessalonians*, PNTC (Grand Rapids: Eerdmans, 2002), 344.

enemy, but warn him as a brother") to be applied simultaneously with the taking public note of the disorderly, not subsequent to the expulsion of the offender. Thus, the caveat of 3:15 would inform the attitude with which the Thessalonians are to carry out the instructions of 3:14. They are not to see the offender as their enemy, to be harshly thrust from the church, but throughout the disciplinary process they are to admonish him as a brother (as Paul instructed them in 1 Thessalonians 5:14). On this understanding, the instructions of 3:14–15 would read something like this: "If anyone does not obey what we say in this letter, take note of that person, and have nothing to do with him, that he may be ashamed. [And as you do so] do not regard him as an enemy, but warn him as a brother."[7]

After a brief section wherein Paul points out the example that he set for them in labor (3:7–13), the apostle broadens his exhortation referring to all that he has said previously in the letter, not just the matter of disorderliness (3:14–15). Paul asserts that the Thessalonians should "not associate" with a person who does not obey his commands (which appears to pick up the earlier command to "keep away" from the disorderly in 3:6).[8]

This disassociation may be defined, for Paul, as not eating with such a person (1 Cor. 5:1–13) and even treating this person as an unbeliever (Matt. 18:15–20; Rom. 16:17–18; Titus 3:10–11).[9] It appears therefore that excommunication is in view here, as the disorderly have already been warned at least twice (1 Thess. 4:11–12; 5:14; 2 Thess. 3:6–12) and rejected the correction both times. However, the church is to warn him as a "brother," since the church has a different relationship with that individual than with a pagan. The hope is that this person will come to repentance and demonstrate true faith in Christ.

As such, there appears to be an intentional ambivalence about how this person is to be treated and regarded. In common with Matthew 18, there is a shunning of correction by the church and thus the need for disciplinary measures. Like the false teachers in the Pastoral Epistles, Paul views these people as perilously close to eschatological judgment (1 Tim. 1:19–20; 2 Tim. 2:17). The church, however, should not give up hope about their repentance and salvation (2 Tim. 2:25–26) and should warn that person as a brother. Thus, the church is called to disassociate from the unrepentant individual with a redemptive goal in mind, namely, so that person might be ashamed to the point of repentance.

---

7. For a thorough exegetical defense of this view, see Charles J. Bumgardner, "'As a Brother': 2 Thessalonians 3:6–15 and Ecclesiastical Separation," *DBSJ* 14, no. 1 (2009): 55–97; idem, "Interpretation and Application of 2 Thessalonians 3:6–15 in the Light of a Pauline Theology of Discipline" (ThM Thesis, Central Baptist Theological Seminary, 2008).

8. Morris, *The Epistles of Paul to the Thessalonians*, 149. See also Green, *The Letters to the Thessalonians*, 354–55.

9. This section is derived mainly from Beale, *1–2 Thessalonians*, 252–55.

Paul then warns the church in Thessalonica not to express hostility toward the disorderly, attacking them because of their lack of conformity to the norms of the group (3:15). Although the person is excluded from the community, some contact continues that gives the members of the church further opportunity to admonish him, in the hope that such warnings will correct his conduct.[10] Therefore, while these people continue to be warned as "brothers" and not outside the realm of salvation, they are warned to repent and to obey the commands given by God through Paul, lest they demonstrate by their continued unrepentant behavior that they are not truly a part of the community of faith and undergo eschatological judgment. This discipline is administered in order that the offenders might be ashamed. This action taken by the church is not out of enmity or condemnation but so that positive change might occur, namely, repentance and restoration. As these disciplinary measures are exacted, the members of the church are called to "not grow weary in doing good" (3:13) as they continue to persevere in faith and obedience.

Summary

While the issue of church discipline is not expounded upon as frequently as other doctrines in the NT, it is certainly cited and holds great importance for the doctrine of the church. Paul is calling for churches to be watchful, exhorting one another, rebuking sin, and seeking to restore the repentant. Even if some consider certain types of "unruly" behavior to be of no real account, Paul encourages the churches to assist one another in persevering in their faith. In each of these NT texts there appears to be a focus in church discipline on eschatological expectations, namely, final salvation. Paul is fully aware that true Christians will endure in their faith, that they are the ones who will stand before God in final judgment and receive eternal life (cf. Phil. 1:6; 2:12–13). Churches should keep this vision before them, so that they humbly and consistently exhort one another and seek to keep far from sin.

REFLECTION QUESTIONS

1. How does Galatians 6:1–3 describe the way in which we should exact discipline within the church?

2. How does the previous context of Galatians 5:16–26 help us in discerning how we should approach the practice of church discipline?

---

10. Green, *The Letters to the Thessalonians*, 356. See also Martin, who stresses that this discipline was not intended as a punishment for enemies but as a restorative measure intended for lovingly confronting the offenders (D. Michael Martin, *1, 2 Thessalonians*, NAC 33 [Nashville: Broadman & Holman, 1995], 287]).

3. What sinful issue was Paul addressing in 2 Thessalonians 3:6–15?

4. How should people respond, based on 2 Thessalonians 3:6–15, to those who will not obey Paul's commands?

5. What other passages in the NT speak briefly to the issue of church discipline?

How Has the Church Practiced Discipline Throughout Its History?

Throughout church history the practice of church discipline has been largely affirmed, though often sporadically applied. Its purpose and significance has also been nuanced in similar, albeit varying ways, often depending on the way in which the church functioned in its particular historical and cultural milieu. In looking at historical trajectories one can note the ways in which the church remained faithful to biblical teaching on the subject, or veered sharply away from such principles. As such, while history is not ultimately determinative in understanding and applying discipline in our churches, there are both helpful and harmful guides and models from which to learn.

Patristic Era (AD 100–500)

While disciplinary action within the church had its controversial and contentious moments, it appears that for the first several centuries the church consistently sought to apply disciplinary measures according to the biblical witness.[1] Indeed, the early church disciplined members both for the propagation of false doctrine and lack of moral purity. It was common practice in the early days of the church to announce disciplinary judgments on Sunday in the context of the church service. Tertullian, describing this event, states, "For judgment is passed, and it carries great weight, as it must among men certain that God sees them; and it is a notable foretaste of judgment to come, if any man has so sinned to be banished from all share in our prayer, our assembly,

---

1. For accounts of the kind of discipline exacted in the early church, see Everett Ferguson, *Christian Life: Ethics, Morality, and Discipline in the Early Church*, Studies in Early Christianity 16 (New York: Garland, 1993); Richard Haslehurst, *Some Account of the Penitential Discipline of the Early Church in the First Four Centuries* (New York: Macmillan, 1921); Henry Charles Lea, *Studies in Church History: The Rise of the Temporal Power; Benefit of Clergy; Excommunication* (London: Sampson Low, Son, and Marston, 1869).

and all holy intercourse."[2] Tertullian, as well as other church fathers,[3] recognized the seriousness of the disciplinary process.

Most churches recognized two kinds of repentance: a one-time repentance accompanied by faith in Jesus Christ for salvation, and a continual repentance of sin throughout one's life.[4] Christians who sinned had to confess their sin before the church if they wished to be restored to fellowship. Eventually, by the third and fourth centuries, restoration to the church became rather difficult. Undergoing "penitential discipline," those seeking repentance were first required to come to the place where they met for church services, but not enter the place of worship. They were to beg for the prayers of those going inside, and after a period of time they were allowed inside to listen to the service in a designated area. The penitents would eventually be allowed to remain during the entire service, though without partaking of communion. Only after these steps were taken could an individual be restored to full membership. This kind of penitential action, along with the continued peace the church experienced after the reign of Constantine, contributed to a shift in ecclesial discipline.

Medieval Era (AD 500–1500)

Church discipline was a difficult practice to keep consistently due to the many challenges the church faced,[5] but dedication to its implementation was strong at first. According to Greg Wills, however, the practice of church discipline eventually declined in the early centuries of the church. He claims:

> After the fourth century, the system of public confession, exclusion, and penitential rigor fell into disuse. Nectarius, bishop of Constantinople from 381 to 398, apparently played an important role in the change. Since the third century Constantinople and other churches had adopted the practice of appointing a special presbyter in charge of administering the church's penitential discipline. When the public

---

2. Tertullian, *Apology*, 39.4, eds. Gerald Henry Rendall and Walter Charles Alan Kerr, trans. T. R. Glover, Loeb Classical Library 250 (Cambridge, MA: Harvard University Press, 1966), 175.

3. See, for example, Augustine, "Letter 185.3.13, The Correction of the Donatists," in Augustine, *The Works of Saint Augustine: A Translation for the 21st Century*, ed. John E. Rotelle, trans. Edmund Hill (Brooklyn: New City, 1990), 187; Clement of Rome, *First Epistle to the Corinthians*, in *The Ante-Nicene Fathers*, eds. Alexander Roberts and James Donaldson (Grand Rapids: Eerdmans, 1950), 1:20; Justin Martyr, *The First Apology*, in ibid., 1:185.

4. See Gregory A. Wills, "A Historical Analysis of Church Discipline," in *Those Who Must Give an Account: A Study of Church Membership and Church Discipline*, eds. John S. Hammett and Benjamin L. Merkle (Nashville: B&H Academic, 2012), 132–39.

5. This includes the severe persecution the church often underwent prior to the time of Constantine, the changing standards regarding the severity of discipline that a person was to undergo, as well as widespread controversies involving the Donatists and Novatianists.

discipline of a deacon at Constantinople for sexual immorality brought considerable public scandal upon the church,
Nectarius abolished the office of the penitential presbyter
and largely abandoned efforts to administer church discipline among the laity. Nectarius did not repudiate the strict
public discipline in principle but he abandoned it in practice. . . . The process of strict public discipline withered in
the Latin-speaking churches of the West just as it did in the
churches of the Greek-speaking East. In its place emerged a
system of private confession and individual penance.[6]

This eventual emphasis on penance transformed church discipline largely
into a private affair between the priest and layperson, and as such the communal role of church discipline dissipated. Thus, church discipline was largely
dispelled, and instead private confession and works of merit were common
fare in the days leading up to the Reformation.[7]

Reformation Era (AD 1500–1750)

Martin Luther, a key figure in the Reformation, is known in the early part
of his career as one who had experienced the weight of the penitential system
and as such questioned much of its validity, particularly in the issuing of indulgences. His criticism of these practices as substitutes for true repentance
and contrition was a necessary catalyst in precipitating the Reformation. This
also allowed for a more biblical comprehension and application of church
discipline by Luther, as well as others such as John Calvin, the Anabaptists,
and later figures like Jonathan Edwards.

Luther wrote three key documents regarding the nature and practice of
church discipline.[8] From these three documents one can observe Luther's
commitment to ecclesial discipline. Unlike the Catholic Church, Luther advocated for the keys of the kingdom to be exercised by the church, rather
than by the Pope solely. While seeking to correct what he deemed as errors

---

6. Wills, "A Historical Analysis of Church Discipline," 140. See also Socrates, *Ecclesiastical
   History*, 5.19, in *Nicene and Post-Nicene Fathers*, eds. Philip Schaff and Henry Wace,
   Second Series, vol. 2 (New York: Christian Publishing Company, 1886), 128; Sozomen,
   Ecclesiastical History, 7.16, in ibid., 386–387.
7. For greater understanding of the development of medieval penitential practices, see John
   T. McNeill and Helena M. Gamer, *Medieval Handbooks of Penance* (New York: Columbia
   University Press, 1938); Sarah Hamilton, *The Practice of Penance, 900–1050* (Rochester,
   NY: Boydell Press, 2001); Abigail Firey, *A New History of Penance* (Leiden: Brill, 2008).
8. Martin Luther, "A Sermon on the Ban," in *Church and Ministry I, LW* 39, ed. Eric W. Gritsch
   (Philadelphia: Fortress, 1970), 3–22; idem, "The Keys," in *Church and Ministry II, LW* 40,
   ed. Helmut H. Lehman (Philadelphia: Fortress, 1958), 321–77; idem, "On the Councils and
   the Church," in *Church and Ministry III, LW* 41, ed. Eric W. Gritsch (Philadelphia: Fortress,
   1966), 3–178.

made by the Catholic Church, Luther still maintained the seriousness of the ban, and emphasized that those who come under discipline were warned of potential eschatological judgment should they not repent. This, however, was the point for Luther, as he viewed church discipline as restorative in nature. He also intended for this measure of discipline to serve as a deterrent to sin for others, in hopes that they would persevere in their faith.

Calvin also advocated for ecclesial discipline in his context in Geneva. Calvin asserted three aims in the use of discipline in his *Institutes*.[9] First, discipline was necessary in local churches so the high honor of God's holy name would not be blasphemed, especially at the Lord's Supper. Second, Calvin advocated for discipline in the church to preserve purity and holiness amongst God's people. And finally, Calvin viewed discipline as a corrective so those under discipline might come to a place of repentance. While much more detail regarding Calvin's views could be elucidated, these are the main purposes for discipline, as he saw it.

The Anabaptists, contemporaries to Luther and Calvin, also protested the corruption of the Roman Catholic Church, particularly regarding penance and indulgences,[10] but went further in seeking to implement what they believed to be biblical reforms, including in the area of church discipline.[11] They believed the church, not the state, should handle matters of ecclesial discipline, and they tightly tied their view of discipline to their convictions regarding the ordinances and regenerate church membership. With their clear ecclesiology, it could be argued that Anabaptists most successfully and consistently upheld discipline in the church and saw the greatest degree of application by their followers. Balthasar Hubmaier, a well-known Anabaptist, wrote several key works on this matter.[12]

---

9. For an overview of the details of Calvin's views of discipline, see especially John Calvin, *Institutes of the Christian Religion*, ed. John T. McNeill, trans. Ford Lewis Battles (Philadelphia: Westminster, 1960), 4.12.1–28. For a summary of his views, including these three key points, see Eric J. Bargerhuff, *Love That Rescues: God's Fatherly Love in the Practice of Church Discipline* (Eugene, OR: Wipf and Stock, 2010), 35–41.

10. Both the Magisterial Reformers and Anabaptists saw that penance, much like the Mass, granted priests, bishops, and the Pope inordinate power in retaining and absolving sins. See Thomas N. Finger, *A Contemporary Anabaptist Theology: Biblical, Historical, Constructive* (Downers Grove, IL: InterVarsity, 2004), 208–9.

11. For a helpful overview of this movement see *A Companion to Anabaptism and Spiritualism, 1521–1700*, eds. John D. Roth and James M. Stayer, Brill's Companions to the Christian Tradition 6 (Boston: Brill, 2007); George Huntston Williams, *The Radical Reformation*, 3rd ed., Sixteenth Century Essays and Studies 15 (Kirksville, MO: Sixteenth Century Journal, 1992).

12. See, for example, Balthasar Hubmaier, "On Fraternal Admonition," in *Balthasar Hubmaier: Theologian of Anabaptism*, eds. H. Wayne Pipkin and John Howard Yoder, Classics of the Radical Reformation 5 (Scottdale, PA: Herald Press, 1989), 372–85; idem, "On the Christian Ban," in ibid., 409–25.

One final figure to consider from this era is Jonathan Edwards, an eighteenth-century pastor in Northampton, Massachusetts. Dealing with one particular case in his own church, Edwards detailed the purposes of church discipline.

> *First.* That the church may be kept pure and God's ordinances not defiled. This end is mentioned in the context: that the other members themselves may not be defiled. 'Tis necessary that they thus bear a testimony against sin. *Second.* That others may be deterred from wickedness. That others may fear. *Third.* That they may be reclaimed, [that their] souls may be saved. [After] other, more gentle, means have been used in vain, then we are to use severe means to bring 'em to conviction and shame and humiliation, by being rejected and avoided by the church, treated with disrespect, disowned by God, delivered to Satan, his being made the instrument of chastising them. This is the last means, with concomitant admonitions, that the church is to use for the reclaiming those members of the church that become visibly wicked; which, if it be'nt effectual, what is next to be expected is destruction without remedy.[13]

Thus, Edwards has the good of the church and of the one under discipline in mind when he considers and practices excommunication. He notes the themes of purity, warning, and reclamation of the erring individual. Edwards's hope in this difficult practice of church discipline is that sinners would be turned from the error of their ways while under judgment and repent, and that others may be deterred from sin and persevere in their faith.

Modern Era (1750–present)

In the early modern era, discipline continued to be a strong emphasis. However, in many denominations, as Enlightenment convictions ascended, including individualism and the inherent goodness of humanity, the practice of discipline generally slipped into decline.[14] There were exceptions to this general trend, but in comparison to the rest of church history, the last two centuries showed a significant decrease in disciplinary activity.

---

13. Jonathan Edwards, "The Means and Ends of Excommunication," in *Sermons and Discourses, 1739–1742*, eds. Harry S. Stout and Nathan O. Hatch, *WJE* 22 (New Haven, CT: Yale University Press, 2003), 78–79.
14. For a specific portrayal of the decline of discipline among Southern Baptist Churches, for example, see Stephen M. Haines, "Southern Baptist Church Discipline, 1880–1939," *Baptist History and Heritage* 20, no. 2 (1985): 14–27; Gregory A. Wills, *Democratic Religion: Freedom, Authority, and Church Discipline in the Baptist South, 1785–1900* (New York: Oxford University Press, 1997).

However, this trend of the decline of church discipline has turned around significantly in recent years. A number of factors can be attributed to this resurgence, but there has been a definite renaissance in teaching about and practicing church discipline. One crucial figure leading the way in this charge is Mark Dever, through his ministry with Capitol Hill Baptist Church and 9Marks.[15] A number of well-written works on ecclesiology have also been penned in recent years, pointing believers back to the importance of this doctrine for the Christian life.[16]

Summary

From the Apostolic Era to the end of the fourth century, church discipline was a standard practice in the church, though not always practiced consistently and morphing due to the increased belief in penance. In the Medieval Era, private confession and individual penance largely did away with any practice of church discipline. The Reformation, however, brought about a desire to recover the practice of church discipline, though, it could be argued, Anabaptists and later Baptists best upheld this doctrine in practice due to their robust ecclesiology. While decline marked the early modern era, one can also note a distinct resurgence in the theology and practice of discipline as pastors and members seek to promote health in their churches.

REFLECTION QUESTIONS

1. What were the key marks and the trajectory of discipline in the Patristic Era?

2. What were the key marks and the trajectory of discipline in the Medieval Era?

3. What were the key marks, different key figures, and the trajectory of discipline in the Reformation Era?

4. What were the key marks and the trajectory of discipline in the Modern Era?

5. What does the overall history of church discipline teach us that will help us as we seek to faithfully live out the call to church discipline in our own local churches?

---

15. See especially Mark Dever, *9 Marks of a Healthy Church* (Wheaton, IL: Crossway, 2004).
16. Many could be named, but see for example, Gregg R. Allison, *Sojourners and Strangers: The Doctrine of the Church*, Foundation in Evangelical Theology (Wheaton, IL: Crossway, 2012); John S. Hammett, *Biblical Foundations for Baptist Churches: A Contemporary Ecclesiology* (Grand Rapids: Kregel, 2005); Michael Scott Horton, *People and Place: A Covenant Ecclesiology* (Louisville: Westminster John Knox, 2008).

Ministry Questions

How Is Discipline Related to Discipleship?

The Great Commission instructs that we are to make disciples of all nations, baptizing them in the name of the Father, Son, and Spirit, and teaching them to observe all that Jesus commanded (Matt. 28:19–20). This passage dominates the mission statements of many churches, and is set apart as a text of great importance. The same cannot always be said, however, for the practice of church discipline. People often identify the Great Commission with importance due to its ongoing relevance to reach all peoples with the gospel. On the other hand, church discipline feels like an outdated practice that communicates condemnation more than it does love.

Church membership and discipline make the gospel visible by fostering a God-centered and supernatural view of salvation, gospel-shaped disciples, a gospel-shaped community, and a clear and unconfused gospel testimony.[1] As such, there is a needful connection to make between discipleship (i.e., the making of disciples in accordance to the Great Commission) and discipline. This chapter will observe the relationship of these concepts, focusing first on their conceptual link and then focusing on how groups of disciples work to make other disciples, with discipline functioning as a crucial part of this process.

Conceptual Relationship between Disciple and Discipline

As one thinks of the terms "disciple" and "discipline," one can note the common etymology in the English language. This is not the case, however, when one considers the terms in the original languages of Scripture, as

---

1. See Bruce Riley Ashford and Danny Akin, "The Missional Implications of Church Membership and Church Discipline," in *Those Who Must Give an Account: A Study of Church Membership and Church Discipline*, eds. John S. Hammett and Benjamin L. Merkle (Nashville: B&H Academic, 2012), 203.

"disciple" (*mathētēs*) and "discipline" (*paideia*) stem from different words. Still, a conceptual link can still be made when thinking of disciples of Jesus and the various ways "discipline" is used in Scripture, especially church discipline.

When studying the Gospels, one can note that there are distinctive emphases in each but that there are also theological themes that cut across all four Gospels. Several of these themes revolve around the nature of the church, including the ethical demands of discipleship in the new Messianic community (Matt. 5–7) and the commissioning of Jesus' followers to carry forward his mission to make disciples to the ends of the earth (Matt. 28:1–20).[2] Clowney identifies disciples as those who are learners of what Jesus taught, servants of God and others, and witnesses of Jesus' person and work.[3] More specifically, disciples of Jesus are not merely to learn cognitive content for right belief. While this is certainly part of being a disciple of Jesus, there is a cost to following Jesus as a disciple (Matt. 16:24–28).[4] Becoming a disciple means embracing all of who Jesus is and what he has done in his life, teaching, death, and resurrection. An all-encompassing embrace of this includes cognitively assenting to the truth he taught, affectively embracing him as our all-satisfying treasure, and volitionally bowing the knee to Jesus in full submission of one's life. A disciple willingly renounces all the world has to offer to fully and unswervingly follow Jesus in every facet of life.

While "disciple" is a prominent term in the Gospels and Acts, the concept of following in God's ways as God's people (i.e., discipleship) is found throughout both the OT and NT. More commonly one can think of God as Father and the people of God as his children. God redeems Israel from Egypt, proclaiming that he is the Father of Israel, his firstborn son (Exod. 4:23). Relating to his people as a Father, God not only redeems and makes covenants with Israel, but also disciplines them when they go astray. He wants to ensure that his people are living out their identity as his sons, and thus he disciplines them to bring them back to a fitting lifestyle of holiness (Deut. 8:5; 2 Sam. 7:13–14; Prov. 3:11–12). This pattern of OT discipline is foundational for understanding the enactment of discipline within the NT church. God is holy, and he requires his people to be holy if he is to dwell in their midst (Lev. 11:44–45; 19:1–2; cf. 1 Peter 1:14–16). While God is also a loving Father, this expectation of holiness grounds God's actions as it relates to his covenant with Israel. God, who is certainly loving and merciful, will not allow his people to dwell in sin for long without enacting dire consequences (Deut. 28:15–68). Holiness means that

---

2. Andreas J. Köstenberger, "The Church According to the Gospels," in *The Community of Jesus: A Theology of the Church*, eds. Kendall H. Easley and Christopher W. Morgan (Nashville: B&H Academic, 2013), 36.

3. Edmund P. Clowney, *The Church*, Contours of Christian Theology (Downers Grove, IL: InterVarsity, 1995), 46–47.

4. See ibid., 46.

God will discipline those in unrepentant sin, though he always does so with an end to love and forgive the one living in sin (Deut. 30:1–10).

As salvation history progresses, the NT will testify to the new covenant of God in Christ and how the idea of the fatherhood of God will find a deeper and fuller expression in the life of God's chosen people (Rom. 8:14–17; Gal. 4:4–7).[5] Divine discipline, therefore, is an encouraging affirmation of God's fatherly love as he disciplines us as sons for our good, so that we might share in his holiness (Heb. 12:5–11).[6] Thus, in thinking of disciples as the people of God, or as his children, one can see that divine discipline and the accompanying fatherhood language is woven throughout Scripture to communicate God's overall redemptive purposes.[7] Divine discipline is used to show God's love in bringing about their full adoption, and family status means a call to live as a son (or disciple) in line with that status.

Disciples Making Disciples through Discipline

God directly disciplines us to bring about purity, and he also has deemed that the church exercise discipline so that disciples of Jesus live out their identity in holiness and righteousness. As holiness was held as a standard for Israel, so it is also required of the NT church (Heb. 12:14). Haslehurst, noting the OT roots of church discipline, maintains, "The apostles when they administered discipline as leaders of the Christian Church were only carrying on a principle with which they had been familiar from childhood."[8] The people of God across the Testaments relate to God as Father and thus are called to follow him as a distinct people, or as disciples.

A culture of discipleship is one where formative discipline is normal, and formal corrective church discipline is practiced. As disciples of Jesus, and as children of God, we joyfully receive instruction and correction so as to

---

5. Grudem brings this progression of fatherhood and a renewed sense of adoption to the fore, saying, "Even though there was a consciousness of God as Father to the people of Israel, the full benefits and privileges of membership in God's family, and the full realization of that membership, did not come until Christ came and the Spirit of the Son of God was poured into our hearts, bearing witness with our spirit that we were God's children" (Wayne Grudem, *Systematic Theology: An Introduction to Biblical Doctrine* [Grand Rapids: Zondervan, 1994], 737).

6. For more on the concept of discipline as explicated in Hebrews, as well as analysis of two key OT texts from the NT passage is derived, see Ched Spellman, "The Drama of Discipline: Toward an Intertextual Profile of *paideia* in Hebrews 12," *JETS* 59, no. 3 (September 2016): 487–506.

7. Bargerhuff helpfully summarizes this point, noting that divine discipline coupled with fatherhood language "characterizes the intimacy, promises, and hope within the covenant relationship, and God's deep desire to restore them fully from sin and show them his steadfast love while bringing about their full adoption as sons" (Eric J. Bargerhuff, *Love that Rescues: God's Fatherly Love in the Practice of Church Discipline* [Eugene: Wipf and Stock, 2010], 104).

8. Richard Haslehurst, *Some Account of the Penitential Discipline of the Early Church in the First Four Centuries* (New York: Macmillan, 1921), 1.

continue growing as disciples and to persevere in our faith until life is done. It is crucial, therefore, that Christians understand their identity as sons of God and as disciples, in order to rightly embrace the call to live a certain kind of life. As disciples we follow Jesus in our mind, affection, and volition, and when we deviate from his path we receive discipline to help us understand how we veered from living faithfully as disciples, and then to repent and pursue the right path by God's grace.

Balthasar Hubmaier, the renowned theologian from the Anabaptist movement, helpfully demonstrates the connection between discipleship and discipline. Hubmaier maintained, in connection with the doctrines of baptism, the Lord's Supper, membership, and discipline, that Christ assigned to the church two ministerial powers: binding and loosing. This power to bind and loose is linked to the keys of the kingdom, as indicated in Matthew 16:19 and 18:18. It is also crucial to note that Hubmaier associated the keys with the practice of baptism and the Lord's Supper.[9] He asserts, "For in water baptism the church uses the key of admitting and loosing, but in the Supper the key of excluding, binding, and locking away, as Christ promises and gives to it the power of the forgiveness of sins."[10]

In other words, disciples live under the Lordship of Christ in ongoing sanctification, celebrating the ordinances together, and—if needs be—corrective discipline. Hubmaier viewed the church as a community of believers who publicly pledged to live as disciples of Christ at baptism and who continued to pledge obedience to Christ at the Lord's Supper, lest they come under the

---

9. Balthasar Hubmaier, "On the Christian Ban," in *Balthasar Hubmaier: Theologian of Anabaptism*, eds. H. Wayne Pipkin and John Howard Yoder, Classics of the Radical Reformation 5 (Scottdale, PA: Herald Press, 1989), 410–11. McMullan concurs and further describes Hubmaier's view: "[The keys] were intricately related to the doctrines of baptism and the Lord's Supper for Hubmaier, and together they authorized the church to receive repentant sinners into a local congregation and to exclude those same ones if they were unwilling to behave in a morally upright way" (William E. McMullan, "Church Discipline as a Necessary Function of the Visible Church in the Theology of Balthasar Hubmaier" [PhD diss., Southeastern Baptist Theological Seminary, 2003], 38).

10. Hubmaier, "Dialogue with Zwingli's Baptism Book," 175. See also, Hubmaier, "A Christian Catechism," 341. McMullan elaborates, "The first key, binding, empowered the church to receive repentant sinners into the congregation through water baptism, and subsequently, by readmitting those who were previously under the ban. The second key, loosing, primarily functioned through the Eucharist, where those who openly professed faith in Christ continually renewed their pledge first made at baptism to live according to the rule of Christ. Subsequently, as to the key to the purity of the church, the second key gave the congregation the authority to exclude obstinate sinners from the fellowship of the Lord's Supper through the ban. . . . Therefore, the proper function of the first key came into use only when the legitimate exercise of the second key, admonition and the Ban, was in place" ("Church Discipline as a Necessary Function in the Theology of Balthasar Hubamier," 76–77).

discipline of the church.[11] This is a model for understanding how discipleship and discipline are linked in the life of the church.

Summary

In thinking of church discipline, one must have an understanding of how the concept of discipleship relates. We are called to make disciples and walk faithfully as disciples in every area of our lives. Knowing we will not walk before God perfectly, we are to repent of our sin and press on toward righteousness. As a loving Father, God disciplines disciples of Jesus, his children. God has also granted the keys of the kingdom to the church to exercise discipline within a local church context. In the call to discipleship and the call to discipline the end goal remains the same, namely, maturity in Christ (Col. 1:28).

REFLECTION QUESTIONS

1. How are discipline and discipleship related conceptually?

2. What characterizes a disciple of Jesus Christ?

3. What does Scripture say about God's fatherly discipline?

4. How is God's fatherly discipline loving?

5. In the process of discipleship and church discipline, what is the goal? How do these actions accomplish that goal in similar and different ways?

---

11. See Hubmaier, "On Fraternal Admonition," 383–85. Here he states, "So all of those who cry: 'Well, what about water baptism? Why, all the fuss about the Lord's Supper? They are after all just outward signs! They're nothing but water, bread, and wine! Why fight about that? They have not in their whole life learned enough to know why the signs were instituted by Christ, what they seek to achieve or toward what they should finally be directed, namely to gather a church, to commit oneself publicly to live according to the word of Christ in faith and brotherly love, and because of sin to subject oneself to fraternal admonition and the Christian ban, and to do all of this with a sacramental oath before the Christian church and all her members."

Who Is in Charge of Administering Discipline?

It is crucial to have a theological foundation for what church discipline is and why it needs to be practiced in our churches. The next several chapters will build on that foundation, while seeking to offer assistance in practical matters that are often dealt with during the disciplinary process. This is crucial to attain not only right understanding regarding ecclesial discipline but also right practice.

In terms of administering discipline, who is responsible for doing so? The answer may differ based on the denomination one is affiliated with, as some may say a presbytery, others the bishop, some the deacon board, and others the pastoral staff of that particular local church. While some extreme cases of longstanding, known sin necessitate discipline to be exacted quickly at the highest level (1 Cor. 5:1–13), the passage that best adjudicates the process for discipline in found in Matthew 18. Here one can see that it is not merely the highest level of leadership or some outside committee that is responsible to enact discipline. Rather, it begins with the individual, and, if necessary, can later include several witnesses, church leadership, and finally the church as a whole.

The Individual

Matthew 18:15–20 outlines a straightforward process when dealing with matters of church discipline, and it begins with church members exhorting other church members on an individual level (Matt. 18:15). A person is to go to his or her fellow Christian brother or sister alone at first to seek to settle a matter of ongoing, unrepentant sin. Leeman astutely notes, "A clear principle that emerges from Matthew 18:15–20 is that Jesus means for the process of correcting sin to involve as few people as necessary for producing repentance. If a one-to-one encounter yields repentance, good. If it takes two or three more, then leave it at that. A matter should only be taken to the whole church when all other avenues have been exhausted."[1] This is a helpful principle to keep in mind as the goal of any measure of church discipline is the repentance of the individual in sin so that they may be restored to the church.

Churches are the temples of the Spirit (1 Cor. 3:16–17; 6:19–20) who constitute a royal priesthood (1 Peter 2:9). All churches are called to be holy (1 Cor. 1:2), are commissioned to make disciples (Matt. 28:18–19), and are tasked with guarding the name and reputation of Christ through church discipline.[2] The church is certainly a corporate entity, but local churches are made up of individuals who must be willing to initiate hard conversations and lovingly rebuke those living in some kind of open sin.

Several Witnesses

Individual Christians in local churches must be willing to rebuke a sinner, just between the two of them, in order to see that person move toward repentance. However, "if he does not listen, take one or two others along with you, that every charge may be established by the evidence of two or three witnesses" (Matt. 18:16). A positive response is envisioned at the end of 18:15, but if the offender does not respond positively to the private personal rebuke, the next step is to bring two or three other church members to serve as a witness to the rebuke and exhort the sinner themselves. This step is exacted seemingly to underline the gravity of the problem and to add their wisdom to its solution[3] In other words, if an individual rebuke has no effect, this inclusion of more people conveys the seriousness and need for discernment in that particular situation.

The addition of "one or two" gives the "two or three" stipulated by Deuteronomy 19:15 (cf. 17:6) which seems to be in view here. The presence of the supporting parties ensures that the initiative is not a confused one, based on a misunderstanding, but is also concerned to enhance in the eyes of the one being approached the seriousness of what is at stake. Nolland observes, "Something nearly analogous to the legal system in Israel is being brought to bear (only nearly analogous because at this stage the matter remains a private

---

1. Jonathan Leeman, *Church Discipline: How the Church Protects the Name of Jesus* (Wheaton, IL: Crossway, 2012), 68. Nolland concurs, saying, "The privacy of the initial contact allows the sin to be dealt with without any need for wider awareness or for public shaming. Insofar as this is possible, the privacy of the initiative protects the dignity of the person, even at the point of serious sin. The matter is to be dealt with at the lowest possible effective level and the circle of knowledge restricted as much as possible" (John Nolland, *The Gospel of Matthew: A Commentary on the Greek Text*, NIGTC [Grand Rapids: Eerdmans, 2005], 746).
2. Jonathan Leeman, *Don't Fire Your Church Members: The Case for Congregationalism* (Nashville: B&H Academic, 2016), 167.
3. David L. Turner, *Matthew*, BECNT (Grand Rapids: Baker Academic, 2008), 445.

initiative—only at the next stage will it become a public church matter—and because this is an initiative aimed at restoration rather than at justice or punishment)."[4] Again, this increase in number outlines the seriousness of the matter and demonstrates that every member serves with the authority of the keys, though the process does not end here.

Church Leadership

It is important here to mention that while all members of the church exercise the authority of the keys, they have also elected leaders to shepherd the flock (1 Peter 5:1–4) and to stand accountable before God for their actions (Heb. 13:17). They are deeply invested in the life of the church in terms of their time, attention, and affection. As such, while Christ does not necessitate that the elders of the church be among the two or three witnesses, or even the final step of discipline, it is wise to inform them at this juncture.

Going through the steps of church discipline involves a concerted effort to assess accurately and effectively the lives of the members and deal with unrepentant sin as it arises. Throughout this process, one can see that as shepherds, the elders—while not the exclusive practicioners of discipline—should have a leading role as they are responsible to oversee church members. Davis maintains that pastors should be made aware of a sin issue after a person has personally confronted the sinning member and there was no repentance. The leaders of the church are in a good position to know two or three reliable witnesses to send along with the person the next time (the witnesses could even be two or three of the elders of the church). Prayer should be made by the elders and the whole church to seek this person's restoration. While the church must take opportunity to confront and ask questions of the offending member, the pastors can offer helpful guidance throughout the process.[5]

The Church

Matthew continues to tell us, "If he refuses to listen to them, tell it to the church. And if he refuses to listen even to the church, let him be to you as a Gentile and a tax collector" (Matt. 18:17). This step in the process is now another attempt to win the offender over, and thus at this point, all of the membership is in charge of administering discipline. The imperative "tell it to the church" is singular, implying that Jesus envisages the person who initiated the process as telling the local church as a whole what had happened (though

---

4. Nolland, *The Gospel of Matthew*, 747.
5. See Andrew M. Davis, "The Practical Issues of Church Discipline," in *Those Who Must Give an Account: A Study of Church Membership and Church Discipline*, eds. John S. Hammett and Benjamin L. Merkle (Nashville: B&H Academic, 2012), 173–75.

it may be wisest for that person to convey to the church leaders what has oc-curred, and they in turn can tell the church).[6] Yet this is still by way of appeal, for Jesus goes on to say what is to be done if he does not heed the church. The implication is that the church will try to bring him to his senses. When the offender sees that the whole group of believers opposes his behavior, surely he will repent. But the possibility remains that he will not. In that case he has cut himself off from the group of people who have eschewed the kind of conduct that he has followed, and from which he refuses to depart.[7]

It is crucial that the entire church membership is involved at this point as they have been given the keys of the kingdom with the authority to bind and loose (Matt. 16:16–19; 18:17). The church leadership is shepherding throughout the process as they are appointed to that position by the church and are certainly among those who are "spiritual" to call people to repen-tance and restoration (Gal. 6:1). As Wellum and Wellum state, final earthly authority goes to the whole church in a number of matters, including church discipline, but the leaders are also called to shepherd the flock faithfully. Thus, in this process, the congregation must recognize and affirm the au-thority and gifting of its leaders based on God's Word, while the leaders also seek out the wisdom of God's people and include them in these matters, as taught by Scripture.[8]

Summary

The administration of church discipline is multifaceted. One should not think of excommunication as the only kind of enactment of discipline. It includes all forms of rebuke and call to repentance, and therefore it is administrated by individuals, small groups, the church leadership, and, if needs be, the entire church. As such, we must not shirk our responsibility to continually repent of our own sin and to help others turn from their sin as well. This is one of the key tasks we must embrace as we seek to oversee one another's discipleship.

REFLECTION QUESTIONS

1. How is the individual Christian in a church involved in administering church discipline?

---

6. Leon Morris, *The Gospel According to Matthew*, PNTC (Grand Rapids: Eerdmans, 1992), 468–69.
7. Ibid., 469.
8. Stephen J. Wellum and Kirk Wellum, "The Biblical and Theological Case for Congregationalism," in *Baptist Foundations: Church Government for an Anti-Institutional Age*, eds. Mark Dever and Jonathan Leeman (Nashville: B&H Academic, 2015), 76–77.

2. Why do we need to bring in one or two more witnesses if there is no repentance? Who should those people be?

3. What does the entire church do if church discipline gets to the point of involving the entire membership?

4. How should church leaders be involved in the process of discipline?

5. What is the proper balance in disciplinary issues as it relates to involving the leadership of the church and the entire congregation?

What Is the Process of Discipline, Restoration, and Forgiveness?

It is important to understand who is involved in church discipline, and Matthew 18:15–20 serves as a helpful guide in understanding those details. However, one must also understand how other NT texts dealing with discipline contribute to our knowledge of the details of the disciplinary process, as well as the length of the process itself. It is needful that Christians understand these details as all members will be involved in this procedure at some point.

The process of ecclesial discipline is not always uniform, though it does consistently contain several key elements. First, there is a call to confront the unrepentant sinner and make that person aware of the issue. Second, one must not only pronounce the fact of sin present, they must also call for the repentance of the individual. This would include both repentance before God, as well as repentance and reconciliation with those who were offended or affected by the sinful actions committed. Third, if repentance does not take place, there must be a formal removal of the sinner from membership. Finally, if the person repents of the sin and seeks restoration, forgiveness must then be extended by the church. As one will see, the timeframe of such a process can vary dramatically.

Confrontation

The first step in the process of discipline is to actually confront the person who is living in unrepentant sin.[1] Christians must maintain awareness of their own sins and commit to repent constantly when things are exposed in their lives. However, the fact that one is sinful and ongoingly repentant should not

---

1. Morris states, regarding Matthew 18:15, "'Go' means taking the initiative; the person in the clear is not to wait for the sinner to come to him" (Leon Morris, *The Gospel According to Matthew*, PNTC [Grand Rapids: Eerdmans, 1992], 467).

negate their call to go and confront another in their sin (Matt. 7:1–5). As fellow church members, we are to be humble and gentle in demeanor, bearing one another's burdens (Gal. 6:1–3), and we are to make clear the specific sin issue that is to be addressed.

Some may object to discipline, especially excommunication, as being unloving and point to the fact that love should cover a multitude of sins (1 Peter 4:8; cf. James 5:20). First, in relation to love covering over sin, this is not referring to one believer atoning for the sins of another believer, but rather a spirit of love offered in the face of sin, particularly in issuing forgiveness.[2] This loving spirit is also the point of the parable following Jesus' instructions on church discipline; the church must be willing to forgive repentant sinners (Matt. 18:21–35). Thus, genuine Christian love is tolerant in that it is forgiving, forbearing, kind (Eph. 4:2), humble-minded (Phil. 2:1–4), and respectful toward people, who are created in God's image.[3] Therefore, we go to one another in a spirit of love.

However, there is also a legitimate sense in which Christian love is intolerant. Strauch states, "It is not tolerant in the sense of approving or accepting that which is immoral or false as defined by God's Word. Love cannot be tolerant of that which destroys people's lives or spreads lies about the gospel."[4] Discipline must take place for unrepentant sin. Thus, love can cover a multitude of sins, but there are other times when love compels a church to act, even to the point of excommunication.

The Call for Repentance

Not only must specific sin be confronted in this process, there must also be a distinct call to repentance before both God and those who may have been affected by the sin. This is crucial to the life of the church, especially when considering that most people view salvation as merely a past-tense experience. Confrontation and the call to repentance within the life of the church is a grace of God, and the aim of such a practice is that God's people would recognize the horror of sin and persist in their faith.[5] The author of Hebrews also commands his readers to exhort one another consistently, and not to neglect meeting together. This exhortation has repentance in mind, namely, to keep us from being hardened by sin and to pursue a life of love and good works (Heb. 3:12–13; 10:24–25). O'Brien comments, "The listeners are to motivate one another to love that is expressed in good deeds. These tangible

---

2. See Thomas R. Schreiner, *1, 2 Peter, Jude*, NAC 37 (Nashville: Broadman & Holman, 2003), 212–13.
3. Alexander Strauch, *A Christian Leader's Guide to Leading with Love* (Littleton, CO: Lewis and Roth, 2006), 161.
4. Ibid.
5. For a balanced approach to the doctrines of union with Christ, perseverance in the faith, and God's preservation of his people, see Marcus Peter Johnson, *One with Christ: An Evangelical Theology of Salvation* (Wheaton, IL: Crossway, 2013), 171–81.

expressions of care had distinguished the congregation in the past (vv. 33–34). Our author now wants this expression of love within their fellowship to be deepened and strengthened."[6]

Again, some may find this call to pushing others toward specific repentance as judgmental and onerous. However, one must consider the biblical narrative. God tasked Adam with imaging him through ruling over creation, but Adam failed. So did Israel. So did Israel's king, David. But then came one who imaged God—perfectly. The good news of the gospel is that God has made a way for us to be restored to God and to his original purpose for our lives—reigning together with Jesus over all creation. He promises a pardon from guilt through the work of his Son, as well as a new law-obeying nature through the work of his Spirit. It's within this framework that church discipline makes sense.[7] The rebuking of sin and the call to repentance is a call to be who we truly are in Christ.

Removal from Membership

If the process proceeds to the last step due to lack of repentance, the call is then to remove that person from the membership of the church. This is why it is so crucial that the church uphold a clear process for regenerate church membership from the outset. A person is committing to the oversight of others and being overseen in terms of their ongoing growth as a disciple. They are submitting to the church and its leadership, in this sense.

Removal from membership does not mean that the person is not allowed to attend services. In fact, if they are willing, the hope is that they will attend, hear the gospel, be brought under conviction, and repent of their sin and seek out restoration. What it does mean is that the person is to be treated as a "Gentile and tax collector" (Matt. 18:17), put out of membership as the church can no longer affirm their testimony of conversion. This also means that the person would not partake of the Lord's Supper, as this is an ordinance to be observed by believers (1 Cor. 11:17–34). Again, this is significant in that the Lord's Supper serves as the renewing oath-sign of the new covenant, and thus the church is declaring by their action of excommunication that potential eschatological judgment awaits the one who is unrepentant. But this act of discipline is also meant to draw them to repentance and serves as a means of perseverance for the saints.

Restoration and Forgiveness

The desire is that a person come to a place of repentance so that restoration can take place. When this happens, forgiveness must be extended

---

6. P. T. O'Brien, *The Letter to the Hebrews*, PNTC (Grand Rapids, Eerdmans, 2010), 370.
7. Jonathan Leeman, *Church Discipline: How the Church Protects the Name of Jesus* (Wheaton, IL: Crossway, 2012), 34.

by the church. This is due to the fact that the church is a gospel-centered institution, and as such we are to forgive one another as God in Christ has forgiven us (Eph. 4:32). Both discipline and forgiveness are a clear testimony of the serious call and power of the gospel, and the church does well to demonstrate their love for the good news of Christ in pursuing these measures consistently.

There is no timetable given in Scripture as to how long a church should take in restoring the person to church membership.[8] Sound wisdom must be present with each case, as various details will have to be factored into the discussion. However, while some time may be taken to sort out the various issues concerning disciplinary cases and restoration to membership, Jeschke asserts, "The perennial temptation of the church is to demand more for restoration than for baptism, to make the conditions for restoration more rigorous than for joining the body of Christ originally."[9] If one looks at the parable Jesus tells immediately after the teaching on church discipline in Matthew 18, one can see that forgiveness of a genuinely repentant individual is paramount (Matt. 18:21–35). As such, while wisdom must be sought, and repentance determined to the best of our ability, the church must stand as a place filled with love and forgiveness, ready to embrace the repentant.

Summary

The process of church discipline is straightforward but complex due to the fact that we are sinful people dealing other sinful people. There is a clear biblical call to confront others in their sin, with humility, love, graciousness, and truth. We are also to call those people to repentance, as we ourselves pursue ongoing repentance in our lives. If the process goes far enough, there is a call for the congregation as a whole to remove that person from membership.

---

8. In the early years of the church there was a struggle over those who lapsed in their faith. This was seen specifically with the Novationists and Donatists, two groups who protested the restoration of those who abandoned the faith during times of persecution. Others, such as Basil of Caesarea and Gregory of Nyssa, advocated for certain periods of time passing before a sinner was restored to the church based on what the offense was (e.g., twenty years for murder, eighteen years for adultery, nine years for fornication). See Basil of Caesarea, "To Amphicolus, Letter 217," in *Nicene and Post-Nicene Fathers*, eds. Philip Schaff and Henry Wace, Second Series (Grand Rapids: Eerdmans, 1989), 8:256; Gregory of Nyssa, "Canonical Epistle to Letoius, Bishop of Melitene," in *The Penitential Discipline of the Primitive Church*, ed. Nathaniel Marshall (Oxford: J. H. Parker, 1844), 188–98. This kind of process sought to ensure continuing righteousness on the part of the offender, though such measures are not found in Scripture. For further details see Gregory A. Wills, "A Historical Analysis of Church Discipline," in *Those Who Must Give an Account: A Study of Church Membership and Church Discipline*, eds. John S. Hammett and Benjamin L. Merkle (Nashville: B&H Academic, 2012), 131–39.

9. Marlin Jeschke, *Disciplining in the Church: Recovering a Ministry of the Gospel*, 3rd ed. (Scottdale, PA: Herald Press, 1988), 101.

This is done in hopes that the person will recognize their sin, repent, and be restored to the community.

In this process wisdom, patience, and discernment are needed. We want to be clear in our doctrine of sin, and to help people see when they veer from God's path of obedience in their attitudes and actions. As a community of members who are committed to know and love one another well, churches must pursue one another's well-being, even when it will be painful to say certain words or bring up certain subjects. Ultimately, we walk through this process for the glory of God's name and the good of our fellow members.

REFLECTION QUESTIONS

1. What is confrontation? How should it be approached according to Scripture?

2. How specific do we need to be when calling someone to repentance? Before whom do they need to repent?

3. Why does someone have to be put out of membership?

4. What are we saying of someone if we do not allow them to partake of the Lord's Supper?

5. How much time should the process of church membership take? What is the church looking for in the restoration process?

How Does the Church Discipline One of Its Leaders?

While members of a local congregation are responsible to oversee and be overseen in their discipleship, leaders are set in place to ensure that discipleship and oversight is pursued with vigilance. The elders of the church, while not the sole enactors of discipline in the church, are responsible for overseeing the process and leading well. As shepherds of the flock, they are the ones who will give an account for the congregation (Heb. 13:17) and work to see that the people of God attain to Christian maturity (Col. 1:28).

However, there are times when a leader in a local church falls into ongoing, unrepentant sin. When this occurs, a church must respond in specific ways so as to maintain its purity and glorify God in all they do. As such, churches must keep in mind that while it is difficult and painful to walk through the disciplinary process with a leader of the church, that leader is a fellow member before he is a leader. The church must then walk through the process of discipline as outlined in Matthew 18 and elsewhere, also taking into account some additional details from 1 Timothy 5.

The Pastor Is Also a Church Member

Pastors/elders are members of the church. This is a key distinguishing mark to hold forth if a church has to walk through discipline with one of its leaders. Those who are put into the position of eldership from their churches have demonstrated that they meet the qualifications outlined in 1 Timothy 3:1–7 and Titus 1:5–9.[1] While looking at the qualifications—consisting of

---

1. Besides the many excellent commentaries available on these passages, see also the discussion in Gregg Allison, *Sojourners and Strangers: The Doctrine of the Church* (Wheaton, IL: Crossway, 2012), 212–18; Alexander Strauch, *Biblical Eldership: An Urgent Call to Restore Biblical Church Leadership*, Rev and Exp (Littleton: Lewis and Roth, 1995), 217–19.

moral, marital and family, and teaching qualifications—one can note how ordinary each of these marks actually are.[2] Elders are not called to be perfect, but to set the pace for the entire congregation in terms of pursuing Christian maturity. As Hammett observes, "Such a person would not need to be perfect (such persons are in very short supply among fallen humanity) but would need a degree of maturity and proven character that would enable him to serve as an effective example, including an example of how to confess and repent when he does stumble."[3] Thus, the character required to be an elder is the character necessary to be an example to the flock.

When an elder—a member of the church who has shown themselves to be qualified to serve as a leader by their example in lifestyle and word—commits sin and shows no repentance, a church must recall that he is first and foremost a fellow member. The elders are not a law unto themselves. Such leaders are not some outside board that the church is incapable of touching. Instead, responsibility to correct the erring member resides with the congregation. This can be a challenge as churches at times can put their leaders on a pedestal, not wanting to believe they are capable of sin, intimidated by their position, or unwilling to upset the status quo within the church. This first principle must be remembered, however, in order to have an objective stance in confronting unrepentant leaders within a church.

There Must Be Two or Three Witnesses

While there are not many passages dealing with the discipline of leaders, 1 Timothy 5:17–22 is instructive.[4] First, Paul considered the situation where a charge is raised against an elder (5:19). Paul reminded Timothy to follow the principle of Deuteronomy 17:6 and 19:15 in church discipline (cf. Matt. 18:16). In effect, Paul urged Timothy to follow this procedure found in Matthew 18 and the OT before the church accepts or acknowledges as correct an accusation against an elder. The process may consist of two or three witnesses bringing an accusation, but normally it would consist of two or three witnesses verifying an accusation that may come from only one individual before it is considered further.[5]

---

2. Carson notes, "almost every entry is mandated elsewhere of *all* believers" (D. A. Carson, "Church, Authority in the," in *Evangelical Dictionary of Theology*, ed. Walter Elwell [Grand Rapids: Baker Academic, 2001], 249 [emphasis original]).

3. John S. Hammett, *Biblical Foundations for Baptist Churches: A Contemporary Ecclesiology* (Grand Rapids: Kregel, 2005), 166.

4. See Benjamin L. Merkle, *40 Questions about Elders and Deacons* (Grand Rapids: Kregel, 2008), 219–26.

5. G. W. Knight, *The Pastoral Epistles: A Commentary on the Greek Text*, NIGTC (Grand Rapids: Eerdmans, 1992), 235.

Capricious and arbitrary accusations should not be taken seriously, for there are almost always people willing to speak a defaming word.[6] There are times when people are simply holding a grudge against a pastor, or have a vendetta against the church as a whole. Unless an accusation can be corroborated by more than one person, it cannot be accepted, and even then, a thorough investigation must take place. One should seek for the repentance of the leader, as they would any other member. As such, this process must be administered with all care.

Deal with It Publicly

If an accusation of sin is verified through this process, then the elder guilty of sin must be rebuked "in the presence of all" (5:20). Lea and Griffin engage three questions derived from this verse.

> First, who were those involved in sinning? Paul's statements did not call them elders, but it is a natural deduction from a context in which he dealt with elders that sinning elders were Paul's concern. The present tense of the word for "sin" suggests that the practice was continuous and not merely an isolated occurrence. Second, who were the persons before whom the public rebuke took place? It could have been either a group of elders or the entire congregation. The word "publicly" (lit., "before all") appears to suggest a group wider than merely the assembled elders. Probably the entire congregation was to learn of the rebuke. Third, who were the "others" who would "take warning"? Some link them with the entire church. Other interpreters refer the term to the remainder of the elders. Probably Paul had the entire church in view. The open rebuke Paul proposed was intended to promote the fear of God within the congregation.[7]

The charges in this case, therefore, are not kept private; rather the whole congregation is informed about the sin of the elder.

One must consider, also, whether every sin committed by a leader in the church bears this kind of public rebuke. No one is perfect in this life, and thus it does not seem that Paul intends for elders to be reproved publicly for every sin they commit. Like any disciplinary case, sins that are publicly known, blatant, and bear no marks of repentance are worthy of discipline. In 1 Corinthians 5,

---

6. Thomas R. Schreiner, "The Biblical Basis for Church Discipline," in *Those Who Must Give an Account: A Study of Church Membership and Church Discipline*, eds. John S. Hammett and Benjamin L. Merkle (Nashville: B&H Academic, 2012), 127.

7. T. D. Lea and H. P. Griffin, *1, 2 Timothy, Titus*, NAC 34 (Nashville: B&H, 1992), 156–57.

for example, sins are to be reproved which are of a public nature and bring reproach on God's name and the church of Jesus Christ.[8] Churches must know that leaders receive no preferential treatment, but are held to a high standard, and must receive the discipline of the church like anyone else.

We receive some illumination from Paul's rebuke of Peter in Galatians 2:11–14. Peter acted hypocritically and ceased eating with Gentile Christians, fearing the disapproval of Jewish believers. Paul reproves Peter before the church (Gal. 2:14) since he was acting in a way contrary to the gospel. A public confrontation was fitting, therefore, since Peter's sin was public and had public consequences (i.e., the Jews and Barnabas followed his example; v. 13). A private word would have scarcely been sufficient since his sinful behavior had influenced others. This fits with 1 Timothy 5:20, as Peter was rebuked so the church was not led astray and so that the rebuke might bring a healthy fear of sin to the rest of the congregation.[9] This is true since one aim of discipline is to serve as a means of perseverance for the church as a whole.

Two final directives from 1 Timothy 5 give further wisdom regarding the discipline of church leaders. First, the church must be impartial in disciplining its leaders (5:21). No elder should receive favoritism because of a special friendship or because he is especially influential. The integrity of the church will be deeply undermined if different standards are applied to different leaders. Second, caution should be exercised as a church looks to appoint elders (5:22). Paul warned Timothy of the danger of making hasty appointments to Christian offices. One need not call the practice here ordination, but it has all appearances of referring to an approval for ministry (e.g., Acts 13:3). Paul hinted that one who participates in such an appointment shares in the sinful results that can easily follow.[10] As such, a church must pray, fast, investigate, and seek godly counsel as it appoints elders in the church.

Summary

Leaders are not exempt from discipline, and they must not be treated with any partiality. They are first and foremost members of the church, and as such they are subject to ecclesial discipline like any other member. However, the church must go through a prescribed process, working from the evidence of two or three witnesses and not merely a disgruntled individual. If leaders are guilty of significant sin, they should confess it before the congregation, be forgiven, and, most likely, be removed from office. The sin of leaders has a public character and affects the entire congregation. As such, it should receive

---

8. Schreiner thus notes, "Hence, an elder may commit adultery on only one occasion or embezzle funds once, but the sins are so egregious that they warrant public rebuke" ("The Biblical Basis for Church Discipline," 128).

9. Ibid.

10. Lea and Griffin, *1, 2 Timothy, Titus*, 157–58.

public rebuke. This is a call for ongoing sanctification in the leader's life, never settling and getting comfortable, but rather constantly seeing and savoring Jesus Christ, growing in holiness and love for God and others.

REFLECTION QUESTIONS

1. Why might it be difficult for a church to practice church discipline on a church leader?

2. Why is it important to view an elder as a member when thinking about the disciplinary process?

3. Why does there need to be two or three witnesses involved before dealing with the sin of a church leader?

4. Why does the rebuke of the leader need to be public?

5. How should the congregation respond to the discipline of the leader?

How Can the Practice of Church Discipline Be Introduced into the Church?

For the health of the church as a whole, church discipline is a necessary and beneficial practice. However, while much can be said about ecclesial discipline and its benefits, the truth is that discipline is a foreign concept in many congregations. It is not that there is ambivalence or resentment held toward the practice; there has simply never really been consideration of such a measure. This is crucial to consider, as the lack of a culture that embraces church discipline could be detrimental to the ongoing life of the church.

Typically, churches that do not practice church discipline are lacking in other key areas that may contribute to its diminished place in church life. Thus, if someone were seeking to implement the practice of discipline in the church, there are other matters that would precede the installation of a specific disciplinary framework. One would need to focus on the points of biblical teaching, regenerate church membership, a culture of discipleship, and a specific plan of action in terms of proper church structure. It is necessary that pastors see the call to discipline as the call to a certain kind of culture, and this must be given due consideration and appropriate measures of time so as not to bring unnecessary pain and confusion to the church.[1]

Biblical Teaching

Pastors function as stewards of God's Word (1 Cor. 4:1–2; 9:17; Eph. 3:2; Col. 1:25; 1 Tim. 3:15; Titus 1:7; cf. Acts 20:17–32). Since God gave us

---

1. For some thoughts on avoiding mistakes in the initiation of practicing discipline, see Jonathan Leeman, *Church Discipline: How the Church Protects the Name of Jesus* (Wheaton, IL: Crossway, 2012), 139–40.

his Word, a pastor should desire to proclaim biblical truths as accurately as possible, which means that exposition would be the primary way in which Scripture would be communicated.[2] This type of preaching and teaching will focus most intensely upon the actual words of Scripture, and will serve as the greatest possible means to being a faithful steward of God's Word. Preaching also, by God's grace, brings about the truths of the gospel in the lives of God's people. Preaching is not only doctrinal and moral instruction, though it includes these; it is also the means by which God, through the Spirit, creates and sustains Christians and churches in their union with Christ.[3] Pastors, therefore, must rightly conceive of their stewardship of God's Word, knowing that by rightly proclaiming the truths of God, His people, under the sovereignty of God, will be transformed progressively into the likeness of Christ (cf. John 6:63; Acts 10:44; 12:24; Phil. 2:14–16; 2 Tim. 2:9; Heb. 4:12; 1 Peter 1:23).

This is true in any number of areas, and certainly applies to the observance of church discipline. If the practice is absent, pastors must ensure that they focus some of their teaching efforts toward educating the congregation in this area. Churches should be taught about God's love, which disciplines (Heb. 12:6) and rejoices in the truth (1 Cor. 13:6). If we keep the commands of Jesus, we will abide in his love (John 15:10), and if we keep the word of Christ, God's love is perfected in us (1 John 2:5). Pastors can help their members abide in Christ's love by teaching the concept of love accurately, correcting erroneous thinking on the subject, and calling the church to obey God. Pastors also need to teach about holiness and repentance. God intends for his people to look different than the world, and he intends for them to live set apart to him as they continually war against their sin. Finally, pastors should teach their people about church discipline itself. Whether in sermons, small groups, or newsletters, there should be a focus on the obvious texts (e.g., Matt. 18:15–20; 1 Cor. 5:1–13), as well as demonstrating how discipline is a major theme that runs throughout all of Scripture. Biblical teaching will set the precedent for the consistent practice of church discipline.

---

2. Certainly various preaching texts espouse different models of preaching, but for a sampling of recent works that argue for the primacy of expository preaching, see Daniel L. Akin, David Lewis Allen, and Ned Lee Mathews, eds., *Text-Driven Preaching: God's Word at the Heart of Every Sermon* (Nashville: B&H Academic, 2010); Bryan Chapell, *Christ-Centered Preaching: Redeeming the Expository Sermon*, 2nd ed. (Grand Rapids: Baker Academic, 2005); Dennis E. Johnson, *Him We Proclaim: Preaching Christ from All the Scriptures* (Phillipsburg, NJ: P&R Publishing, 2007); John MacArthur, *Rediscovering Expository Preaching* (Dallas: Word, 1992); Jason C. Meyer, *Preaching: A Biblical Theology* (Wheaton, IL: Crossway, 2013); R. Albert Mohler, *He Is Not Silent: Preaching in a Postmodern World* (Chicago: Moody, 2008); Ramesh Richard, *Preparing Expository Sermons: A Seven-Step Method for Biblical Preaching* (Grand Rapids: Baker, 2001).

3. Michael Scott Horton, *People and Place: A Covenant Ecclesiology* (Louisville: Westminster John Knox, 2008), 253.

Regenerate Church Membership

A church won't be willing to put someone *out* of the church unless they understand that there is an *in* and an *out*.[4] While much has been said in previous chapters on this point, it is important to emphasize that in a church not practicing church discipline, regenerate church membership is a step that must be taken previously. Again, pastors must teach clearly on this matter, helping their congregation to understand that membership is a church's public affirmation of an individual Christian's profession of faith in Jesus. The individual Christian is also choosing to submit to the oversight of the church in their ongoing discipleship.

As the church rightly understands membership, they will then have a better reference point for discipline. People join a church by the authority of its members, and they are put out of a church by the authority of its members. Membership is the front door of the church, and discipline is the back door. One cannot separate these two practices; both are needed for a healthy church.

Culture of Discipleship

Churches must be taught what it means to be a disciple of Jesus. Harper and Metzger rightly observe that a focus on biblical discipleship leads us to "encourage people to guard against depending upon the faith of their parents or their own past merits and rituals to carry them spiritually; instead they must be encouraged and challenged to respond personally and repeatedly to Christ's call on their lives."[5] This discipleship occurs both privately and corporately, through personal spiritual disciplines and the life of the church.

In order to engage culture and not merely be shaped by and conformed to it, discipleship must be holistic and deeply embedded in the DNA of the church.[6] Members of the church must be correcting and teaching each other from Scripture (Col. 3:16; 2 Tim. 3:16–17), and this must be normative culturally. Formal and informal relationship structures should be built, sample questions can be offered for ongoing discipleship,[7] and individuals should learn to invite and give correction and encouragement. When this kind of accountability environment permeates the church, formal church discipline makes more sense.

Proper Church Structure

When seeking to enact discipline in a local church context, pastors should organize the structure of their church to accommodate such a practice. Over

---

4. Leeman, *Church Discipline*, 127.
5. Brad Harper and Paul Louis Metzger, *Exploring Ecclesiology: An Evangelical and Ecumenical Introduction* (Grand Rapids: Brazos, 2009), 143.
6. See Timothy Keller, *Center Church: Doing Balanced, Gospel-Centered Ministry in Your City* (Grand Rapids: Zondervan, 2012), 185–86.
7. See, for example, the "X-Ray Questions" in Timothy S. Lane and Paul David Tripp, *How People Change* (Greensboro. NC: New Growth Press, 2006), 163–65.

time one must ensure that as they have taught on discipline and built a culture where discipline makes sense, they also look to have their documentation in line with the practice. Whether a church is dealing with a constitution, bylaws, or a church covenant, the practice of discipline must be in writing so people are not surprised by the expectations. Leeman asserts that these documents should communicate the following: what is expected of members in terms of beliefs and behavior, how the church's authority structures operate, what to expect for the receiving and dismissing of members under normal circumstances, and how church discipline works under extraordinary circumstances.[8]

Churches should also ensure they have the proper legal foundations in relation to discipline, and that they have a handle on church membership rolls. One of the most effective ways to protect a church against lawsuits in matters of ecclesial discipline is to adopt biblical policies that comprehensively describe how your church will exercise discipline over unrepentant members. Informed consent must be established so that court of law could see that the person who brought the complaint was in fact fully aware of the church's policies. These policies should be in writing and explicitly taught in the process of an individual joining a church for membership.[9]

Finally, in order to practice church discipline effectively, one must know who the church is. As such, faithful records must be kept and constantly updated so as to be aware of who is a covenant member of the church. There will likely be more attenders than there are members, and when it comes to handling the formal business of the church, including cases of church discipline, one must know who the members are. When first coming to a church, this will require some level of research. Some people will have moved away due to job relocation, others will not have attended for months or even years. Deliberation will need to take place, and churches will need to make clear who members are and what is expected of them. This is worthwhile work as it will assist in building a church that embraces both regenerate church membership and discipleship.

Summary

If church discipline is not in place, proper action must be taken. The leadership of the church must faithfully teach on the subject, champion regenerate church membership, build a culture of discipleship and accountability, and order the structure of the church so as to normalize the practice of discipline. This is the kind of environment that will image a God of love and holiness.

---

8. Leeman, *Church Discipline*, 133.
9. For helpful resources, both in a general sense of resolving conflict within the church and the specifics of dealing with legal issues, see Ken Sande, "Informed Consent: Biblical and Legal Protection for Church Discipline," 9Marks E-Journal, September/October, 2009, https://9marks.org/article/informed-consent-biblical-and-legal-protection-church-discipline/; idem, *The Peacemaker: A Biblical Guide to Resolving Personal Conflict*, 3rd ed. (Grand Rapids: Baker, 2004).

REFLECTION QUESTIONS

1. What should a pastor teach on specifically, in preparing a church to embrace the concept of church discipline?

2. How can a church effectively build a culture of discipleship?

3. In what ways, if any, does the church membership process in your church address the realities of church discipline?

4. What documents in your church contain teaching about church discipline? What is taught there specifically? Does anything need to be added?

5. Does your church have a system for maintaining and updating the membership rolls of the church? What updates need to be made in that area?

Practical Questions

Why Do Some Churches Not Practice Church Discipline?

Some churches do not practice discipline because they are unaware of the biblical mandate, or because they are unsure how to start the process. Other churches, however, have other concerns about the potential consequences of such a practice. They know what Scripture teaches on the matter, but remain unconvinced as to the legitimacy or pragmatic viability of ecclesial discipline.

Churches can hold to a number of reasons for rejecting the practice of church discipline. Some believe that the practice does not comport with the biblical concept of love. Related to that idea, some will point out that none of us are perfect, and therefore we should not be focused on getting rid of people when they sin. Still others maintain that the church can err in their practice of church discipline, since the church is filled with fallible, sinful human beings. Finally, some maintain such a practice is far too invasive of private lives. These objections will be considered and answered.

Discipline Is Unloving

Many look at any form of discipline as arrogant, cruel, and unloving. Love is meant to look past sin and let things go; it covers a multitude of sin (1 Peter 4:8). However, ultimately knowing that sin leads to death (Rom. 6:23), the church must understand that discipline is in fact a loving act. As a declarative sign of potential eschatological judgment, discipline is meant to serve as a call to repentance and a means to persevering in the faith.[1] What may seem unloving is in fact meant to demonstrate the greatest kind of love, pointing someone to eternal life.

---

1. This thesis is defended in Jeremy M. Kimble, *That His Spirit May Be Saved: Church Discipline as a Means to Repentance and Perseverance* (Eugene, OR: Wipf and Stock, 2013).

Bargerhuff concurs with this point, arguing that the church "as an embodiment of Christ empowered by the Holy Spirit, is authorized and obliged to exercise discipline as an expression of God's fatherly love toward the company of his redeemed children."[2] Here one can observe that God demonstrates his love through disciplinary acts (Heb. 12:3–11; cf. 1 Cor. 11:17–32), as he seeks to turn the hearts of his people toward holiness. God has delegated this divine authority to the church as well, so as to discipline for the same purposes (Matt. 16:16–19; 18:15–17). A long-term view is in mind, as the goal is to see members of the church pursuing maturity in godliness. God makes it clear that his people will be marked by holiness (1 Peter 1:15–16; cf. Heb. 12:14). Discipline is a means to pursuing holiness; therefore discipline, done as God directs, is a loving act.

The Church Is Filled with Sinners

Others will object to discipline in the church since everyone is guilty of sin. The argument here is that discipline is a hypocritical act due to the fact that no one is guiltless; we are all marred by sin. Again, while this is true, it does not negate the obvious texts in Scripture that call for church discipline to be exercised. While it does not negate the practice of ecclesial discipline, the presence of sin should chasten our approach.

Consider, for example, Matthew 7:1, wherein the reader is told, "Judge not, that you not be judged." Interestingly, in our present-day culture, the idea of judging another person is seen as arrogant and narrow-minded, and this verse is often used as ammunition against a concept like church discipline. This, however, would be a misreading of the text. We are specifically told to judge one another within the church (though not in the final way that God judges); Jesus' words in Matthew 18, Paul's in 1 Corinthians 5–6, and other passages clearly show that the church is to exercise judgment within itself.[3] Thus, there is a sense in which judgment in this context is necessary and appropriate, but it must be done in a certain way, or else it is sinful (cf. Matt. 7:2–5; Gal. 6:1).

The church is certainly not to condemn others unjustly. The imagery in Matthew 7:1–5 (the speck and log in one's eye) in fact suggests that we must be self-critical when it comes to our own sin, but this is done not for the purpose of excluding the judgment of others altogether, but as a prerequisite to judging.[4]

---

2. Eric J. Bargerhuff, *Love That Rescues: God's Fatherly Love in the Practice of Church Discipline* (Eugene, OR: Wipf and Stock, 2010), 183.
3. Mark E. Dever, "Biblical Church Discipline," *SBJT* 4, no. 4 (2000): 29.
4. Bruce Ware brings out this point and helpfully connects it to church discipline: "After Jesus says what is commonly quoted ('do not judge lest you be judged'), he proceeds with instructions precisely about how properly to bring an erring brother to account. Recall that he warns to 'take the log out of your own eye, and then you will see clearly to take the speck out of your brother's eye' (7:5). What is often missed in this is that once the log is removed, one has the obligation then to help remove the speck from his brother's eye. In other words,

This fits with Galatians 6:1, which tells us we who are spiritual should seek to restore those who have sinned. We are to do so with a spirit of gentleness and to keep watch on ourselves, lest we too be tempted to sin. Thus, Jesus and Paul have not condemned judging altogether but have rather called the church to be above reproach in the way they do so by examining their own hearts first.

The Church Can Err

Some will question the legitimacy of the church's authority in issuing a warning to unrepentant sinners.[5] If the church is not infallible, will the judgment rendered against a sinning individual always be correct? This is a crucial question to answer since this view of discipline potentially speaks to a person's eternal state and because local congregations can err in their judgments.

When considering the legitimacy of such a pronouncement coming from the church, one must take into consideration key passages from Matthew 16 and 18. These deal specifically with the authority given through the keys of the kingdom, as well as the concomitant power granted to the church in binding and loosing (Matt. 16:19; 18:18). Jesus does not give *carte blanche* to the church to do as it pleases and assume his blessing on all actions. This is a stern warning to churches not to abuse this principle and practice. Jesus is giving a promise concerning a very specific situation: the maintenance of the integrity of the body of Christ.[6] As such, if the church is to possess the authority as stated in Matthew 16:19 and 18:18, the community must act in accord with the truth of Scripture and distinct details of each disciplinary situation.[7]

Thus, when a church—no matter how large and influential, or small and seemingly inconsequential—acts in accordance with God's Word, their authority is real, albeit mediated. The church possesses a kind of power, wherein, there is the heavenly recognition of earthly transactions when handled

---

Jesus expects us to be used in the lives of others to help them advance in holiness, just as they may be used likewise in our lives to help us to grow. Church discipline is, most essentially, the formal structure that grows out of a healthy practice of corporate accountability" (Bruce A. Ware, "Perspectives on Church Discipline," *SBJT* 4, no. 4 [2000]: 87).

5. This section is derived from Kimble, *That His Spirit May Be Saved*, 135–37. Used by permission of Wipf and Stock Publishers (www.wipfandstock.com).

6. Lauterbach maintains, "[Jesus] is building his church and care must be taken in that process. When the church acts according to his will, as described in his Word, then he is at work in its actions. Consider it his hand working through the glove of the church" (Mark Lauterbach, *The Transforming Community: The Practise of the Gospel in Church Discipline* [Ross-shire, Scotland: Christian Focus, 2003], 201).

7. See Wray, who asserts, "The church is not by this text made infallible, nor is the holy God by it engaged to defend their errors. The only fact to be established at this point, however, is simply that the Lord Jesus Christ *does* indeed intend his church to govern its members even to the extent of disciplinary measures when these become necessary" (Daniel E. Wray, *Biblical Church Discipline* [Carlisle, PA: Banner of Truth, 1978], 3).

according to divine directions.[8] Exercising discipline in the church, then, is a most delicate affair. Vanhoozer helpfully summarizes the proper interpretation of these passages, saying, "Ultimately, only God can judge the human heart. At the same time, the church has received a dominical and apostolic commission to preserve the truth and to pursue holiness."[9] The church, therefore, must humbly and discerningly apply their mediated authority granted by Christ.

Church discipline is thus a "warning," not a "pronouncement." This is significant in that there is recognition that God is the ultimate judge of all things, not the church. Warning, therefore, connotes a proper tone of serious admonition, while also granting final authority to God. Discipline, therefore, is a warning of "potential" judgment. Eschatological judgment is not unerringly certain, due to the fact that the church is filled with sinners. It is, however, a sign of potential judgment, and as such should be taken with all seriousness. Thus, while the fallibility of the church must be taken into account, this particular understanding of ecclesial discipline still holds.

Discipline Is Overly Invasive

One final objection that may be raised is over the issue of individualism. Discipline seems to be too far-reaching, invading the privacy of people's lives and turning their sin into a public spectacle. To exact discipline, some would argue, would bring about humiliation over details that ought not to be known by the public.

This objection may feel right in a culture that so highly values autonomy and individual expression, but it goes against the grain of the Bible's teaching. Faith involves the end of self-enthronement. At the heart of faith is the idea of submitting to the authority of another. Specifically believers are called to submit to God, his kingdom rule, the local church, and its leadership.[10] Submission to Christ's kingdom means a submission to the present earthly outpost of his kingdom, namely, the church. In becoming a member of this new covenant kingdom community, we submit ourselves to the divinely mediated discipline of the church.

Summary

Many objections will arise in thinking of the practice of church discipline. It seems rather unloving to remove someone from membership. The church

---

8. See Roy Knuteson, *Calling the Church to Discipline: A Scriptural Guide for the Church That Dares to Discipline* (Nashville: Thomas Nelson, 1977), 36–37.

9. Kevin J. Vanhoozer, *The Drama of Doctrine: A Canonical-Linguistic Approach to Christian Doctrine* (Louisville: Westminster John Knox, 2005), 424.

10. Jonathan Leeman, *Political Church: The Local Assembly as Embassy of Christ's Rule*, Studies in Christian Doctrine and Scripture (Downers Grove, IL: IVP Academic, 2016), 326–27. See also Oliver O'Donovan, *The Desire of the Nations: Rediscovering the Roots of Political Theology* (Cambridge: Cambridge University Press, 1999), 117.

is filled with people who are themselves sinners, and therefore they can err in their judgment. Finally, discipline can seem overly invasive, looking too closely into the private affairs of others. However, as has been demonstrated, discipline is not an unloving, invasive act, perpetrated by wicked people. Bonhoeffer observes, "Nothing can be crueler than the tenderness that consigns another to his sin. Nothing can be more compassionate than the severe rebuke that calls a brother back from the path of sin."[11] As such, discipline must be exacted in the church and done humbly, gently, and carefully, always aiming for love in pointing someone to repentance and life in Christ.

REFLECTION QUESTIONS

1. If someone were to tell you discipline is an unloving act, how would you respond?

2. How should sinful people pursue disciplining other sinful people?

3. If the church can err, what steps can be taken to ensure that disciplinary measures line up with God's will?

4. Why is biblical church discipline not overly invasive in nature?

5. What does submission look like in a local church? To whom do we submit? How far does this extend practically?

---

11. Dietrich Bonhoeffer, *Life Together*, trans. John W. Doberstein (New York: Harper & Row, 1954), 107.

What Is the Goal of Church Discipline?

At times, people truly struggle to see the point of ecclesial discipline or what good it will accomplish. However, church discipline is not some pointless measure used at the whim of heartless leaders and churches. Instead, discipline is God's tool to bring about transformation, repentance, and renewal. It is intended to accomplish specific results in the lives of people within a local church.

Dever acknowledges a variety of purposes for church discipline: "Finally, church discipline should be practiced in order to bring sinners to repentance, a warning to other church members, health to the whole congregation, a distinct corporate witness to the world, and, ultimately, glory to God, as his people display his character of holy love (see Matt. 5:16; 1 Peter 2:12)."[1] Each of these goals could be taken up in great detail over many pages. This chapter will focus on three key goals of discipline: (1) that God's people would repent, (2) pursue sanctification, and (3) receive warning so as to endure in their obedience to him.

Repentance

The biblical notion of repentance refers to the radical turning away from anything which hinders one's wholehearted devotion to God, and the corresponding turning to God in love and obedience.[2] In the OT the verb "repent" (*niham*) occurs about thirty-five times. The background of the NT idea of repentance lies not primarily in *niham* (except in Job 42:6; Jer. 8:6; 31:19), however, but rather in *šûb*, meaning "to turn back, away from, or toward" in the religious sense.[3] In the OT, the people of God who had entered into covenant with him were to reflect God's nature (Lev. 19:2; 20:22–26; Deut. 10:12–13).

---

1. Mark Dever, "The Church," in *A Theology for the Church*, rev. ed., ed. Daniel L. Akin (Nashville: B&H Academic, 2014), 634.

2. J. M. Lunde, "Repentance," in *NDBT*, eds. T. Desmond Alexander and Brian S. Rosner (Downers Grove, IL: InterVarsity, 2000), 726.

3. C. G. Kromminga, "Repentance," in *EDT*, ed. Walter A. Elwell, 2nd ed. (Grand Rapids: Baker Academic, 2001), 1012.

Their turning away in unbelief and unfaithfulness shows a personal rejection of God (Deut. 4:23; 11:16; 1 Sam. 15:11; 1 Kings 9:6; 2 Chron. 7:19, 22; Ps. 51:4; Jer. 11:10) and results in God's turning away from them and bringing about the realization of the covenant curses (Deut. 4:15–28; 30:15–20; Dan. 9:11–14). This divine discipline, however, is meant to move his people to repentance as he calls them to remember his promises of blessing (Isa. 55:1–3).[4]

In the NT *metanoia* (noun) occurs twenty-three times and *metanoeō* (verb) thirty-four times. Repentance is the theme of the preaching of John the Baptist (Matt. 3:1, 8; Mark 1:4). Baptism in water unto repentance is accompanied by confession of sins (Matt. 3:6; cf. 1 John 1:8–9). Jesus continues John's theme but adds, significantly, "The time is fulfilled" (Mark 1:15). His coming is the coming of the kingdom in person and is decisive (Matt. 11:20–24; Luke 13:1–5). All life relationships must be radically altered (Matt. 5:17–7:27; Luke 14:25–35; 18:18–30). Sinners are called to repent (Matt. 9:13; Mark 2:17; Luke 5:32), and heaven rejoices over their repentance (Luke 15). Repentance can thus be said to denote that inward change of mind, affections, convictions, and commitment rooted in the fear of God and sorrow for offenses committed against him, which, when accompanied by faith in Jesus Christ, results in an outward turning from sin to God and his service in all of life.[5] Godly sorrow is also an ongoing fact of life that works in the lives of Christians, bringing about repentance (2 Cor. 7:10). And discipline is an essential means of bringing about repentance, whether it be for a believer who was briefly erring or a person who has demonstrated that they were not truly part of the new covenant community and in need of salvation.

Sanctification

In keeping with repentance, Christians should bear fruit and continue to grow in their sanctification. The term "sanctification" comes from the same root for "holiness" or "consecrate." It refers to that which is set apart and pure. God is holy; "separate" from nature, other gods, and sinners; unapproachable except by mediation and sacrifice (Isa. 6:3–5). Men and women "sanctify" God by obeying his commands (Lev. 22:32; Isa. 8:13; 1 Peter 3:15). Israel is inherently holy, separated by God from "the peoples" to be his own. Paul refers to the people of God in the NT as "saints," those who are set apart to God (1 Cor. 1:2; Eph. 1:1; Phil. 1:1; Col. 1:1). Yet, the people of God are also called to become holy, working out their own salvation with fear and trembling as God works in them to will and to work for his good pleasure (Phil. 2:12–13).[6]

Sanctification has a twofold sense, connoting both a status conferred and a process to be pursued. Christ is our righteousness (1 Cor. 1:30) and by union

---

4. Lunde, "Repentance," 726.
5. Kromminga, "Repentance," 1012.
6. R. E. O. White, "Sanctification," in *EDT*, 1052–53.

with him we are sanctified and declared to be holy before God.[7] Based on this status, we are also to increasingly become who we already are in Christ. Christians are to strive for holiness or sanctity (Heb. 12:14). So Paul prays that the Thessalonians be sanctified wholly—spirit, soul, and body being kept sound and blameless—as something still to be accomplished (1 Thess. 5:23–24). Sanctification is the will of God for them, especially in the matter of sexual purity (1 Thess. 4:3–4). Similarly, the Romans are exhorted to present their bodies holy in their worship (12:1); and in 1 Corinthians 6:13–14 the body of the Christian must be kept from immorality because every Christian is a sacred ("sanctified") person, belonging to Christ.

Discipline is a means God uses to remind people of their status, namely, children of God who are in Christ. It is also a tool used by God to continue to grow his people in godliness. Christians are called to grow in holiness and increase in godly character (2 Peter 1:3–9), and discipline, rightly applied, can yield the peaceful fruit of righteousness.

Endurance

One final goal of ecclesial discipline is to see God's people persevere in the faith. Church discipline is a means God uses to preserve his people in faith to the end. It is a warning of potential eschatological judgment and thus functions in this way. Similarly, the Bible is filled with warnings addressed to God's people. These biblical warnings and admonitions serve as the means used by God in calling the saints to persevere in their faith.[8] Thus, a connection seems to exist between the warning passages in Scripture and the warning that comes through ecclesial discipline.

True Christians will persevere in their faith, and those who reject Jesus after seeming conversion demonstrate that they were not truly part of the people of God (1 John 2:19; cf. Matt. 13:1–23). Church discipline reminds church members that they should be characterized by ongoing repentance and the pursuit of holiness. The warning exists both for the erring member and the church as a whole. The erring member is reminded of his or her need to repent, and the church is exhorted to continue persevering in the faith and to investigate their own lives for sinful patterns. While this may sound onerous and oppressive, church discipline is actually a gracious means given

---

7. For an extended treatment of our status of sanctification, see David Peterson, *Possessed by God: A New Testament Theology of Sanctification and Holiness*, NSBT (Grand Rapids: Eerdmans, 1995). Beale elaborates, "Sanctification in the NT conveys the idea of a believer who continues increasingly to be set apart from the old creation to the new creation, and who bears fruits in keeping with being a part of the new creation" (G. K. Beale, *A New Testament Biblical Theology: The Unfolding of the Old Testament in the New* [Grand Rapids: Baker Academic, 2011], 933).

8. Thomas R. Schreiner and Ardel B. Caneday, *The Race Set Before Us: A Biblical Theology of Perseverance and Assurance* (Downers Grove, IL: InterVarsity, 2001), 38–45.

by God to assist us in our endurance.[9] Discipline, therefore, is a needful practice for the perseverance of the saints.

Summary

Church discipline is not some whimsical practice to assuage the masochistic tendencies of a select few people in a local church. The heart of discipline is grace and love. The goals of discipline include enacting repentance in one's life, assisting in the pursuit of sanctification, and serving as a warning so as to stimulate ongoing perseverance in the faith. These goals are formative in nature and have the best in mind for individuals who are lovingly confronted in unrepentant sin.

This is a needful perspective to adopt, so as to see discipline for what it truly is. Culture will likely not appreciate a strong stance by the church on discipline. However, the church must regain its biblical footing, recognize what God teaches us from his Word, and proclaim to the world that a truly flourishing life conforms to the truths of Scripture. Discipline is meant to point us in a direction that leads to an abundant life in Christ (John 10:10).

REFLECTION QUESTIONS

1. What are the goals of church discipline?

2. What is repentance? How can church discipline be one way that God brings repentance about?

3. What is sanctification? How can church discipline be one way that God brings sanctification about?

4. Some may view discipline as cruel or unloving, but how is discipline actually a gracious act?

5. How does God use church discipline as a means of perseverance in our lives?

---

9. Mathis rightly asserts, "Providing regular, gracious words of correction can seem like such a small thing in community life. It's so easy just to let little sins go and mind your own business. But the long-term effect of such active grace, administered in loving humility, can have eternal implications (James 5:19–20)" (David Mathis, *Habits of Grace: Enjoying Jesus through the Spiritual Disciplines* [Wheaton, IL: Crossway, 2016], 194).

What Is the Benefit of Discipline for the Person under Discipline?

Church discipline greatly benefits the person who is experiencing confrontation due to unrepentant sin. This may not seem to be the case at first glance, but once one understands the theology of the church and the finality of God's coming final judgment, discipline is certainly beneficial. As such, one must possess a robust ecclesiology, doctrine of God, and understanding of judgment to appreciate this practice. If erring sinners will repent and recalibrate their minds to see these features, they will see how discipline served them.

Mutual Watchfulness

As the people of God, the NT church is called to take care of each other at various levels. One key way we care for each other is by overseeing one another's discipleship. If regenerate church membership is held as a conviction in a local congregation, we then labor to the best of our ability to ensure that those who enter the church as members are in fact believers. Once they join in membership, they become part of a people who covenant to oversee one another and ensure that each person is living properly as a member of the new covenant community. Historically, this idea was termed "mutual watchfulness."

The early settlers of New England, for example, sought to exact a fairly strict practice of church discipline.[1] In 1644, John Cotton explained

---

1. For general discussion of church discipline and deviance leading up to and in colonial New England, see Theodore Dwight Bozeman, *The Precisianist Strain: Disciplinary Religion and Antinomian Backlash in Puritanism to 1638* (Chapel Hill: University of North Carolina Press, 2004); Kai Erikson, *Wayward Puritans: A Study in the Sociology of Deviance*, rev. ed., Allyn & Bacon Classics (Boston: Allyn and Bacon, 2005).

that church discipline represented the "key of order." Such a key "is the power whereby every member of the Church walketh orderly himself . . . and helpeth his brethren to walk orderly also." In 1648, Puritan minister Thomas Hooker explained the necessity of church discipline: "[God] hath appointed Church-censures as a good Physick, to purge out what is evil, as well as Word and Sacraments, which, like good diet, are sufficient to nourish the soul to eternal life." Hooker explained that church members must watch over one another, "each particular brother (appointed) as a skillful Apothecary, to help forward the spiritual health of all in confederacy with him." Disciplinary practices helped to ensure that the early settlers, as well as subsequent generations, stayed on their godly paths.[2] While the intensity of mutual watchfulness gradually settled into decline,[3] early American religion was profoundly shaped by the reciprocal care displayed within the church.

While culture and the pace of life have changed from the early days of America, the need for mutual watchfulness is as great as ever. We must address sin in our churches (1 Cor. 5:1–5; Gal. 6:1–5; 1 Tim. 1:20). Ordinary church members must address one another's sin. Turning a blind eye is not an option. To be sure, there are situations where wrongdoing is so slight that love leaves it unaddressed (Prov. 19:11). And there are situations where lack of relationship or the right circumstances make it unproductive to approach a brother about sin.[4] But those caveats aside, a culture must be built that values the loving confrontation of sin. We want our churches to stand in amazement at what God has chosen to do through the gospel. When they treasure salvation as undeserved grace, they will take seriously their responsibility to watch over one another and guard each from sin. The more amazed we are at our own salvation, the more we will foster a culture of honest, grace-filled conversation about sin, and this is an amazing benefit to an erring, unrepentant sinner.[5]

Tangible Manifestation of Love

We are called by God to love our neighbor as ourselves (Matt. 22:39). This command—along with loving God with all our heart, soul, mind, and strength—summarizes the Law and the Prophets (Matt. 22:40) and is referred

---

2. This section was derived from Monica D. Fitzgerald, "Drunkards, Fornicators and a Great Hen Squabble: Censure Practices and the Gendering of Puritanism," *Church History* 80, no. 1 (2011): 41–42.
3. For more on the decline of mutual watchfulness and its effects on the ministry of Jonathan Edwards, see Jeremy M. Kimble, "That Their Souls May Be Saved: The Theology and Practice of Jonathan Edwards on Church Discipline," *Themelios* 39, no. 2 (2014): 251–67.
4. Mark Dever and Jamie Dunlop, *The Compelling Community: Where God's Power Makes a Church Attractive*, 9Marks Books (Wheaton, IL: Crossway, 2015), 173.
5. Ibid., 182.

to as the fulfillment of the law (Rom. 13:8–10). We can do amazing feats for God, but if we do not have love for him and his people, it profits us nothing (1 Cor. 13:1–4). Love is essential to the Christian life and is connected to the practice of church discipline. However, many will think this a mistaken conclusion because they hold to a faulty view of love.

In our individualistic, skeptical, anti-authority, and God-forsaking age, we are often instinctively repulsed by being bound or limited by anything. As such, many have redefined the idea of God's love in a way that makes it more palatable to the masses. Leeman notes that we have erected an idol and called it "love." He continues, "And this idol called love has two great commands: 'Know that God loves you by not permanently binding you to anything (especially if you *really* don't want to be),' and, following from it, 'Know that your neighbor loves you best by letting you express yourself entirely and without judgment.'"[6] This view of love, however, is idolatrous and deviates from the norms of Scripture.

God's love is God-centered. Thus, in a certain sense, God loves everyone because God beholds his own handiwork, image, and glory in everyone. On the other hand, God's God-centered love bears a posture that opposes everything that opposes God.[7] This is so because God's love is a holy love. Holiness is the purity of love's devotion to God.[8] God loves himself with infinite purity, and he calls a people to love him with heart, soul, mind, and strength (Deut. 6:4–5). He also calls these people to love others in holiness (Eph. 5:1–2), which includes both forbearance as well as truths declared in membership and discipline. In holy-love, the church receives individuals who have turned from idols to love the only true God in holiness. Discipline, as we will see, pronounces coming judgment, due to lack of conformity to the holy-love of God. Thus, discipline demonstrates mercy, kindness, and true love, which seeks to conform to the holiness of God.

Tangible Manifestation of a Future Reality

Church discipline serves as a declarative sign of eschatological judgment. Judgment is a comparatively simple topic, but it bears upon every aspect of biblical theology. The OT emphasizes judgment within history, while the NT emphasizes eschatological judgment, filling out the concept of the day of the Lord (Amos 5:18) with the large perspectives of the day of

---

6. Jonathan Leeman, *The Church and the Surprising Offense of God's Love: Reintroducing the Doctrines of Church Membership and Church Discipline* (Wheaton, IL: Crossway, 2010), 74 (emphasis original).
7. Ibid., 85–86. For more on the multifaceted nature of God's love, see D. A. Carson, *The Difficult Doctrine of the Love of God* (Wheaton, IL: Crossway, 2000), 16–21.
8. Ibid., 100.

Christ (2 Thess. 1:5–10; 2 Peter 3:7–13).[9] In the last day the Lord Jesus will stand as judge over all, and everyone will receive either eternal life (Matt. 25:34, 46) or eternal judgment in fire (Matt. 25:41, 46). There is no third option on that day, God will glorify himself through eternal salvation of the redeemed and eternal judgment of those who never received his grace.

Church discipline serves as a tangible sign and reminder of that in-evitable future judgment.[10] Discipline serves as an anticipatory act, judgment by a local congregation that foreshadows the even greater judgment to come. This act is beneficial to the person under discipline, because it serves as a gracious warning of the greater judgment. While appreciation and gratitude may not be welling up in the hearts of those who are confronted in their unrepentant sin, this is a means of calling people back to repentance, faith, and holiness. While church discipline, at any level, will feel unpleasant, it is far better to receive the rebuke of your local church and be called to repentance than to fall under the eternal judgment of God where there will be no second chance of repentance (Heb. 9:27). This practice serves as a great benefit to the one under discipline, as it serves a loving act, calling the sinner to repentance so as to be in right standing when final judgment comes.

Summary

For a person under discipline, the act of confrontation or even being put out of a church will likely feel overly harsh, unloving, and ungracious. These feelings are exacerbated by a culture that so highly values autonomy and an anti-authoritarian spirit. Ecclesial discipline will likely be interpreted as bigoted, arrogant, and intolerant, bringing harm to the one on the receiving end of discipline.

However, as has been discussed, discipline is of great benefit to the person in sin. The practice of mutual watchfulness within the church is of great help, knowing that we all need to continue to grow in holiness. Discipline, as ironic as it sounds, serves as a tangible manifestation of love. Love is imbued with holiness and therefore aims to point people toward the standard of life that conforms with God's character. Finally, discipline is a tangible manifestation of the future reality of final judgment. Present judgment aims to point people toward repentance by reminding them of the finality of future judgment so that, ultimately, they will avoid future judgment by their repentance.

---

9. See J. A. Motyer, "Judgment," in *NDBT*, eds. Brian S. Rosner and T. Desmond Alexander (Downers Grove, IL: IVP, 2000), 612.

10. Horton rightly maintains, "The church's acts are not final—they do not coincide univocally with the eschatological realities, but they are signs and seals. Christ's performative speech is mediated through appointed officers" (Michael Horton, *People and Place: A Covenant Ecclesiology* [Louisville: Westminster John Knox, 2008], 243).

REFLECTION QUESTIONS

1. What would you say to someone who believes that church discipline in no way benefits the person under discipline?

2. Is mutual watchfulness a part of your present church culture? How could that reality be more readily applied?

3. What is love, according to Scripture?

4. How is the practice of church discipline a loving act?

5. What is the relationship between church discipline and final judgment?

What Is the Benefit of Discipline for the Church as a Whole?

Church discipline is of great benefit to the person under discipline, as ultimately the intent of discipline is to see the person turn from the error of their ways and be restored to the fellowship of the church. It is a beautiful moment when one can observe manifest repentance, and when a church can welcome back the repentant individual with open arms. The process of discipline has worked to the full in that instance, in that we have gained our brother (Matt. 18:15).

Discipline is not only beneficial to the person in sin, however, but also to the congregation as a whole. God gave the practice of discipline to the church not so they could be meanspirited, nor to become increasingly calloused and condemning. Rather, discipline reminds the church of the connection between doctrine and practical Christian living. Discipline brings a host of theological truths to mind, and shows how practical theology truly is. Discipline also serves as a benefit to the congregation in that it encourages humility and perseverance. Finally, discipline, done rightly, will produce a healthy church culture that glorifies God and acts for the good of others.

Reminder of How Doctrine and Life Intersect

Church discipline is a practical theological implication that directly impacts the lives of those involved. This is not unique for doctrine since, as Frame so aptly states, "Doctrine is the Word of God in use to create and deepen one's knowledge of God, and to encourage an obedient, rather than disobedient, response to his revelation. Or, more briefly, doctrine is the application of God's Word to all areas of human life."[1] It makes sense,

---

1. John M. Frame, *The Doctrine of the Christian Life*, A Theology of Lordship (Phillipsburg, NJ: P&R, 2008), 9.

then, that church discipline is a natural outflow from the doctrine of ecclesiology for the life of the church. However, there are many other doctrines that bear on the practice of church discipline and have direct impact on our Christian living. Here the focus will be on three primary doctrines: (1) Scripture, (2) God, and (3) sin.

First, the Bible is God's Word to his people, in which he communicates a revelation of his person and his works.[2] These writings contain factual historical information and doctrinal content, as well as commands and promises. In all of these different ways, God is seeking to communicate with his people.[3] Scripture is to be understood as the revelation of God, inspired by God, and thus, based on his own character, inerrant, infallible, and authoritative for us. This specific characterization of the Word of God means that we are to be submissive to the precepts and commands that we find therein. Churches and individual Christians are compelled, therefore, to study the Word of God, to know its contents, and apply those contents to real life. We must seek to learn and obey as we encounter the words of God in Scripture.[4] Churches, therefore, must be committed to the objective words of Scripture, specifically in this instance about church discipline and what constitutes such an action by the church.

Secondly, God exists as the self-existent one, all-powerful, all-knowing, sovereign, and majestic. Calvin maintained, "No man can survey himself without forthwith turning his thoughts towards that God in whom he lives and moves; because it is perfectly obvious that the endowments which we possess cannot possibly be from ourselves; nay, that our very being is nothing else than subsistence in God alone."[5] In other words, we simply cannot know ourselves our world, or anything else apart from the right knowledge of the Creator. He is transcendent, existing in the fullness of his infinitely glorious Trinitarian unity and apart from the finite spatio-temporal creation he freely brought into existence. God is also immanent, as he freely enters into the realm of the creaturely existence that he designed and made.[6] Transcendence and immanence also give rise to the fact that God is both holy and loving.

---

2. For more on a theology of Scripture, see John Frame, *The Doctrine of the Word of God* (Phillipsburg, NJ: P&R, 2010); Peter Jensen, *The Revelation of God* (Downers Grove, IL: IVP Academic, 2002); Timothy Ward, *Words of Life: Scripture as the Living and Active Word of God* (Downers Grove, IL: IVP Academic, 2009).

3. See Kevin Vanhoozer, *First Theology: God, Scripture, and Hermeneutics* (Downers Grove, IL: InterVarsity, 2002), 159–203.

4. See Ward, *Words of Life*, 175.

5. John Calvin, *Institutes of the Christian Religion*, ed. John T. McNeill, trans. Ford Lewis Battles, (Philadelphia: Westminster, 1960), 1.1.1.

6. Bruce Ware, *God's Greater Glory: The Exalted God of Scripture and the Christian Faith* (Wheaton, IL: Crossway, 2004), 35.

We can cite many other attributes of God, but these four characteristics serve as summary statements of who God is. As such, we serve a God who has chosen to relate to us covenantally in love but stands apart as a God of perfect purity, Creator of all things. As we live as Christians in the church, a proper doctrine of God keeps us grounded, knowing that we cannot simply compare ourselves to others, or make up our own criteria for right and wrong. Rather, we will all stand before God to give an accounting of our lives (2 Cor. 5:10). As such, we are compelled to recognize who God is and align disciplinary standards in the church with his character and commands.

Finally, the doctrine of sin reminds us of how doctrine intersects with discipline in the church. Adam and Eve rebelled and sinned against God, causing all of humanity to come under the condemnation of sin and death (Gen. 3; cf. Rom. 5:12–21). The result is that we are still image-bearers (e.g., Gen. 9:6), but that image is now deeply marred. Sin, as Carson notes, is rebellion against God's very being, against his explicit word, against his wise and ordered reign. It results in the disorder of his creation and in the spiritual and physical death of his image-bearers.[7] God in his grace established covenants with his people, and the climactic covenant given is the new covenant (Jer. 31:31–34; Ezek. 36:25–27; cf. Heb. 8:1–13). Only through the life, death, and resurrection of the God-man, Jesus Christ, can we as sinners experience redemption (Rom. 3:21–26).[8] Sin is an absolute reality in the lives of individuals and the culture at large, and it must be dealt with in the way God prescribed. God intends church discipline to highlight the egregiousness of sin as well as his gracious redemption.

Warning to Persevere and Stay Humble

Much has already been said regarding perseverance, but it bears repeating that this serves as a great benefit for the church as a whole. The local congregation is not merely to condemn or make light of the sin in their midst. Rather, they are to observe the consequences for sin, recognize the fact that one is being handed over to Satan for the destruction of their flesh (1 Cor. 5:5), stand in fear of such discipline (1 Tim. 5:20), and persevere in their faith. There is no arrogance involved in such an approach to discipline; the church stands in humility as they deal with disciplinary issues.

---

7. D. A. Carson, "Sin's Contemporary Significance," in *Fallen: A Theology of Sin*, eds. Christopher W. Morgan and Robert A. Peterson (Wheaton, IL: Crossway, 2013), 23.

8. In relating sin, salvation, and the Christian life, Carson asserts, "Whether one considers the theme of God's wrath or the particular objects of his saving love, whether God thunders over Sinai or the particular Jerusalem, whether we focus on individual believers or the covenantal identity of the people of God, whether one stands aghast at the temporal judgments poured out on Jerusalem or stands in rapt anticipation of the glories of the new heavens and the new earth, the substratum that holds the entire account together is sin and how God, rich in mercy, deals with sins and sinners for his own glory and for his people's good" (ibid).

This fits the overall biblical witness. God is the great Creator who dwells in heaven, and he looks to the one who is "humble and contrite in spirit and trembles at my word" (Isa. 66:1–2). We are told that God opposes the proud, but gives grace to the humble (Prov. 3:34; James 4:6; 1 Peter 5:5). People who are humble and reverent toward God's Word, stand in awe before the King of Kings who made the heavens and the earth. They deeply respect what God has said, take it seriously, internalize it, make it part of their worldview, and then they implement it in their daily walk and thinking.[9] Church discipline should be one of the ways God continually works humility within us; this is beneficial not only for our own lives as individual Christians, but also for the culture of the church as a whole.

Healthy Church Culture

Sin undealt with in the church is likened by the apostle Paul to yeast in dough. Yeast represents the unclean and spreading nature of sin (1 Cor. 5:6–8). Since Christ has died as our Passover Lamb, we are to clean out the old bread and be a new batch of dough that has no yeast (i.e., sin). Sin that remains in the church will damage the overall culture of the church, and so we must repent and cleanse the church through biblical discipline.

This commitment to discipline will yield a culture of mutual accountability, love, and gospel witness. To ensure this culture is manifest, discipline must be present. We are to be a community of holiness (1 Peter 1:15–16), who speak the truth in love (Eph. 4:15), and shine as gospel witnesses before men (Matt. 5:16). A church pursuing biblical discipline will yield a healthy culture that also bears corporate witness to the world of the holiness and love of God.

Summary

Church discipline is truly a beneficial practice to the church. It reminds the church how the Christian life is informed by its doctrine. It also calls the people to endurance in their faith and a posture of holiness. Finally, it produces a culture wherein holiness, love, and the witness of the gospel are all taken with utmost seriousness.

As we think about the benefits of discipline for the person in sin, as well as the overall congregation, we must also recognize that ultimately we practice church discipline for the same reason we do all things in life, namely, to glorify God (1 Cor. 10:31; Col. 3:17). God does all that he does for his glory (Isa. 48:9–11); he made us to glorify him (Isa. 43:6–7); and, therefore, we discipline within the church so that he receives the praise he is due. We are called to delight in this God (Ps. 16:11), which brings him glory (Phil. 1:20–24), and thus discipline is calling us to forsake sin and rejoice in the Lord always (Phil. 4:4).

---

9. Gary V. Smith, *Isaiah 40–66*, NAC 15b (Nashville: B&H, 2009), 730.

REFLECTION QUESTIONS

1. In thinking of the various doctrines of the Christian faith, how do these doctrines inform our practice of church discipline?

2. Is your church committed to learning doctrine? How will a deep study of doctrine affect the overall life of the church?

3. Why should church discipline develop a posture of humility in the church?

4. How does discipline contribute to the corporate witness of the church?

5. In what ways does discipline work for the glory of God?

What Kind of Sins Require Church Discipline?

Some are fearful of church discipline because of the kind of exposure it may bring. Linked to this fear is the question about the legitimacy of ecclesial discipline, given the fact that everyone sins regularly. It seems inconsistent at times to discipline the way we do, since in reality everyone is guilty before God.

It is important to distinguish these points, as one thinks about what kinds of issues require church discipline. One must note that all sin is wrong in the eyes of God, though some sins bring about more serious consequences in life than others. Crucial to this discussion also is the understanding that discipline refers to a number of practices—from preaching, to personal confrontation, all the way to excommunication. Sin requires church discipline, but not always at the same level. Finally, sins require church discipline when people show signs of not belonging to the new covenant community.

All Sin Is Wrong

There are times as Christians when we can categorize sin and distinguish various transgressions from those which are egregious before God to sins that one views as virtually permissible.[1] However, in terms of our legal standing before God, any one sin, even what may seem to be a very small one, makes us legally guilty before God and therefore worthy of eternal punishment.[2] Through Adam and Eve's one trespass condemnation came to all (Rom. 5:16). Everyone is under the curse of the law because we do not abide by all things

---

1. For helpful commentary on sins we often overlook and deem as lesser evils, see Jerry Bridges, *Respectable Sins: Confronting the Sins We Tolerate* (Colorado Springs: NavPress, 2007).
2. Wayne Grudem, *Systematic Theology: An Introduction to Biblical Doctrine* (Grand Rapids: Zondervan, 1994), 501.

written there (Gal. 3:10). And whoever keeps the whole law, and yet fails in one point, has become guilty of all of it (James 2:10–11).

So legally, all sins stand as equally offensive before God. On the other hand, Grudem states, "some sins are worse than others in that they have more harmful consequences in our lives and in the lives of others, and, in terms of our personal relationship to God as Father, they arouse his displeasure more and bring more serious disruption to our fellowship with him."[3] In this sense there does seem to be gradation regarding sin (Ezek. 8:6, 13, 15; Matt. 5:19; 23:23; John 19:11). In general, one may say that some sins have more harmful consequences than others if they bring more dishonor to God or if they cause rampant harm to ourselves, others, or the church. Moreover, those sins that are done willfully, repeatedly, and knowingly, with a calloused heart, are more displeasing to God than those that are done out of ignorance and are not habitual (Lev. 4:2, 13, 22; 5:17; Num. 15:30; James 3:1).[4] Underlying this kind of iniquity, the sin of unrepentance is especially serious.

Thus, in regard to church discipline, we are all indeed guilty of sin. But we must also recognize that there are some sins that are so blatant, ongoing, and harmful to the church, that they must be dealt with directly by the process of church discipline. This distinction is crucial so that we do not neglect all discipline, nor exercise discipline for every instance of sin.

Loss of Credibility in a Person's Confession of Faith

Many people, however, still might believe that only certain sins are worthy of discipline, such as adultery or embezzlement. However, the kind of sin is not necessarily the issue, but rather what the sin is saying about the person's status as a child of God. Sin has become pervasive and there has been no sign of repentance, prompting the question of whether or not this person is truly part of the new covenant community. These kinds of sins that call for discipline can take many forms, but generally could be private and personal offenses that violate Christian love—divisiveness and factions that destroy Christian unity, moral and ethical deviations from biblical norms, or the teaching of false doctrine.[5]

Again, one must be clear that everyone sins, but that repentance is characteristic of Christians. For instance, consider the lies of two different professing Christians. One brags about receiving a job promotion that he never actually received. Later he becomes convicted about this deceit and confesses his lie. The second person build his entire career on a falsified resume.

---

3. Ibid., 502.
4. Ibid., 502–3.
5. Ted G. Kitchens, "Perimeters of Corrective Church Discipline," *BSac* 148, no. 1 (1991): 211–12.

It is later discovered and he is confronted, but he refuses to acknowledge it and persists in his fabrications. The first example is one that we expect from Christians, where occasional sin does come up, but repentance follows. The second lie is not something we expect from a Christian, as there is no conviction, fighting sin, or repentance.[6] If there is a loss of credibility in a member's confession of faith, corrective discipline must be sought out, whether the sin be adultery, addiction, gossip, abuse, desertion of a spouse, lying, or nonattendance.

Using All the Tools for Skillful Shepherding

Dealing with sin issues in the church does not necessitate that a congregation will immediately seek to excommunicate everyone that has committed sin. When recognizing that all are sinful and all are in need of God's grace, it is amazing to see that God has instructed the church to act in accordance with spiritual danger that various members may find themselves facing. Pastors and churches would do well to consider all of these tools as we deal with various issues of sin in our midst.

First, even if a member is living fruitfully, recognize they can potentially be in danger of not persevering and thus encourage them in the faith (1 Thess. 4:1; Phil. 2:29). Second, if a member is lacking information and is doctrinally ignorant, seek to teach and instruct them (Acts 18:26; 1 Cor. 12:1; 1 Thess. 4:13). Next, if a member is lazy and neglectful, exhort and spur them on (2 Cor. 9:4–5; Heb. 5:11–12; 6:12; 10:24). If someone in your church is suffering through trials and experiencing discouragement, seek to comfort and console with the Word and prayer (2 Cor. 1:4; 7:6). If you see a member starting to go astray and developing new sin patterns, warn, correct, and admonish them (1 Cor. 4:14; Titus 3:10). Sixth, if a member is determined to wander and they are committing habitual sin, rebuke them (Gal. 2:11; Titus 1:11–12; Rev. 3:18–19). Finally, if there is stubborn unrepentance in a member of the church and they refuse to make things right, the church will need to excommunicate them (Matt. 18:17; 1 Cor. 5:5).[7]

All of these tools should be used in the church so as to ensure the body of Christ is admonishing the idle, encouraging the fainthearted, helping the weak, and exercising patience with all (1 Thess. 5:13). This is a holistic approach to the matter, and not merely reactionary to the sins we consider to be culturally taboo. It will be strange at first to implement such an intentional and robustly aware church context, but it will communicate the seriousness with which the church takes sin and the glorious nature of the gospel.

---

6. This example was derived from Leeman, *Church Discipline*, 49–50.
7. Andrew M. Davis, "The Practical Issues of Church Discipline," in *Those Who Must Give an Account: A Study of Church Membership and Church Discipline*, eds. John S. Hammett and Benjamin L. Merkle (Nashville: B&H Academic, 2012), 172.

Summary

Sin is real, pervasive, and deadly. We must be aware of the dangers and not seek to categorize sin to such a degree that we neglect much of what goes on in our churches. Sin makes us all legally guilty before a holy God. Apart from the atoning work of Jesus Christ, there is no hope for anyone, and thus in that sense there is equality in relation to sin. It must also be noted that different sins can have different consequences and can be committed by those with little knowledge of the truth or a great deal of understanding regarding biblical truths. All of this must be considered in our church contexts.

Sin can be so pervasive and the person show such signs of stubbornness in terms of repentance, that their profession of faith is called into question. This is not only the case for one or two specific sins. A lack of fruit and repentance is a reason for a church to begin investigating the merits of that person's conversion. This is one of many tools at the church's disposal as a culture is propagated that seeks to foster and promote the growth of the member's holiness. All of these tools should be used in relation to people's needs.

REFLECTION QUESTIONS

1. Is all sin equally egregious in the eyes of God?

2. Are there some sins that are "worse" than others? How so?

3. Regardless of the sin issue, what is at root and signals when a church should begin the disciplinary process with a person?

4. What tools can be used to help members continue in their growth in godliness?

5. How will you respond when someone says we all sin and therefore we should not practice church discipline?

Should a Believer Associate with Someone Under Church Discipline?

Excommunication may happen at your church, and when it does the church has to know how to relate to someone put out of the church. Can you talk to them when you see them at a store? Have dinner together at someone's house? Go on a trip together? Or are all of these kinds of activities now considered to be out of bounds because of their status in the church?

Some churches hold a view much like Bathasar Hubmaier, the distinguished Anabaptist theologian. He maintains, regarding the ban, that the excommunicant, "must be avoided and shunned so that the whole outward church may not be ill spoken of, shamed, and disgraced by fellowship with him or be corrupted by his evil example, but rather that it will be frightened and filled with fear by this punishment and henceforth die to sin."[1] Thus, Hubmaier believes it is needful, sometimes completely to cut off the "corrupt and stinking flesh" together with the "poisoned and unclean members" so that the entire body might not thereby be "deformed, shamed, and destroyed."[2] While churches must be aware of the corrupting influence of sin, this still begs the questions of whether total shunning and avoidance is needed. Other churches, if they practice discipline, may not see a real need to change anything in regard to their treatment of that person (especially if they practice open communion).

When thinking through this matter, one must take several considerations into account. First, the status of the person who is under excommunication is that they are no longer a member of the church, and by this act the church can no longer affirm them as a member of the new covenant community. As

---

1. Hubmaier, "A Christian Catechism," in *Balthasar Hubmaier: Theologian of Anabaptism*, eds. H. Wayne Pipkin and John Howard Yoder, Classics of the Radical Reformation 5 (Scottdale, PA: Herald Press, 1989), 353.
2. Hubmaier, "On Fraternal Admonition," in ibid., 374.

such, they are no longer to receive the Lord's Supper, and we do not relate to them as though everything continues as if nothing ever happened. Instead, we relate to them in a way that calls for faith and repentance.

They Are No Longer Members

Membership, as has been stated, is a privilege afforded to those whom the whole church has recognized as being part of the new covenant community. In other words, they have heard the person's testimony of conversion and concluded that the testimony is authentic. Because of the nature of the new covenant, where all within the covenant will know the Lord (Jer. 31:34), the church—as a picture of the coming kingdom of God—must labor to ensure to the best of their ability that the membership of the church is made up of regenerate people.

Discipline is a visible sign of eschatological judgment which signifies a reality existing in the not yet visible kingdom of God. Webster remarks, "The church is a human gathering; it engages in human activities . . . it has customs, texts, orders, procedures, and possessions, like any other visible social entity. It does and has these things, and so it is what it is, by virtue of the work of the Holy Spirit. Only through the Spirit's empowerment is the church a human assembly; and therefore only through the same Spirit is the church visible."[3] The Spirit indwells the people of God upon conversion (Ezek. 36:27; 1 Cor. 3:16; 6:19–20), and the pattern of the NT is to see Spirit-indwelt believers in Jesus Christ gather into local churches, becoming visible manifestations of new covenant. A person who lives as though they are not truly converted cannot be counted among the membership of the church, as that would cut against the grain of covenantal truths that God has brought about.

They Do Not Receive the Lord's Supper

As those under excommunication are put out of membership, this also means they are not to participate in the Lord's Supper as it is taken during a church gathering.[4] Scripture speaks of the Lord's Supper as a commemoration

---

3. John Webster, "The Visible Attests the Invisible," in *The Community of the Word: Toward An Evangelical Ecclesiology*, eds. Mark Husbands and Daniel J. Treier (Downers Grove, IL: IVP Academic, 2013), 101.

4. Regarding whether those who are excommunicated can attend worship services, Allison offers helpful commentary: "Some have seen in this expression [in Matthew 18:17] the permission to encourage the excommunicated person to continue to attend church worship services so that he or she can be exposed to the gospel, and, as a pagan, be converted. True, Jesus was a friend to sinners and tax collectors and often made such people the heart of his ministry (e.g. Matt. 9:10–13; 11:19; Luke 18:9–14). But 'Gentile' can also refer to one who was outside of the covenant community . . . and 'tax collector' can also denote one who, as a traitor siding with the enemy, was an outcast from his own people. Considering the context of Jesus' instructions about church discipline, the latter interpretation is far more plausible. Accordingly, severe measures are demanded at this last stage of the disciplinary

and proclamation of Christ's death and the establishment of the new covenant (Matt. 26:26–29; Mark 14:22–25; Luke 22:14–23), a participation in Christ and all his salvific benefits (1 Cor. 10:14–22), an expression of unity (1 Cor. 11:17–34), and the anticipation of an eschatological feast with the triumphantly returned Messiah (Rev. 19:6–9).[5] Unlike baptism, which is a one-time initiatory rite, the Lord's Supper is an ordinance that is observed repeatedly. Hammett also maintains that baptism can be pictured as a wedding ceremony wherein a believer publicly professes his or her commitment to Christ, and the Lord's Supper is similar to an anniversary celebration where the wedding vows are renewed.[6]

Therefore, an organic link exists between baptism, church membership, and the Lord's Supper. One must be a part of the body of Christ as a covenant member to enjoy all of its privileges, and this includes the partaking of the Lord's Supper. As an ongoing sign of the realities of the new covenant, those who partake of the Lord's Supper demonstrate a clear line of distinction between the church and the world. The excommunicant is removed from partaking of the Lord's Supper for their own sake, so as not to receive further discipline from the Lord (1 Cor. 11:27–32) and because they are not bearing fruit that would allow them to remain in membership.

We Communicate for the Sake of Their Repentance

Luther comments, regarding discipline, the Lord's Supper, and our relationship to the excommunicated, "he who is put under the ban is forced to live without the common sacrament and association with men; nevertheless he is not abandoned on that account by their love, intercession, and good works."[7] In other words, while the unrepentant sinner is no longer participating as a member of the church, this does not mean the congregation is completely shunning the individual. Discipline is always seeking the restoration of the individual, and the church serves as an important means of this restoration, both during the disciplinary process and after excommunication has been pronounced. We do not relate in the same way to that person, but we

---

process. Moreover, part of the responsibility of the church at worship is to acknowledge its identity as the called out and sent people of God who are together engaged in the *Missio Dei*. . . . Retention of excommunicated members of the church at worship obscures who are genuine Christians and who are not" (Gregg Allison, *Sojourners and Strangers: The Doctrine of the Church* [Wheaton, IL: Crossway, 2012], 186). This is a complex topic as we would typically allow other unbelievers to attend our services, but the texts dealing with discipline do demarcate those who are excommunicated in specific ways that render further meaning regarding their involvement in church life.

5. Ibid., 394–95.
6. John S. Hammett, *Biblical Foundations for Baptist Churches: A Contemporary Ecclesiology* (Grand Rapids: Kregel, 2005), 277.
7. Martin Luther, "A Sermon on the Ban," in *Church and Ministry I, LW* 39, ed. Eric W. Gritsch (Philadelphia: Fortress, 1970), 9–10.

do seek to communicate with them at various points with the hope that they will repent of their sin.

Leeman gives pertinent advice on how members are to interact with those who are under excommunication:

> The New Testament addresses this matter in a number of places (1 Cor. 5:9, 11; 2 Thess. 3:6, 14–15; 2 Tim 3:5; Titus 3:10; 2 John 10). The basic counsel the elders of my own church give is that the general tenor of one's relationships with the disciplined individual should markedly change. Interactions should not be characterized by casualness but by deliberate conversations about repentance. Certainly family members should continue to fulfill family obligations (see Eph 6:1–3; 1 Tim 5:8; 1 Pet 3:1–2).[8]

While various details could be cited regarding the application of discipline, the point is that we do not relate as before with casual meals, vacations, and a relationship that assumes mutual faith in Christ. Instead our interactions are scarcer, highly intentional, and marked with pleas for repentance. When we see them at work, in the store, or at the gas station, our interactions are intentional as we lovingly speak the truth to them. If they were to try and join another church, through the membership process the hope is that the excommunication would become known and that church would insist the issue be made right. We also pray specifically for the unrepentant sinner that God would work in their hearts. The hope is that this person feels a sense of shame and isolation from the church and from Christ, and that this acts as a catalyst to return to the Lord in repentance. This is a sober point, and one we must continue to speak to them about.

Summary

When excommunication happens, the church must be clear how it will respond and interact with the person. Theological truths must inform these relational components. First, it must be acknowledged that this person has been removed from membership, which communicates what the church believes their status to be in relation to God. There is a removal from partaking of the Lord's Supper as this is an ongoing ordinance for believers. These realities pave the way for how we should relate to the unrepentant individual: in sobriety, with prayer, speaking the truth in love, and seeking for their repentance and restoration.

---

8. Jonathan Leeman, *Church Discipline: How the Church Protects the Name of Jesus*, 9Marks (Wheaton, IL: Crossway, 2012), 76.

REFLECTION QUESTIONS

1. Why is a person removed from membership when they undergo excommunication?

2. How is church membership linked to membership in the new covenant?

3. Why is a person removed from receiving the Lord's Supper when they undergo excommunication?

4. How is someone to relate to a person who is under excommunication?

5. If someone was under excommunication at a different church and then came to your church and sought to join, how should your church handle that situation?

What Should Be Done When Someone under Discipline Repents?

Another question to consider deals with the procedure for restoring someone to church fellowship after they have been disciplined.[1] The goal is repentance and restoration, and if that occurs, the church again must be cognizant of their responsibilities. Is this an immediate reinstatement, or is there some kind of probationary period? As churches become more faithful in implementing the process of discipline, this question will become increasingly relevant, and therefore demands thoughtful attention.

Churches must be willing to do the hard work of investigation. When the person returns in repentance, the church wants to ensure in some way that the repentance is in fact genuine. When they assess that this person's repentance is sincere, the church is called to forgive and receive the individual into membership. Congregations may have been profoundly hurt by the actions of the individual. Nevertheless, the church must continually forgive, as God in Christ forgives us (Eph. 4:32).

Assess the Repentant Individual

When a person comes seeking to be restored to the church, the leaders should remind the congregation that such a restoration is biblical and desired (2 Cor. 2:6–8). Restoration can be defined as the forgiveness of an excommunicated individual by the church after they have repented and also an affirmation of his or her "citizenship" in God's kingdom and the new covenant community. Restoration and forgiveness should be extended to individuals under discipline, but it is also key that, to the best of the church's ability,

---

1. Portions of this chapter are derived from Jeremy M. Kimble, *That His Spirit May Be Saved: Church Discipline as a Means to Repentance and Perseverance* (Eugene, OR: Wipf and Stock, 2013), 143–45. Used by permission of Wipf and Stock Publishers (www.wipfandstock.com).

assessment of the genuineness of the person's repentance and thus their alignment with kingdom citizenship is made.

As there is a process for church membership, so it will be a process to receive someone into membership who has been previously excommunicated. When an excommunicated sinner repents and comes back to the elders of the church expressing a desire for reinstatement, the elders should examine the individual thoroughly to determine if genuine repentance has occurred. The repentant sinner should plainly repudiate the sinful acts that led to the excommunication, and be willing to say so in front of the whole church. Before the individual speaks to the church, the elders should investigate the life of the person, asking relevant persons—friends, family, neighbors, coworkers, and other church members—for evidence of the individual's repentant life.[2] If there were specific people in the congregation who bore the brunt of the sinful offense, the repentant individual should also go to them and seek restitution. All of these are tangible ways a church can assess the authenticity of the repentance.

Forgive and Receive Them into Membership

Once the assessment of the individual in question occurs, forgiveness, restoration, and concentrated discipleship must take place. Adams asserts, based on 2 Corinthians 2:6–8, that restoration requires three factors: The repentant offender must be forgiven; he must be assisted to avoid that sin in the future; and he must be reinstated in love. He gives no timeframe for this process, but along with assessment, it would certainly take some time to work through it all effectively.[3] Thus, there would be some formal gathering of the whole church,

---

2. Andrew M. Davis, "The Practical Issues of Church Discipline," in *Those Who Must Give an Account: A Study of Church Membership and Church Discipline*, eds. John S. Hammett and Benjamin L. Merkle (Nashville: B&H Academic, 2012), 179.

3. See Jay Edward Adams, *Handbook of Church Discipline* (Grand Rapids: Ministry Resources Library, 1986), 91–97. Davis likewise maintains, regarding restoration as seen in 2 Corinthians 2:6–8, "Having thus ascertained the genuineness of the repentance, the individual should ask for the church's forgiveness . . . and express sorrow over the sins that led to the excommunication. The church should then reinstate the individual . . . and express in many ways the delight they have at what God has done to restore this person. It would also be wise for an elder to be assigned to meet with the individual regularly for concentrated discipleship and counseling after that person has been reinstated" ("The Practical Issues of Church Discipline," 179). Davis mentions the role of elders in church discipline, which is another question that arises, particularly in congregationally governed churches. He maintains that "the elders are in the best spiritual position in the church to act both as witnesses against the sinning church member and (even more importantly) as mature shepherds of souls, skillfully wooing one of Christ's wandering sheep back to repentance" (ibid., 170–72). This is certainly true, but the entire congregation is responsible to exercise the keys of the kingdom to bind and loose. A careful balance must be struck in the elders' leadership and the church's authority. For works that advocate a leading role for elders while also recognizing congregational authority, see Benjamin L. Merkle, *40 Questions about Elders and Deacons* (Grand Rapids: Kregel, 2008); idem, *The Elder and Overseer: One Office in the Early Church*, SBL 57 (New York: Peter Lang, 2003).

where a deliberative decision would be approved and carried out, at least by the majority of the congregation.[4] And the goal is long-term perseverance in the faith, which calls for concentrated counseling and discipleship.

Again, the timeframe is not specifically expressed, but these principles should be maintained in any scenario wherein a person under excommunication is seeking restoration to the local church. We related to the unrepentant sinner in a certain way so as to ascertain their repentance. We removed them publicly, and now we restore them publicly. We relate to them as a brother or sister in Christ, fully restored, and ready to participate with them in worship.

Keep on Forgiving

Through the process of discipline, excommunication, and restoration, forgiveness must be upheld as a preeminent value. Church discipline is messy. People get hurt, and animosity and bitterness can reign in our hearts if left unchecked. This seems to be the reason why Jesus calls his listeners to forgiveness immediately after he teaches about the process of church discipline (Matt. 18:15–35). Jesus knew the hearts of humanity, and understood that in many instances it would be difficult to forgive someone who has undergone discipline once, let alone multiple times.

Jesus is commanding the people of God to forgive a person who confesses and repents of his or her sin in matters of church discipline. Chamblin rightly asserts, "Failure to forgive fellow believers (none of whose debts to each other could compare with those incalculable debts that God has canceled) shows that one has never really understood God's forgiveness. The judgment threatening such a person is just as real and final (v. 34) as that which threatens the offender (cf. vv. 14–20)—strong incentive for offering genuine, not just apparent, forgiveness (v. 35b)."[5] At this point in the process the church is in a place where, if they do not forgive the repentant sinner, they may themselves be demonstrating a lack of fruit that brings their own membership status into question. The gospel must reign supreme in our hearts; we must forgive as God in Christ forgave us (Eph. 4:32).

This call to forgiveness brings to mind a passage such as Matthew 6:14–15. There Jesus warns his followers, "For if you forgive others their trespasses, your heavenly Father will also forgive you, but if you do not forgive others their trespasses, neither will your heavenly Father forgive your trespasses." It appears that these verses are citing forgiveness as a fruit by which we know that we belong to God. If we are an unforgiving people toward repentant sinners, we are proving that we are not truly forgiven by God, and thus we

---

4. Murray J. Harris, *The Second Epistle to the Corinthians*, NIGTC (Grand Rapids: Eerdmans, 2013), 228.
5. Knox Chamblin, *Matthew Volume 2 (Chapters 14–28)*, A Mentor Commentary (Ross-shire, Scotland: Mentor, 2010), 745.

ourselves could be subject to church discipline based on that particular sin. A person who has been forgiven by God through salvation must certainly confront and judge others who disobey the commands of God, but it is also very clear that we must forgive the repentant.[6]

Summary

It is a thrilling experience to see a sinner turn from the error of his or her ways. The angels in heaven, and God himself, rejoice over sinners who turn to Jesus Christ in faith (Luke 15:1–32). This coincides with the goal of church discipline. We are not seeking to cast someone out of our presence forever and simply be done with that person; rather, we pray for them and speak to them that they might repent and be restored.

When repentance occurs, church leaders—and the congregation as a whole—should seek to assess the true status of their repentance. Churches want to ensure there is sincerity, not merely outward conformity. As this is confirmed, the church will gladly forgive and receive this individual back into their midst as a member of the church with all the privileges it yields. Since this may not be a one-time occurrence, churches must continue to forgive. In so doing, they are a manifestation of the truths of the gospel, forgiving other people as a people forgiven by God.

REFLECTION QUESTIONS

1. What is the process for restoration?

2. How can a church, to the best of its ability, ensure the sincerity of an individual's repentance?

3. What are we saying of the individual when we receive them back into membership?

4. Though not specified in Scripture, how long might this whole process take?

5. How does this process of forgiveness and restoration connect to the realities of the gospel?

---

6. For further thoughts on this particular subject, see Everett Ferguson, *The Church of Christ: A Biblical Ecclesiology for Today* (Grand Rapids: Eerdmans, 1996), 372; Thomas R. Schreiner and Ardel B. Caneday, *The Race Set Before Us: A Biblical Theology of Perseverance and Assurance* (Downers Grove, IL: InterVarsity, 2001), 77.

What Kind of Culture Does Biblical Discipline Produce in the Church?

Church discipline is an essential part of church life. If a church applies the biblical principles that relate to formative and corrective discipline, it will yield a certain kind of culture. However, in many churches, this culture must be nurtured and built from the ground up. Discipline has simply not been part of the vocabulary or value system of the church as a whole, and this will have certain overarching consequences.

Discipline should not begin with the whole church. It must begin in the discipleship culture of the church. Members must first learn to love and trust one another enough to share tough and encouraging words with one another.[1] As individuals in the church learn to do this faithfully, they will find that the entire church benefits. The expectation of making disciples and pursuing discipleship increase. Members learn how to both give and receive truthful and loving words that seek to bring about correction. And in all of this, as God is glorified in the church's pursuit of holiness and love, there is a deep-rooted, God-centered joy.

High Expectations of Discipleship

We do not want to propagate a kind of milieu wherein "cheap grace," as Dietrich Bonhoeffer once called it, abounds. He states, "Cheap grace is preaching forgiveness without repentance; it is baptism without the discipline of community; it is the Lord's Supper without confession of sin. . . . Cheap grace is grace without discipleship, grace without the cross, grace without the living, incarnate Jesus Christ."[2] This cannot be the case in our churches. There

---

1. Jonathan Leeman, *Don't Fire Your Church Members: The Case for Congregationalism* (Nashville: B&H Academic, 2016), 179–80.
2. Dietrich Bonhoeffer, *Discipleship*, eds. Geffrey B. Kelly and John D. Godsey (Minneapolis: Fortress, 2001), 30.

is only costly grace, grace that is purchased at a cost and that is powerful to change us.[3] We have been saved by grace through faith in Jesus Christ—not by our works, but to do good works (Eph. 2:8–10). Works do not save us, but we are called to bear fruit as evidence of true faith in Jesus Christ.[4]

With this teaching in mind there is, therefore, a high call to discipleship within the local church. Jesus has called us, as disciples, to make more disciples of him and to live in a particular way in the world. Jesus makes demands of his disciples, a life that displays the worth of his person and the effect of his work. We are to connect what he commands with who he is and what he has accomplished on our behalf.[5] The obedience Jesus demands is the fruit of his redeeming work and the display of his personal glory. These demands include repentance, love, abiding, taking up our cross, worship, prayer, humility, faith, righteousness, generosity, integrity, and giving testimony to Christ's work.

Thus, there is a high expectation when it comes to discipleship. Churches are groups of disciples of Jesus. When disciples come together, there must be intentional synergy bent toward making and growing disciples. The demands of discipleship are set out for us in Scripture, and our calling is to continually and increasingly conform to God's ways by God's grace. This should be an expectation within the church and should be made known to prospective members. The church is not a place where laxity reigns; we work diligently to see godliness reign and grow in our midst, recognizing that it is the grace of God and the work of his Spirit within us bringing about these results (1 Cor. 15:10; Phil. 2:12–13).

Honest, Loving Words

As difficult as it may be at first, churches need to recognize that "Better is open rebuke than hidden love" (Prov. 27:5) and "Faithful are the wounds of a friend" (Prov. 27:6). Part of love is correction. We steep ourselves in the words of Scripture for our own spiritual growth but also so that we can speak fitting words to those who are in need of hearing them. We speak these words in all humility, recognizing we have our own sins to deal with, but we work to repent of personal sin and help others in pursuing holiness as well (Matt. 7:1–5).

Ephesians 4:15 upholds this calling to speak honest, loving words to one another: "Rather, speaking the truth in love, we are to grow up in every way into him who is the head, into Christ." Paul is not exhorting his readers to truthfulness in general or speaking honestly with one another, however appropriate or important this may be. Rather, he wants all of them to be members of a "confessing" church, with the content of their testimony to be "the word of truth,"

---

3. Ibid., 31.

4. For more on works serving as an evidence of salvation, see Thomas R. Schreiner, *Faith Alone: The Doctrine of Justification* (Grand Rapids: Zondervan, 2015), 191–206.

5. John Piper, *What Jesus Demands from the World* (Wheaton, IL: Crossway, 2006), 19.

the gospel of their salvation (1:13; cf. Gal. 4:16).[6] We are new creations (2 Cor. 5:17), a new humanity (Eph. 2:11–22), meant to speak these words so as to live rightly within the new covenant community.[7] The truth as proclaimed should not be dissociated from love or promoted at the expense of love. And a life of love should embody the truth of the gospel. As we speak loving words of gospel truth to one another, we will forsake sin and grow in Christlikeness.

Humble Reception of Exhortation and Rebuke

Not only must we as church members be able to initiate in giving truthful, loving words to others, we must also be willing and able to receive such words. We will not live the Christian life in perfection, and we will often be blind to some of the sin issues in our lives. We need people in community who are loving enough and full of conviction who can speak the truth of the gospel to us in such a way as to help us see the error of our ways. If we are to grow up in every way into Christ, we must be receptive to such words.

Proverbs is replete with statements that show the wisdom of such an approach.

- Whoever loves discipline loves knowledge, but he who hates reproof is stupid (Prov. 12:1).
- Whoever ignores instruction despises himself, but he who listens to reproof gains intelligence (Prov. 15:32).
- Listen to advice and accept instruction, that you may gain wisdom in the future (Prov. 19:20).
- He who is often reproved, yet stiffens his neck, will suddenly be broken beyond healing (Prov. 29:1).

Foolish people simply cannot receive correction. They mock, ridicule, excuse, deny, and thwart any attempt at exhortation and rebuke. However, the wise person will hear such exhortation, take it to heart, repent of the sin, and learn from his or her mistakes. Our first response may be to get defensive and live in denial when we are rebuked in our sin, but a church must work to build this formative culture in order to cultivate continual, corporate growth into the head, Jesus Christ (Eph. 4:15–16).

God-Centered Joy

Church discipline, if pursued and exacted in a biblical manner, will ultimately produce a culture within the church of God-centered joy. We are

---

6. See P. T. O'Brien, *The Letter to the Ephesians*, PNTC (Grand Rapids: Eerdmans, 1999), 311.
7. For more on speaking the truth in love within Christian community, see Peter J. Gentry, "Speaking the Truth in Love (Eph 4:15): Life in the New Covenant Community," *SBJT* 10, no. 2 (2006): 70–87.

commanded by God, as a fruit of conversion, God's ongoing grace, and the work of the Spirit, to obey him, and this obedience glorifies God.[8] God is infinitely committed to his own glory, fame, and renown being known and displayed throughout all of creation (Isa. 48: 9–11; Hab. 2:14). We were made to glorify God in every facet of our lives; this is our purpose (Isa. 43:7; 1 Cor. 10:31; Col. 3:17). And there is no greater joy to be had in life and death than to live for God's glory (Ps. 16:11; Phil. 1:20–24).

Jonathan Edwards, who thought a great deal on these matters, states the preceding points in the following way:

> God is glorified within himself these two ways: (1) by ap-
> pearing or being manifested to himself in his own perfect idea,
> or, in his Son, who is the brightness of his glory; (2) by enjoying
> and delighting in himself, by flowing forth in infinite love and
> delight towards himself, or, in his Holy Spirit. So God glorifies
> himself towards the creatures also two ways: (1) by appearing
> to them, being manifested to their understandings; (2) in com-
> municating himself to their hearts, and in their rejoicing and
> delighting in, and enjoying the manifestations which he makes
> of himself. . . . God is glorified not only by his glory's being
> seen, but by its being rejoiced in, when those that see it delight
> in it: God is more glorified than if they only see it; his glory is
> then received by the whole soul, both by the understanding and
> by the heart. God made the world that he might communicate,
> and the creature receive, his glory, but that it might [be] re-
> ceived both by the mind and heart. He that testifies his having
> an idea of God's glory don't glorify God so much as he that
> testifies also his approbation of it and his delight in it.[9]

God made us to glorify him, and we do so with both mind and heart, thought and affection. As a church ponders the greatness of the glory of God and seeks to rejoice in the Lord always (Phil. 4:4) and increasingly know and understand him (Jer. 9:23–24), there is a corresponding desire to forsake sin in all of its forms. As such, church discipline, rather than producing a dour, negative atmosphere, will instead aim at joy that is rooted deeply in God and his manifest glory.

---

8. See Wayne Grudem, "Pleasing God by Our Obedience: A Neglected New Testament Teaching," in *For the Fame of God's Name: Essays in Honor of John Piper*, eds. Sam Storms and Justin Taylor (Wheaton, IL: Crossway, 2010), 272–92; John Piper, *The Pleasures of God: Meditations on God's Delight in Being God*, rev. and expanded (Sisters, OR: Multnomah, 2000), 241–67.

9. Jonathan Edwards, "End of the Creation," in *The Miscellanies: A-500, WJE* 13, ed. Thomas A. Schafer (New Haven, CT: Yale University Press, 1994), 495.

Summary

The acceptance and practice of church discipline in an ecclesial context will produce a certain kind of culture. First, it will raise the bar on discipleship and the expectations we set for members of the church. As we continue to make disciples and help them grow in Christian maturity, we demonstrate that this is not a passive faith but one that is engaged in the works that God prepared for us before creation (Eph. 2:10). A church that values discipline will also produce a context wherein loving and truthful words are esteemed and spoken for the good of others.

Not only will we speak such words to others for their good; we will also learn to receive correction when we have fallen into sin. As difficult as this may be at first, it is necessary for us to live a life of wisdom and grow in Christlikeness. Finally, the pursuit of discipline will produce a culture of God-centered joy. This is so because God's aim to be glorified and our aim to be satisfied are the same path. We glorify God by enjoying him and obeying his commands, and one of the means by which this happens is the church and the discipline it produces.

REFLECTION QUESTIONS

1. What is the culture of your church presently? Does it value discipline?

2. What does your church do in relation to discipleship? Is the bar set high in this area, in regard to expectations of disciples?

3. What hinders you from being able to speak truthful, loving words of exhortation to others in your church?

4. What hinders you from receiving truthful, loving words of exhortation from others in your church?

5. How does discipline in the church produce God-centered joy?

PART 4

CONCLUDING QUESTIONS ABOUT
MEMBERSHIP AND DISCIPLINE

What Is the Significance of Church Membership and Discipline for Theology?

Membership and discipline have profound theological implications. One key purpose of church discipline is to serve as a declaration of potential eschatological judgment.[1] This is done both to warn offenders of their need to repent, and, by implication, to exhort church members to persevere in their faith.[2] As such, church discipline is a means God uses to save and preserve his people, members of the church, and the new covenant community to the end.[3] It should be noted that only God can make ultimate pronouncements

---

1. This chapter is derived from Jeremy M. Kimble, *That His Spirit May Be Saved: Church Discipline as a Means to Repentance and Perseverance* (Eugene, OR: Wipf and Stock, 2013), 112–33. Used by permission of Wipf and Stock Publishers (www.wipfandstock.com).

2. It must be acknowledged that there are a variety of purposes for church discipline. Dever helpfully summarizes, "Finally, church discipline should be practiced in order to bring sinners to repentance, a warning to other church members, health to the whole congregation, a distinct corporate witness to the world, and, ultimately, glory to God, as his people display his character of holy love (see Matt 5:16; 1 Pet 2:12)" (Mark E. Dever, "The Doctrine of the Church," in *A Theology for the Church*, rev. ed., ed. Daniel L. Akin [Nashville: B&H Academic, 2014], 809). For more on church discipline being a "sign of eschatological judgment," see Michael Scott Horton, *Covenant and Eschatology: The Divine Drama* (Louisville: Westminster John Knox, 2002), 272.

3. A similar argument is made by Thomas R. Schreiner and Ardel B. Caneday in *The Race Set Before Us: A Biblical Theology of Perseverance and Assurance* (Downers Grove, IL: InterVarsity, 2001). They argue that biblical warnings and admonitions serve as the means used by God in calling the saints to persevere in their faith. While this work is quite thorough in the exegesis of various texts on perseverance, particularly in the NT, there is relatively little data regarding church discipline, though there seems to be a very close connection between the warning passages in Scripture and the warning that comes through ecclesial discipline (ibid., 38–45).

concerning the salvific status of individuals; the church is simply a messenger and steward of the message he has given. While this is the case, it must also be acknowledged that Christ has given his church authority and, though not ultimate, this authority is to be used as a warning to unrepentant sinners and as a means to restore them.

Taken from this vantage point, church membership and discipline are theologically connected to the concepts of eschatological judgment and the perseverance of the saints. The key issue here is to demonstrate what connection actually exists so as to highlight the theological significance of membership and discipline. This chapter will demonstrate that church membership and discipline serve as a helpful test case whereby several strands of theological inquiry can be analyzed, demonstrating the importance of ecclesiology in general.

Eschatological Judgment

The concept of final judgment is thoroughly biblical and intrinsically connected to the concepts of church membership and discipline. Motyer depicts final judgment and states, "The Lord Jesus spoke plainly about the dreadful aspects of the last day (Matt 10:28; cf. 5:29; 23:33; Luke 12:5), and placed himself at the center of the eschatological events. His coming signals the ingathering (Mark 13:26–27) and 'out-gathering' (Matt 13:41–42)."[4] He continues, "All will stand before him, to receive either eternal life (Matt 25:34, 46) or eternal fire (Matt 25:41, 46)."[5] There are no exceptions; this truth applies to all people in the earth throughout the course of history (2 Cor. 5:10). Eschatological judgment, therefore, denotes a fact that all of humanity will face, though not all will face the same eternal destiny.

When surveying the passages detailing the final judgment, it should be noted that individuals are judged in accordance with what they have done (e.g., Matt. 25:31–46; 2 Cor. 5:10; Rev. 20:13). As such, to be accurate to Pauline language, we are justified by faith and judged according to works.[6] This point, though it remains a difficult paradox to explicate exhaustively, is what connects church discipline to the perseverance of the saints. Believers are called to persevere in a faith that works itself out in love (Gal. 5:6), for it is this kind of life that demonstrates true faith (James 2:14–26). Conversely, if a church member is not persevering in this kind of faith, and instead indulges in habitual, unrepentant sin, the disciplinary process should be applied.

---

4. J. A. Motyer, "Judgment," in *NDBT*, eds. Brian S. Rosner and T. Desmond Alexander (Downers Grove, IL: IVP, 2000), 615.

5. Ibid.

6. See Dane Ortlund, "Justified by Faith, Judged According to Works: Another Look at a Pauline Paradox," *JETS* 52, no. 2 (2009): 323–39. Ortlund provides a helpful taxonomy of views regarding this matter and ventures to understand this difficult tension via a robust understanding of our union with Christ.

In this time where the kingdom of God has been inaugurated, the business of the church is receiving and delivering the message of salvation.[7] Thus, the message proclaimed by the church is encapsulated in the gospel of Jesus Christ, and the keys granted by Christ to the church (Matt. 16:18–19; 18:15–20) designate the church's authority to bind and loose, to receive in and to shut out. Horton continues,

> Through preaching, baptism, and admission (or refusal of admission) to the Communion, the keys of the kingdom are exercised. After all, it may be said that the "binding and loosing" involved in church discipline is at issue in every liturgical absolution, sermon, baptism, and Communion. On all of these occasions, the age to come is breaking into this present age: both the last judgment and the final vindication of God's elect occur in a *semi*realized manner, ministerially rather than magisterially. The church's acts are not final— they do not coincide univocally with the eschatological realities, but they are signs and seals. Christ's performative speech is mediated through appointed officers.[8]

As the church, therefore, seeks to maintain its doctrinal fidelity and pursue holiness, it must examine prospects for church membership to ensure they are converted and be willing to remove a sinning, unrepentant member from fellowship, participation in the ordinances, and also "from the company of players if not from the play itself."[9] In other words, the practice of church discipline, specifically excommunication, warns of eschatological divine judgment for those not showing fruit in keeping with conversion as members, and thus while one is justified by faith alone, it is crucial to also note the importance of the obedience that comes from faith (Rom. 1:5).

Perseverance of the Saints

One other category to define is the biblical concept of perseverance. Understood simply as enduring in one's faith until the end, there is disagreement over whether apostasy is a genuine possibility for believers. The debate centers particularly on the severe warnings in the NT that threaten judgment for those who apostatize (e.g., Rom. 11:22; Gal. 5:2–6; 2 Tim. 2:11–13; Heb. 6:4–8; 10:26–31). Preserving the tension between assurance and warnings is

---

7. Michael Scott Horton, *People and Place: A Covenant Ecclesiology* (Louisville: Westminster John Knox, 2008), 242.
8. Ibid., 243.
9. Kevin J. Vanhoozer, *The Drama of Doctrine: A Canonical-Linguistic Approach to Christian Theology* (Louisville: Westminster John Knox, 2005), 425.

necessary to be faithful to the biblical witness.[10] This tension is key in not allowing believers to become lethargic in their faith, and also to not live in constant fear and doubt.

Schreiner and Caneday survey four differing views on the topic of perseverance.[11] First, some assert that it is possible for believers to lose their salvation and apostatize from the faith. They maintain that the Bible's warnings and admonitions make it clear that heirs of God's promise can fail to persevere in faithfulness and thus forfeit the inheritance of salvation. Current proponents of this view would include I. Howard Marshall[12] and Scot McKnight,[13] who would both be classified in the Wesleyan/Arminian camp. While it may appear that this reading may be the most straightforward as it relates to these warning passages, it seems to do away with the tension that must be held between warning and assurance, as stated previously.[14]

Schreiner and Caneday document three other views: the loss of rewards, test of genuineness, and hypothetical loss of salvation. The first and third, while advocated by a number of proponents,[15] do not seem to do justice to the tenor of the biblical texts. Neither seems to deal with the force of these texts in a satisfactory manner.[16] The test of genuineness view advocates that biblical warnings are addressed to people who profess faith in Jesus Christ, but who prove to be false in their confession. Supporters of this view, such as John

---

10. Thomas R. Schreiner, "Assurance," in *DTIB*, ed. Kevin J. Vanhoozer, et al. (London: SPCK, 2005), 71.

11. These four views can be found in Schreiner and Caneday, *The Race Set Before Us*, 19–45. See also Thomas R. Schreiner, "Perseverance and Assurance: A Survey and a Proposal," *SBJT* 2, no. 1 (1998): 32–62.

12. I. Howard Marshall, *Kept by the Power of God: A Study of Perseverance and Falling Away* (Minneapolis: Bethany Fellowship, 1983).

13. Scot McKnight, "The Warning Passages of Hebrews: A Formal Analysis and Theological Conclusions," *TJ* 13, no. 1 (1992): 21–59; idem, "Apostasy," in *NDBT* (Downers Grove, IL: IVP Academic, 2000), 78–80.

14. For an excellent example of how one can refute the Arminian reading of Hebrews 6, arguably the most difficult warning passage for non-Arminians to explain, see Wayne Grudem, "Perseverance of the Saints: A Case Study from the Warning Passages in Hebrews," in *Still Sovereign: Contemporary Perspectives on Election, Foreknowledge and Grace*, eds. Thomas R. Schreiner and Bruce A. Ware (Grand Rapids: Baker, 2000), 133–82.

15. For the loss of rewards view see Michael A. Eaton, *No Condemnation: A New Theology of Assurance* (Downers Grove, IL: InterVarsity, 1997); Zane Clark Hodges, *The Gospel under Siege: Faith and Works in Tension* (Dallas: Redención Viva, 1992); R. T. Kendall, *Once Saved, Always Saved* (Chicago: Moody Press, 1985); Robert N. Wilkin, *Confident in Christ: Living by Faith Really Works* (Irving: Grace Evangelical Society, 1999). Regarding the hypothetical loss of salvation view, see Homer Austin Kent, *The Epistle to the Hebrews: A Commentary* (Grand Rapids: Baker, 1972); B. F. Westcott, *The Epistle to the Hebrews* (Grand Rapids: Eerdmans, 1973).

16. While outside the purview of our immediate discussion here, one can analyze the arguments more definitively in Schreiner and Caneday's work.

MacArthur,[17] maintain that perseverance in holiness is essential for salvation because perseverance is the necessary evidence that belief is genuine.

Schreiner and Caneday's own view is most similar to the position just mentioned, though unique in its own right. They assert that God's promises and warnings do not conflict; rather, the warnings serve the promises, for the warnings urge belief and confidence in God's promises. Biblical warnings and admonitions are the means God uses to save and preserve his people to the end.[18] They also seek to hold the tension of an already/not-yet salvation, wherein we are already saved and we still await eschatological salvation. As such, they seek, as much as possible, to do justice to the biblical texts with a view to understanding them within their textual and canonical context.

While a complex discussion and worthy of much inquiry, regardless of one's interpretation, all would agree that good works are *evidence* of genuine saving faith (cf. James 2:14–26). The view of Schreiner and Caneday presents the best case, understanding the warnings in Scripture to serve as means for believers to persevere in their faith. This understanding appears to best fit with the biblical data and also helps to make sense of the tension one sees in membership, church discipline, and final judgment. Discipline serves a redemptive purpose, but, if not properly acknowledged by repentance (i.e., lack of perseverance), it can be a strong indicator that those under discipline will not inherit eschatological salvation at the final judgment.

The Interrelatedness of Membership, Discipline, Judgment, and Perseverance

As one can see, while they are not always highlighted as related doctrines, church membership, ecclesial discipline, eschatological judgment, and enduring faith are intricately connected. White and Blue accurately claim, "Church discipline is anything the body of Christ does to train Christians in holiness, calling them to follow their Lord more closely."[19] While this is a broad definition of discipline, it encompasses the fact that enduring holiness, or perseverance in the faith, is the goal, and at times this will require correction to warn and admonish others to remove the sin in their lives.[20]

---

17. John MacArthur, *The Gospel According to Jesus: What Is Authentic Faith?*, rev. and exp. ed. (Grand Rapids: Zondervan, 2008).

18. Schreiner and Caneday, *The Race Set Before Us*, 40. For further details on this last view see Christopher W. Cowan, "The Warning Passages of Hebrews and the New Covenant Community," in *Progressive Covenantalism: Charting a Course between Dispensational and Covenantal Theologies*, eds. Stephen J. Wellum and Brent E. Parker (Nashville: B&H Academic, 2016), 189–213.

19. John White and Ken Blue, *Healing the Wounded: The Costly Love of Church Discipline* (Downers Grove, IL: InterVarsity, 1985), 112.

20. Rosner helpfully elaborates on this point, and states, "Exclusion from the community and salvation are linked in 1 Corinthians 5:5b, but the former does not lead to the loss of the latter. On the contrary, the express purpose of this expulsion is the offender's salvation.

One can observe that exclusion from the church does not necessarily mean that final salvation is unavailable. Instead, this judgment is meant to foster repentance and perseverance. However, assurance of salvation depends in part on ethical progress. Most of the texts that refer to an eschatological judgment also emphasize the need for growth in godliness of church members during the present age. This is in keeping with their new covenant status. NT writers never consign holiness to the future with the idea that the lives of believers here and now do not matter. Believers are not and cannot be perfected now, but they are to advance in holiness until the final day (1 Thess 3:12–13).[21] Thus, ecclesial discipline is needed to ensure that, to the best of the church's ability, sin is shunned and righteousness is pursued, such that members show their kingdom status is not fraudulent.[22]

Summary

Church membership, discipline, the perseverance of the saints, and eschatological judgment are interrelated doctrines. Though the confrontation involved in church discipline may seem unpleasant, it is necessary and, when done rightly, brings about a greater pursuit of holiness in the life of the

---

Paul's ultimate aim in excluding the man is his own good. How is this purpose to be understood? Paul assumed (see 6:9–11) that those who persist in flagrant sin have no future with God; in this sense 6:9–11 clarifies 5:5b. Yet he is confident that God's faithfulness will confirm believers 'until the end . . . blameless on the day of our Lord Jesus' (1 Cor. 1:8). However, future salvation is not a forgone conclusion for one 'who calls himself a brother but is sexually immoral' (v. 11). The passage does not teach that ethical failure results in the loss of salvation, but that assurance of salvation depends in part on ethical progress; cf. 6:11: 'that is what some of you *were.*' Paul does not answer the question of whether the man is currently 'saved.' His point is that so-called brothers who engage in blatant sexual misconduct will be finally saved 'on the day of the Lord' only if 'the sinful nature is destroyed.' According to 5:5b exclusion is undertaken not only to benefit the community and the individual in the present, but also to secure the salvation of the sinner in the future" (B. S. Rosner, "Exclusion," in *NDBT* [Downers Grove, IL: IVP Academic, 2000], 474–75).

21. Thomas R. Schreiner, *Run to Win the Prize: Perseverance in the New Testament* (Wheaton, IL: Crossway, 2010), 61.

22. This position is not in any way suggesting that works contribute to our salvation. Ortlund asserts, regarding the idea of salvation and works, that "obedience is not merely evidential but is rather built into the very fabric of salvation itself, yet without contributing to justification." Justification and judgment are linked not so much in cause and effect or by linear progression, as it is that they are organically unified. This organic bond, says Ortlund, is union with Christ, in which one is not only declared righteous but also indwelt by the Spirit. "Justification and obedience both sprout from the seed of union with Christ. For this reason the category of those who are justified by faith is coextensive with those who will be justified on the last day after a whole life of perseverance. Those who are justified will, for reasons other than any kind of earning, do the law." While the church cannot definitively know the state of one's soul, the spiritual fruit of one's life must be examined and, therefore, discipline should be exercised to maintain perseverance and demonstrate the validity of one's justification (Ortlund, "Justified by Faith, Judged According to Works," 338).

membership. We are not saved by our works, but one should affirm the fact that we were created for good works (Eph. 2:10) and they are evidence of genuine faith (James 2:12–26). Church discipline is needful in that it is a warning of potential eschatological judgment and a means by which the saints are called to endurance in their faith, showing the veracity of their membership. Therefore, church membership and discipline serve as test cases whereby several strands of theological inquiry can be analyzed.

REFLECTION QUESTIONS

1. What is one key purpose of church discipline, as cited in this chapter?

2. How does church discipline relate to the perseverance of the saints?

3. What are the various views regarding perseverance of the saints, and which seems most compelling biblically?

4. How does church discipline relate to eschatological judgment?

5. How can we speak of the importance of works in the Christian life and still maintain that we justified by faith alone?

What Is the Significance of Membership and Discipline for the Christian Life?

After looking at the concepts of church membership and church discipline, one can observe that these concepts are not merely theoretical. These matters are not only significant theologically; the theological conclusions regarding membership and discipline render concrete applications for the Christian life. This must be remembered for all exegetical and theological inquiry. We are not merely to be hearers of the Word but also doers (James 1:22–25), and in this case that means applying the truth learned about membership and discipline to practical living.

While a number of points of significance can be highlighted, this chapter will focus on four key areas of practical application for life. The first is that membership and discipline are significant for the Christian life, in that they demonstrate that theology matters beyond just cognitive awareness. Second, these matters remind us that sin is real, and that God metes out real consequences for sin. Next, these doctrines remind us of our future salvation and also make clear that future realities affect the way we live presently. Finally, church membership and discipline are practical reminders that the church is a profoundly important matter in the life of the Christian.

Theology Matters Practically

If we want to live a consistent Christian life, have a ministry that will have lasting impact, and see churches that are healthy, we must first do our theology well. While one may not be involved in a variety of ministries in the local church, the point is that sound theology is needful for ministry effectiveness. Similarly, but on a more basic level for the Christian life and the church, Jamieson affirms doctrine as crucial and practical in reading the Bible accurately, as well as pursuing holiness, love, unity, fitting worship, effective witness, and God-centered joy.[1]

Church membership and church discipline are two facets of ecclesiology, the doctrine of the church. These concepts have real ramifications for practical Christian living, dealing with the nature of true conversion, membership processes, congregational involvement, elder leadership, an understanding of sin, repentance, forgiveness, holiness, love, and much more. Often we limit ourselves to conceptual data when it comes to theology. However, one should observe first how various doctrines are interrelated, and then how those doctrines press on the way one lives as a child of God. A kind of seamlessness exists when one thinks about the loci of theology: Scripture, God, man, sin, Christ, salvation, Holy Spirit, church, and last things. Theological thinking shapes our worldview, which in turn brings about biblical wisdom and affects the way one thinks, feels, and acts. As such, membership and discipline are good reminders that theology matters practically.

There Are Real Consequences for Our Sin

Sin is real, and profound consequences result from our sin. Church membership recognizes redemption is as real as sin, and while someone is not perfected in this life, they are fighting sin well (Rom. 8:13). Church discipline is a means by which the congregation can hold one another accountable to keeping the commands of God; and excommunication, therefore, is a loving way to warn the offending sinner of potential judgment due to their continual sin and lack of repentance. Thus, membership and discipline are tightly linked, as we are called under the new covenant to be a people who are forgiven and persistently obedient to God (Jer. 31:31–34).[2]

Church membership reminds us of what we have been saved from as we join a church formally (1 Cor. 6:11). And church discipline reminds us that the unrighteous will not inherit the kingdom of God (1 Cor. 6:9–10). Sin does not disqualify us from membership, but discipline is there to keep members accountable and call them to ongoing repentance and perseverance, knowing that the consequences for sin are real.

Future Salvation Affects the Way We Live Presently

The apostle Peter reminds us of the great salvation we have in Christ, describing it as a living hope, and an inheritance that is imperishable, undefiled, unfading, and kept in heaven for us (1 Peter 1:3–5). Believers rejoice in this salvation, even though they will face trials of various kinds (1 Peter 1:6–7).

---

1. See Bobby Jamieson, *Sound Doctrine: How a Church Grows in the Love and Holiness of God* (Wheaton. IL: Crossway, 2013).
2. See James M. Hamilton Jr., *God's Glory in Salvation through Judgment: A Biblical Theology* (Wheaton, IL: Crossway, 2010), 567–68.

Hope and joy and love are rooted in Christ, no matter what comes up in this life. More specifically, Schreiner notes, "The [present] love and joy of believers is rooted in the hope of eschatological salvation. They know, therefore, that despite present sufferings they will see Jesus Christ when he is revealed and enjoy him forever."[3] This great eschatological hope of salvation is then followed by a call to holiness (1 Peter 1:13–16); in fact, much of 1 Peter speaks to the issue of holiness based on this great salvation.

The point in 1 Peter, and the rest of the Bible, is that when one is saved by God and awaits their future hope, this affects the way they live presently. As members of the church, we seek to continually become who we already are, namely, saints, adopted children of God, united to Christ, Spirit-indwelt, inheritors of the kingdom of God, and members of the new covenant community. While we will not be perfect, our identity will shape our reality. And when a member falls out of step with what is fitting for a member with this kind of identity, the church is called to confront and exhort that individual so they see the error of their ways, repent, and realign with their identity in Christ. Therefore, our identity bought through salvation in Christ shapes the way we live in the present.

The Church Matters

Finally, in looking at membership and discipline, one must recognize the worth and weight of the church, both doctrinally and practically. At times, ecclesiology can receive short shrift when compared with other doctrinal heads, and certainly we must recognize this in light of such doctrines as the Trinity and atonement. However, readers have seen that, theologically, membership and discipline connect to other doctrines such as eschatological judgment and perseverance in the faith. Ecclesiology, in many ways, manifests the practical qualities of other key doctrines. The church is the gospel made visible and as such serves an important place in our theological inquiries.[4]

Membership and discipline also show that the church matters practically. Greg Wills writes that, to many Christians in the past, "A church without discipline would hardly have counted as a church."[5] This would also certainly be the case for membership (especially in Baptist circles). However, at times, not only are membership and discipline seen as optional in church life, even regularly attending a local church is challenged as being a necessity for Christians. One of the main intentions of this study has been to show that the church is one of the primary means God uses to demonstrate who is truly part of the

---

3. Thomas R. Schreiner, *1, 2 Peter, Jude*, NAC 37 (Nashville: Broadman & Holman, 2003), 71.
4. For further commentary on this statement, see Mark Dever, *The Church: The Gospel Made Visible* (Nashville: B&H Academic, 2012).
5. Gregory A. Wills, *Democratic Religion: Freedom, Authority, and Church Discipline in the Baptist South, 1785–1900* (New York: Oxford University Press, 1997), 33.

faith and to sustain people in their faith. To neglect the church is neither right nor safe; rather, we embrace and commit to biblical community, both theologically and practically.

Summary

Church membership and discipline function as crucial practices for the life of the church. They serve as a reminder that theology is not merely esoteric; it truly affects the way one lives the Christian life. These practices also remind us of the consequences for sin. God disciplines those whom he loves, and sin will also bring about negative consequences in our relationships on earth. Membership and discipline also remind us that our future inheritance of salvation should impact the way we live our lives presently. And finally, membership and discipline remind us of the importance of the church in general, both theologically and practically.

Christ loves his bride, the church (Eph. 5:22–25), and desires that the church be washed with the water of the Word and presented to him spotless. Our objective righteousness is rooted in Christ's work on our behalf (2 Cor. 5:21). And based on this objective work we are also called to forget what lies behind and strain forward to what lies ahead, to reach the goal and align ourselves increasingly with who we already are in Christ (Phil. 3:12–14). This is the calling of the church, and church membership and discipline are needful elements for pursuing this goal.

REFLECTION QUESTIONS

1. How does theology relate to practical Christian living?

2. In what way does membership and discipline relate to the doctrine of sin?

3. How should our future inheritance affect the way we live now? How do membership and discipline help us in this process?

4. Why does the church matter theologically? Practically?

5. What lessons about church membership and church discipline have been most important in your learning from this book? What needs to be done based on what you have learned?

Selected Bibliography

Adams, Jay Edward. *Handbook of Church Discipline*. Grand Rapids: Ministry Resources Library, 1986.

Allison, Gregg R. *Sojourners and Strangers: The Doctrine of the Church*. Wheaton, IL: Crossway, 2012.

Bargerhuff, Eric J. *Love That Rescues: God's Fatherly Love in the Practice of Church Discipline*. Eugene, OR: Wipf & Stock, 2010.

Brower, Kent E., and Andy Johnson, eds. *Holiness and Ecclesiology in the New Testament*. Grand Rapids: Eerdmans, 2007.

Clowney, Edmund P. *The Church*. Contours of Christian Theology. Downers Grove, IL: InterVarsity, 1995.

Cox, Don. "The Forgotten Side of Church Discipline." *Southern Baptist Journal of Theology* 4, no. 4 (2000): 44–58.

Dever, Mark. *Nine Marks of a Healthy Church*. Wheaton, IL: Crossway, 2004.

_____. *The Church: The Gospel Made Visible*. Nashville: B&H Academic, 2012.

_____, ed. *Polity: Biblical Arguments on How to Conduct Church Life*. Washington, DC: Center for Church Reform, 2000.

Dever, Mark, and Jamie Dunlop. *The Compelling Community: Where God's Power Makes a Church Attractive*. 9Marks Books. Wheaton, IL: Crossway, 2015.

Dever, Mark, and Jonathan Leeman, eds. *Baptist Foundations: Church Government for an Anti-Institutional Age*. Nashville: B&H Academic, 2015.

Easley, Kendall H., and Christopher W. Morgan, eds. *The Community of Jesus: A Theology of the Church*. Nashville: B&H Academic, 2013.

Ferguson, Everett. *The Church of Christ: A Biblical Ecclesiology for Today.* Grand Rapids: Eerdmans, 1996.

Hammett, John S. *Biblical Foundations for Baptist Churches: A Contemporary Ecclesiology.* Grand Rapids: Kregel, 2005.

Hammett, John S. and Benjamin L. Merkle, eds. *Those Who Must Give an Account: A Study of Church Membership and Church Discipline.* Nashville: B&H Academic, 2012.

Harper, Brad, and Paul Louis Metzger. *Exploring Ecclesiology: An Evangelical and Ecumenical Introduction.* Grand Rapids: Brazos, 2009.

Haslehurst, Richard. *Some Account of the Penitential Discipline of the Early Church in the First Four Centuries.* New York: Macmillan, 1921.

Horton, Michael S. *People and Place: A Covenant Ecclesiology.* Louisville: Westminster John Knox, 2008.

Husbands, Mark, and Daniel J. Treier, eds. *The Community of The Word: Toward an Evangelical Ecclesiology.* Downers Grove, IL: IVP Academic, 2013.

Jamieson, Bobby. *Going Public: Why Baptism Is Required for Church Membership.* Nashville: B&H Academic, 2015.

Kitchens, Ted G. "Perimeters of Corrective Church Discipline." *Bibliotheca Sacra* 148, no. 590 (1991): 201–13.

Lauterbach, Mark. *The Transforming Community: The Practise of the Gospel in Church Discipline.* Ross-shire, Scotlnd: Christian Focus, 2003.

Leeman, Jonathan. *Church Discipline: How the Church Protects the Name of Jesus.* 9Marks. Wheaton, IL: Crossway, 2012.

_____. *Church Membership: How the World Knows Who Represents Jesus.* 9Marks. Wheaton, IL: Crossway, 2012.

_____. *Don't Fire Your Church Members: The Case for Congregationalism.* Nashville: B&H Academic, 2016.

_____. *Political Church: The Local Assembly as Embassy of Christ's Rule.* Studies in Christian Doctrine and Scripture. Downers Grove, IL: IVP Academic, 2016.

_____. *The Church and the Surprising Offense of God's Love: Reintroducing the Doctrines of Church Membership and Discipline*. Wheaton, IL: Crossway, 2010.

Marshall, Nathaniel. *The Penitential Discipline of the Primitive Church*. Oxford: J. H. Parker, 1844.

Sande, Ken. *The Peacemaker: A Biblical Guide to Resolving Personal Conflict*. 3rd ed. Grand Rapids: Baker, 2004.

Travis, William G., Bruce A. Ware, Donald A. Carson, and Ben Mitchell. "Perspectives on Church Discipline." *Southern Baptist Journal of Theology* 4, no. 4 (2000): 84–91.

Verbrugge, Verlyn D. "Delivered Over to Satan." *Reformed Journal* 30, no. 6 (1980): 17–19.

_____. "The Roots of Church Discipline: Israelite and Jewish Practice." *Reformed Journal* 30, no. 5 (1980): 17–19.

White, John, and Ken Blue. *Church Discipline That Heals: Putting Costly Love into Action*. Downers Grove, IL: InterVarsity, 1992.

_____. *Healing the Wounded: The Costly Love of Church Discipline*. Downers Grove, IL: Intervarsity Press, 1985.

White, Thomas, Jason G. Duesing, and Malcolm B. Yarnell, eds. *Restoring Integrity in Baptist Churches*. Grand Rapids: Kregel, 2008.

Wills, Gregory A. *Democratic Religion: Freedom, Authority, and Church Discipline in the Baptist South, 1785-1900*. New York: Oxford University Press, 1997.

Wray, Daniel E. *Biblical Church Discipline*. Carlisle, PA: Banner of Truth, 1978.

Scripture Index